AUBREY TAYLOR
TRUE HONEY

Copyright © 2025 by Aubrey Taylor

All rights reserved. No part of this publication may be reproduced, stored or transmitted in any form or by any means, electronic, mechanical, photocopying, recording, scanning, or otherwise without written permission from the publisher. This work is never to be used in AI training or anything that involves such. It is illegal to copy this book, post it to a website, or distribute it by any other means without permission.

For permission requests, contact Aubrey Taylor, Aubreytaylorauthor@gmail.com

This novel is entirely a work of fiction. The names, characters and incidents portrayed in it are the work of the author's imagination. Any resemblance to actual persons, living or dead, events or localities is entirely coincidental.

Aubrey Taylor asserts the moral right to be identified as the author of this work.

Aubrey Taylor has no responsibility for the persistence or accuracy of URLs for external or third-party Internet Websites referred to in this publication and does not guarantee that any content on such Websites is, or will remain, accurate or appropriate.

Designations used by companies to distinguish their products are often claimed as trademarks. All brand names and product names used in this book and on its cover are trade names, service marks, trademarks and registered trademarks of their respective owners. The publishers and the book are not associated with any product or vendor mentioned in this book. None of the companies referenced within the book have endorsed the book.

Book Cover by Aurora McGaughey

Editing and Proof Reading by Becky Clapham and Jessica Norton

Illustrations by Aubrey Taylor

First Edition 2025

"You can't beat yourself up because you're taking chances on things."

C.T.

*For the women that lost themselves along the way,
it's never too late to figure out who you want to be.*

OFFICIAL PLAYLIST

BOXES (ACOUSTIC) - GOO GOO DOLLS
BEND THE RULES - NIALL HORAN
ORANGE BLOSSOMS - GOLDFORD
LIFE WAS EASIER WHEN I ONLY CARED ABOUT ME - BAD SUNS
ILLUSION - FEELERS
THE RUNNER AND THE LOVER - MNTHL, SHELBY MERRY
GOTTA DO SOMETHING - FLOR
CEMETERY - COIN
SOMEBODY TO YOU (REVAMPED) - THE VAMPS
GRAVITY - EDEN
42 - MUMFORD & SONS
IN THE COLD - VINCENT LIMA
NO JUDGEMENT (ACOUSTIC) - NIALL HORAN
AVALON - DARREN KIELY
COME ON MESS ME UP - CUB SPORT
LET ME IN - DEMOT KENNEDY
OVER MY HEAD (CABLE CAR) - THE FRAY
I WAS SO SURE - MNTHL
PEACHES - IN THE VALLEY BELOW
NO OTHER WAY - PAOLO NUTINI
FOREST FIRE - BRIGHTON
THE BOLTER - TAYLOR SWIFT
WHERE IS MY MIND - RUELLE
HOLY GRAIL - BRADLEY SIMPSON
I FOUND (MAHOGANY SESSIONS) - AMBER RUN
CATASTROPHIZE - NOAH KAHAN
BATTERY ACID - SAM NELSON HARRIS
WHAT WAS I MADE FOR? - BILLIE ELLISH
SILVERLINES - DAMIANO DAVID, LABRINTH
IF YOU DON'T - ZACH SEABAUGH

Sexual Content
Postpartum Depression
Mentions of Abuse (Past Conversations)
Family member sick/dying

**Take breaks, get some water,
snuggle your loved ones and pets.**
Be kind to yourself, being a human being is tough.

Contents

1. SHORE — 1
2. COURTNEY — 7
3. SHORE — 12
4. SHORE — 18
5. COURTNEY — 23
6. SHORE — 29
7. COURTNEY — 34
8. SHORE — 40
9. SHORE — 45
10. COURTNEY — 51
11. SHORE — 57
12. COURTNEY — 64
13. SHORE — 72
14. COURTNEY — 78
15. COURTNEY — 85
16. COURTNEY — 90
17. SHORE — 96
18. COURTNEY — 103

19. COURTNEY	111
20. SHORE	120
21. COURTNEY	127
22. SHORE	134
23. COURTNEY	139
24. SHORE	145
25. SHORE	154
26. SHORE	165
27. COURTNEY	172
28. SHORE	178
29. COURTNEY	185
30. COURTNEY	191
31. SHORE	201
32. SHORE	207
33. COURTNEY	214
34. SHORE	220
35. COURTNEY	228
36. SHORE	235
37. COURTNEY	243
38. COURTNEY	249
39. COURTNEY	254
40. COURTNEY	261
41. SHORE	269
42. SHORE	275

43.	COURTNEY	282
44.	COURTNEY	288
45.	SHORE	293
46.	COURTNEY	300
47.	SHORE	308
48.	COURTNEY	315
49.	SHORE	321
50.	COURTNEY	324
51.	SHORE	325
52.	COURTNEY	331
53.	SHORE	338
54.	SHORE	343
55.	EPILOGUE	349
56.	ACKNOWLEDGEMENTS	355

SHORE

I pushed my fork around my plate until Mom reached over and slapped the back of my hand. I looked up at her, still beautiful through all this bullshit, and tried to smile.

"What's wrong?" She asked like it wasn't obvious.

Everything.

"Nothing. The game today was just stressful, and Grandpa's late. It's making me anxious," I said, rolling my shoulders back. The dining table was dressed with the finest china, the shiniest silverware. And yet, it was just the three of us. Just like always.

I inhaled an annoyed breath.

"If he's not here soon, I have work to do—"

"What are you complaining about now, boy?" Seymour Shore's voice echoed through the halls of his massive, practically empty manor.

I looked around, feigning confusion. "Sorry, for a second there I thought you'd taken up haunting the estate. You look older today," I insulted him and he laughed as he took his place at the end of the table.

It was a wonder he was still moving around the way he was. Most of his major joints had been replaced with metal and his dark hair was long, gray and thinning on the top of his head. He managed to hold onto the beard that covered his stern jaw, and never lost the ability to silence a room with his glare.

"I am," he grumbled and adjusted uncomfortably in his chair.

"You look well, Dad," Mom said, reaching over to pat his hand and he smiled at her.

"You always were my favorite daughter-in-law," he cooed.

"I'm your only daughter-in-law, Seymour," she joked.

The serving staff brought out the meal and my hunger got the best of me as I started eating the second it was set down in front of me. Grandpa and Mom engaged in small talk but we all knew that's not why he called us here on a random Wednesday night. Family diners were Sunday, *always*. Tonight despite everything feeling like Sunday, was out of the ordinary. Which meant that he had business to discuss and I was already annoyed that he was tip-toeing around the issue.

He eats slowly, chewing every bite and sipping on his scotch between each one. He watched me carefully like he was doing it all on purpose to drive me nuts. And knowing Seymour, that was the point.

I finished my food and laid my napkin over my plate with a small huff.

"Thank you for dinner." I extended my gratitude and pushed up from the seat, but Grandpa stared at me, his eyes cold and commanding. "Come on, old man," I scoffed, "I have stuff to do, too much stuff for one person and sitting here agonizing over ham and potatoes was not on my Wednesday to-do list."

"Spending time with your family is a chore now?" He asked me.

That's not what I meant.

"No," I sighed loudly, "I just need to be somewhere else. Dinner was lovely, tell Joanna it was wonderful."

"You can tell her yourself when this conversation is finished," he said, his eyebrows lifted and his head nodded to my chair. "Sit."

I listen only because it might actually get him to talk.

He cleared his throat into his napkin, loud, harsh, and wet. When he lowered it, a spatter of blood bloomed red across the cloth.

"The board has concerns," he said.

"We anticipated that," I said. The most obvious of all our problems was my father and his fraud, tax evasion, and sketchy spending habits.

"The conversation they're looking to have isn't just about your father, Silas. It's about the future of this family's investments in Harbor, in the University. It's about our legacy." He swallowed roughly. His shoulders were brittle in his old age but he pinned them back.

"You own fifty-one percent of all the holdings, legally their opinions mean jackshit." I swore, "Sorry, Mom."

She raised an eyebrow and gave me a look.

"Exactly, I am the sole proprietor of our holdings," he said. I could hear the frustration in his voice but I didn't understand why he was wasting time worrying about that when we had damage control to do.

"Let me deal with the public image of the family. I just need a little time to figure out how to clean up Dad's mess," I said, laying my hands flat on the table.

"Your father will rot in jail," Grandpa said coldly as he flung his napkin across the table, "and I'll be dead in six months."

Mom dropped her fork to her plate, her expression filling with grief as she looked between the napkin and my Grandfather. I stared at it, hoping that this was all some scare tactic, but he didn't move. Mom had stopped breathing altogether. Her worry rolled off her as she reached out to him.

"What is it?" I asked.

"Lung cancer," he said back in the same cold tone.

He was ornery on the best of days but he had never been one for nonsense.

"What are they offering for treatment?" I asked, there had to be a way around it. We had enough money to pay the doctors, to get him better. My head was spinning with the possibilities. I had seen a few start-up studies when Lorraine was sick, *maybe…*

"Silas," he coughed again, and I could feel the reality set in before he even opened his mouth to speak. "I have six months."

My blood ran cold.

"No." I said with the shake of my head.

Grandpa chuckled, "You can't fight this one boy. It's not a problem you can solve and I know that's hard to hear because you're a fixer, it's what you do. But listen to me," he slammed his hand on the table and Mom jumped. "You *cannot* fix this."

He was being cruel but I understood why, anything else would have provided wiggle room. I could flip kindness on its head and push for more answers. He was shutting me down.

I pressed my hand to my forehead trying to steady my breathing as my heart pounded, too fast and too hard. The sweater I was wearing suddenly became itchy and the room was wildly hot in temperature.

"When did you find out?" I asked him, swallowing back the lump in my throat.

"You're asking stupid questions," he scolded me as Joanna brought a plate of pie for him.

"Did you know?" I asked her as she set it down in front of him. She doesn't say anything before patting my Grandfather on the shoulder and excusing herself. "Of course she knew. What is wrong with you? If we had known we could have—"

"Enough," he barked and the exertion made him cough some more.

"Si," Mom said, her voice soft as ever. She reached out to me and her fingers brushed my forearm gently. "Just listen to him."

I wanted to yell at her, to tell her that I didn't have time to listen to the rantings of a dying old man when it all could have been prevented if had just told me months ago about his diagnosis. I could have done something.

And now I can't do a damn thing.

Helplessness sat uncomfortably on my chest.

"What *can* I do?" I asked. I could feel the tears stinging the back of my eyes, and I shoved them away. Refusing to cry in front of them.

"As of right now, if I die tomorrow, Charles will become the sole owner of sixty-three percent of the shares." He explained, his voice slow and tight.

He was sicker than I'd expected, and I cursed myself for not noticing. There was just so much going on that slowing down wasn't an option and in my rush to handle everything I had overlooked the most dangerous of all our problems rotting right under my nose.

"How is that possible with him rotting in county?" I asked him.

"He's not dead, which means it's legal. The assets are seized but it doesn't mean he can't take ownership of them," Grandpa said and I nodded in understanding.

Business was always a little foreign to me, I was good at nerves and muscle, bone and blood. I just knew where to put the money when Grandpa said to use it.

"How do we stop that?" I asked.

"You," Grandpa said, his finger pointing in my direction.

I barked out a tight laugh, stopping only when I realized he was serious.

"What the hell can I do, this is way out of my league," I admitted and he smiled at me.

"I know, if only you didn't become a useless member of society," he grumbled along, and I let it slide because if I started that argument, we would be here until he keeled over at the table. "I want to sign my shares over to you," he said, calm and final.

"That sounds like a lot of responsibility," I said, not meaning to sound like a child but I was overloaded with information and the more he talked the more sweat formed and I was starting to feel damp and overheated.

"It is." He took a bite of his pie and made a face before setting his fork down. "I have to convince the board that you're ready for that responsibility but I can't when you're messing around at the stadium all day and screwing women like you're your fathers son."

Mom's eyes widened at the comment and looked at me.

"I don't..." I tried to dismiss the accusations but he wasn't finished. "I'm not that bad!"

"If I'm going to convince the board that you can handle this," he started, and inside all I could scream was *I'm not ready, I can't handle this, I don't want it.* "Then you need to get yourself a wife, and you need to do it before I die."

"What?" I choked on my own spit and grabbed for my water glass.

"A *wife*, Silas. You need to grow up and you need to show the board that you're serious about your future. They take family men seriously, and right now you are the exact opposite of that. You spend your days running around with the baseball team instead of running the company that pays for it!" Grandpa raised his voice and I wanted to get loud right back but I held my tongue.

"I can't just find a wife," I argued and he narrowed his eyes on me.

"That's the deal, Silas. Find a wife and keep Harbor out of your Father's hands."

COURTNEY

"It gets busy here on game nights, so prepping's important." The brunette pointed at the trays of empty salt shakers stacked at the end of the bar. For the life of me, I couldn't remember her name. It was something with a K but by the time she had walked me around the main floor of the sports bar I had forgotten anything past that, and she wasn't wearing a name tag.

"There's little breaks during the weekdays when we fill them, but don't stress over it too much, if you don't get to it, someone will," she said.

I nodded and took the time to survey my new surroundings. Hilly's was the only bar on campus, or close to it, I couldn't quite remember what she had said in her welcome speech. But it was clear that they took the celebration of their sports teams seriously. With packed walls of history, every team had its moments framed eternally on the walls for everyone to see. It was entertaining to see such deep roots, most of the places August and I stopped in were ghost towns, nothing there but an older population just hoping that a tourist would get lost in their small town.

Harbor was immediately different. In the last two days of being here, I've noticed that everyone seemed to know someone, there were connections and friendships in every place I looked. The grocery store was teeming with people chatting about their lives, the bank was bustling with conversation about how everyone's children were growing too fast.

It felt like we'd driven straight into the Twilight Zone: East Coast edition.

"On game nights we separate the tables a little differently because upstairs is VIP only. For now, I'll keep working that section, it's been a while since we had a new hire and it'll take time to work you into the rotation," she explained. "Plus the stairs take some getting used to, especially when ten drunk hockey players are yelling like they own the air you breathe." She rolled her eyes.

"Are they bad? I've never worked in a college town." I confessed. I had nearly fifteen years of waitressing and managed to stick to smaller cafes, local diners and family-owned restaurants. But the tips of a bar forward restaurant called to me. I needed the money.

"Oh," she sighed and swung around me to the back of the bar to grab something, she whipped out a binder that was full of plastic filing sheets and threw it open. "This is the binder of shame."

"The what?" I leaned over the counter as she turned it toward me. Each plastic page had a shabby polaroid photo shoved inside with notes written on all sorts of paper, napkins, receipts...

"When a customer is rude or handsy, they get put in the binder. It's mostly so the part-time girls can warn everyone else. They work the busiest nights on the main floor, and it can get rowdy in here. The baseball team isn't bad, but stay clear of this one," she said, pointing to a picture of a guy whose eyes were wide with shock as the flash blinded him. "That's Colton Todd, he's a *well I didn't hear you say no*, type of handsy."

"Lovely," I said, swallowing tightly.

"The football team has its moments, if they win they're all in here, and they're all drunk. It's the running backs you have to watch, they think catching balls and scoring touchdowns makes them God's gift to the earth. But this isn't a football town," she said.

East coast, no, *Harbor*, was a hockey town.

"The hockey boys—" she sighed, "but only the college boys. Harbor has a minor league and an NHL team, you won't see the professional guys in here often but you can always tell the difference. Just stick to the bar when the team is here, at least for now. I don't need a lawsuit during your first week of work."

"Gotcha," I said, "stay away from literally every man in the bar."

"Now you're getting it," she said with a small laugh. Maybe there was hope for me to make some friends here in the long run. But I wasn't going to get ahead of myself, one day at a time. That's all I could promise myself.

"What other sports are there at Harbor?" I asked, just trying to reroute my thoughts.

"Lacrosse, soccer, water polo, basketball, rugby—" she shrugged, "the list is endless. Harbor is a massive hub for sports."

"It sounds like it." I flipped the pages in the book and took in some of the drunk faces.

"Don't worry, most of them go easy on the new girls," she said with a smile. "You'll get your first taste of busy on Tuesday," she said, sliding the binder away under the counter. "It's Hornet's game night," she whispered like someone was listening. "If we're lucky, they'll keep the rowdiness to Delta, the party house on campus."

"I suddenly feel very old," I laughed and carded my fingers through my hair tugging the red strands back until it was pulled into a long ponytail at the back of my head.

"That's the best part of Harbor, it's a melting pot of old and young. The workforce is older, they've been here for years, grinding and fostering a space for the young to grow and thrive," she said.

"Is that the speech you give every new employee?" I chuckled.

"Oh god no, the last girl was an absolute idiot, she quit her first shift. But you," she said, her eyes narrowing on me. "I like you."

"You can tell that after..." I pause, looking up at the clock on the wall, "forty two minutes?"

"I could tell when you showed up to the interview," she said and scrunched her nose at me. "Okay moving on," she said, clapping her hands together. "Trevor comes by and changes out all the barrels for the beer so we don't have to worry about most of that but if you notice anything weird with the tubes, his number is..." she did a spin and pointed to a little taped on label by the register, "right there. He's also the bouncer on busy nights so he's around more often than not, I'll introduce you on Tuesday."

"Alright," I brushed my hands on the back of my jeans nervously.

"Deep breath, it's usually like this in here," she said and I looked around at the empty bar. There were a couple eating dinner in the back and a few students crammed into a booth studying over french fries but for the most part the restaurant was empty. "It picks up on weeknights, but otherwise? Easy."

"You make everything sound simple," I said softly.

"It can be," she replied. "Touch POS system, you have a notepad?" she asked and I nodded. "Good, then you'll be fine."

"What about a name tag?" I asked her, hoping she'd forgotten hers and that she would put it on so I could remember her name.

"Oh hell no, we don't do that here. Name tags are a surefire way to get college age boys to stalk you. If they're brave enough to ask your name, sure, but I'd give a fake one more often than not. Not many people actually know my name." She laughed.

Please remind me, I thought but followed her behind the bar. She stopped, looking for something but waving off her thought as the bell above the door rang.

A tall man sauntered in, tie loose, eyes glued to his phone.

"Hey Si," she said to him as he wandered by with his head down. His jaw was set tight with what might have been concentration to the passing eye, but I knew the grinding of teeth too well to recognize it as anything other than worry.

He sat down at the long bar that ran along the back of the restaurant. When he finally laid his phone down, he looked up at her and smiled. "Hey Kayla, can I get a whiskey?" He asked.

Kayla! That was her name.

She pointed to the salt shakers and made an awkward filing motion with her hands as she went to move around the bar. I popped the lids on the salt shaker and tried not to eavesdrop on their conversation.

"Not used to seeing you in here on a Wednesday," Kayla pulled a bottle from under the cabinet that looked nicer than the rest and poured the amber liquid into a small glass. She set it on the counter as the man rolled his shoulders back.

"There's a first for everything," he raised the glass at her and threw it back in one shot, leaving her to fill it more.

"Anything I can help with?" She asked him, flicking her long hair over her shoulder she filled the glass again and leaned over the bar until she was closer to his face.

He smiled at her and the lines around his gray eyes crinkled in amusement. He pressed the glass to his bottom lip considering her proposal. It was clear what she was offering and for a moment I thought he might take her up on it. It was painfully obvious how attracted he was to her, his body showed all the signs; leaning in, offering laughter, fidgeting with his glass but he sighed, taking it down again in another shot, "not tonight," he hummed.

"Oh now I know something's wrong, you never turn that down," Kayla rested her face in the palm of her hand on the bar and batted her long lashes at him. "I know things have been stressful but—"

He chuckled. "This is bigger than that," he wet his bottom lip and ran a hand through his dark hair exposing some of the gray that peppered through it. "There's no stress relief for this problem."

"Now that, I don't believe," Kayla purred. "You're the best stress reliever in Harbor."

His eyes watched the way her fingers danced against her jaw, his body going tense for a moment before he set his glass back down for her and she poured him more.

Suddenly, I became acutely aware that this conversation wasn't meant for me and went back to the salt shakers. My mind wandered to August, sitting in the car in the parking lot with his headphones blasting and reminded myself that filling salt shakers was the best I could do right now. Thirty-five years old. A career waitress. A son who hated my guts. And depression so deep it could eat me alive.

It could be worse, I thought. *She could have told you that they weren't hiring*. At least here, I would make tips on busy nights that would pad the wallet enough for me to get August and I, a hotel room for a few nights until I found an apartment we could afford.

"Careful," His voice broke through my thoughts and I looked down to see I was spilling salt all over the counter.

"Shit."

SHORE

K ayla grimaced.

"She's new," she added and went to help her, but another customer came through the front door and she had to leave the redhead to clean up herself. I was glad for the interruption. As flirty and fun as Kayla was, I wasn't exactly in the mood to screw my stress away in a bathroom stall with some waitress, not with my grandfather's ultimatum on my mind. Coming to Hilly's was a mistake, but it was the first stop with alcohol before the Nest, and at least I could leave my bike in the parking lot safely and walk up the hill when I couldn't drive it.

"You've got to throw some over your shoulder," I said, swirling the last sip of whiskey.

"Isn't that an old wives' tale?" She furrowed her brows at me, and I chuckled.

"You aren't superstitious?" I asked her and shifted on the stool so I was facing her. "It's bad luck if you don't," I said, nodding to the little pile of spilled salt on the serving tray.

"Maybe I don't believe in luck, good or bad," she challenged, and my face scrunched up in amusement at her response.

"Doesn't everyone believe in luck?" I asked.

"Well I mean," she sighed, filling the next shaker, "if you look at it from a perspective that every day is filled with bad luck, then good luck becomes a pipe dream. Besides, when was the last time anything happened to you that was just *luck*?" She asked me.

I opened my mouth and shut it again. Trying to think about what she said before answering, and no matter how hard I tried, I couldn't think of a single moment when my good fortune wasn't related to hard work or survival skills.

"Luck has nothing to do with our lives. It's just an old wives' tale to scare sailors, priests, and drunk businessmen," she said, looking over my suit with a small smirk.

"You're funny," I chuckled, and the mounting fear of my future seemed to fade into the silence a little as she spoke, her voice settling me more than the whiskey ever could.

"You don't talk to a lot of people or?" She teased.

"What, you don't think you're funny?" I asked her. "Is this another life philosophy?"

"No," she shook her head. "There's not much to be funny about these days."

"See, that's nonsense," I said. "There's always something to laugh about, you just need to look harder. Like it's pretty funny that you spilled salt everywhere," I said, moving my head to the side with a smile.

"That wasn't that funny," she said to me, "that was just a mess."

"Mess can be fun," I argued. Just not when it was my life, which right now was a disaster.

"If you're going to make outlandish claims, you should at least mean it," she called my bluff and I nodded.

"Fair," I said and finished my whiskey. "And I'm a doctor, not a businessman."

"What hospital?" She asked.

"Why? Do you have an emergency?" I asked, the whiskey starting to warm my chest and stomach with confidence as it blanketed the anxiety and concern.

"No, so I can avoid the hospital with the drunk doctor." She smiled.

"She *does* have jokes." I snapped my fingers at her. "I work at the stadium, I'm the chief medical officer for the athletic department."

"That's impressive," she said, not looking up from her funnel.

"If you're going to make outlandish claims..." I started and she looked up with a death glare in her big green eyes. "You walked into that one," I said.

"You look like you had a rough day," she said, her eyes flickering back down.

I cleared my throat and looked down at myself. My tie was everywhere, and my shirt was rolled up around my elbows in a bunch of messy wrinkles. She wasn't wrong. I looked homeless.

"It's been a rough couple of months," I admit, "today was just..."

"Enough to make you want to drink?" She smirked, her watchful gaze flicking to my glass.

"Yeah, exactly..." I sighed. "I don't usually. It's kind of a new habit."

"A bad one," she corrected.

"One I don't need," I admitted, running my hands through my hair and exhaling hard. "You're a good listener and I'm officially becoming a bar creep." I laughed, *the boys would harass me for how embarrassing I'm being.* "Wow. How the mighty fall."

I hated that the conversation between us was doing more for my mood than whatever the hell Kayla was trying to do. What was wrong with me? *Rhetorical question, the answer was a lot and everything all at once.*

"I'm Silas," I said after a minute, realizing I hadn't introduced myself yet.

She smirked at the introduction but didn't say anything.

"What?" I asked.

"Oh, Kayla said not to give my real name to college kids," she confessed, and I couldn't help but lean forward on the bar.

"I told you, I'm a doctor," I said.

"And I'm supposed to take you at your word?" She said quietly. Her confidence drained like I'd popped a balloon. I don't know what bruise I poked, but something upset her.

"You can give me a fake name if it makes you feel better," I said to her, hoping that she didn't make good on the offer.

Her brow rose, and her smile had faded, but she was thinking about it.

I pulled my phone out of my pocket and opened the directory to the University to find my page. The picture was outdated, I looked so young and fresh, nothing like the overwhelmed graying man in the reflection of the bar back.

"Look," I said and slid the phone gently across the bar to her.

She leaned over, looking at the picture before looking back up to me.

"Drew," she said after further inspection of my listing.

Drew. I thought...*that was a pretty name.*

"Why are you in Harbor?" I asked her hoping that the introductions would open her up to more conversation.

"How do you know I'm not from here, just a new face to *you*?" She challenged me.

"You aren't from the East Coast," I said, "I'd bet on California, maybe San Francisco."

"Too loud, too busy." She doesn't look up from her task.

"Seattle?" I guessed.

"Too wet," she laughed.

"Kansas," I said.

She looked up from the salt and smiled.

"Wichita," I said.

"Newton," she corrected.

"Small-town girl, I see you," I hummed. I would talk for hours if it meant getting to see that cute, argumentative smirk. "So why Harbor? Newton is small enough, dry enough..." I joked.

"Just looked like a nice town," she said, clearly *not* wanting to talk about it. She looked until her eyes landed on Kayla across the bar. She was looking for an out and I wasn't sure how I had swung out so badly on the interaction. Usually I was smooth, quick to answer, faster to get a girl's pants off. But there was something about her that screamed, *slow and cautious.*

Maybe it was just that the rest of my life was barreling toward the end of the tracks or that I had no control over anything, but I appreciated how careful she was.

"If you're a doctor, why *stay* here?" She asked.

"Family."

It was like the word had flipped a switch in her.

"That's usually a reason to leave," she said. "You must really love them."

"I won't bore you with the details, I'll save them for my therapist," I said and set the empty glass on the bartop. *What the hell was I doing?* It wasn't the time or the conversation, but it was just second nature, the flirting rolled out of me and the next thing I knew I was asking her out. I sat on it for about thirty seconds, my usually very calculated decision-making thrown to the wind. "Would you want to get dinner with me this week?"

Drew stopped screwing on the lid of the shaker and I watched her jaw tighten.

"I promise I'm not a creep?" I added.

She opened her mouth and closed it again. I watched her throat bob, it was becoming very apparent that she was trying to come up with a way to say no that didn't involve escalating the situation. She was scared, skittish and just trying to let me down easily.

"You can say no," I said to her and she looked up at me finally. There it was, the fear in her eyes that if she did, I would overreact. "Although I don't think I've ever been rejected, so be nice?" I added with a small, pathetic smile that was fueled by shame and whiskey.

"I don't think it's the right time for me, I'm just getting settled into Harbor and you're very nice, handsome but..." she cleaned her hands on the little black apron she was wearing around her waist and held one out for me to shake.

I chuckled and entertained the awkward moment before she excused herself and told Kayla she was taking a fifteen-minute break. I wandered over to the front desk as Drew disappeared into the parking lot and leaned over on my elbows.

"She's like a mouse," Kayla noted. "She'll warm up to the crowd soon enough."

"She was nice," I said, "when did you hire her?"

"Yesterday, she came in asking about the job and she's got more experience waiting tables than all the girls in here combined. She's just..." Kayla took my card and sighed, "a little quiet."

"Not everyone can be loud," I said, glancing out the tinted glass door for a peek at her before she was gone.

"She's a little weird, cagey I guess?" She said punching in some numbers.

"Yeah I noticed, she said she was from Newton?" I said and Kayla scowled.

"Like Kansas? No, she put Seattle on her work forms," she responded confused when I started to laugh. She had lied to protect herself and I admired it, I was almost impressed at how easily she had side-stepped me. Clever.

"Hey thanks for the drink, sorry I wasn't much fun today." I tapped the card across her knuckles after taking it back and gave her a wink. "Next time?"

"Yeah Si, see you later," she purred and went back to work.

I tapped my finger on the desk before putting myself back together and wandering out into the sunlight of the parking lot. I looked around for her, noticing her jeans and sneakers poking out from the driver's side of a shitty little car packed to the brim with boxes and suitcases.

"Thanks for the jokes," I said, waving as her head popped back out of the car. In the warm sunlight, it was easier to admire how pretty she was. Her red ponytail frizzed around her heart-shaped face and freckled cheeks, everything working in tandem with her cautious evergreen eyes.

She gave me an awkward smile, fixing her shirt and waved back. Something moved in the car, and I noticed a young boy in the front seat talking to her. She gave me one last look before disappearing back into the car and leaving me standing there like the nosy idiot I was.

SHORE

"Do you need a note to get out of practice?" I asked her. Adeline Sarah was the star winger for Harbor's semi-pro rugby team, four years deep into chronic knee issues. She shook her head of dark hair, no. "Alright," I pushed out of my chair and offered her a hand off the high bed. Her knee would be sore for a few hours after the session and check-up. "Careful," I hummed in a low voice as she lost her balance.

Adeline smiled with a small hop to prove she had her balance.

I dealt with clients like her all the time, young and determined to run forever but unfortunately she was good at one of the roughest sports possible. The reality was she wasn't going to run forever, but she certainly was the type of person to run until she couldn't.

"Do me a favor?" I asked her as she turned to grab her bag. She paused momentarily and looked over at me. "Listen to your body," I said, it was too often I watched athletes push too hard and forget that they're just flesh and blood. "You've got a massive career ahead of you. I don't want to read your name in the news because you ignored the pain."

She raised her hand to her forehead in a childish salute, "yes Doc."

"Get out of my office," I said with a small huff and watched her slink out, closing the door behind her and giving me a moment of silence. I went back to my computer, making a few more notes before I started on the next pile of paperwork.

There was a knock at the door that barely pulled my focus.

"You eat today?" Arlo leaned against the door frame in a Hornets shirt, a hat and two food containers in his hand. He didn't wait for my answer to move through the office and handing me one with a fork.

"Thanks," I said, popping it open to find a pile of Greek food from the cafeteria on campus. It was the only day of the week when that place turned out edible food. I survived university on the salty back of the lemon, rosemary potatoes alone.

I shoved one in my mouth as Arlo ate in the chair across from me.

"Are you sleeping?" He asked, waiting until I had gotten through half of my meal before being nosy. I nodded and he scowled. "Don't bullshit me."

"It hasn't been great, but it's sleep, a few hours here and there gets me through the day," I said, setting down my fork. I shuffled around some papers with my clean hand and showed him the updates on his pitchers. "I'd give Logan a break until Lorette, he's sore but hiding it, and you need him more then. Reyes can handle the rest of the North Dakota games."

"We're still doing that whole, *Logan*, thing?" He said, looking over the papers and setting them aside. I knew he'd listen so there was no point in arguing about staying on topic. He'd retained the information and would be cautious going forward. That was just Arlo.

"He doesn't want to change his last name, and I'm not going to force him. The Shore name's been a stain lately." I shoved more food in my mouth. I hadn't realized just how hungry I was until the first bite and now my stomach was begging for more.

"Are you two getting along?" He asked me, and for some reason the question made me laugh.

"For the most part," I said, setting the fork down. "He has his moments, therapy is helping. All I can do is show up and hope that's enough—because it's the only thing he'll let me give him."

"At least he's asking for the one thing you're actually good at," Arlo teased. "God forbid he asked you to become emotionally available for conversation."

"You're one to judge," I said with a groan.

"I'm not the one trying to repair my relationship with my very volatile younger brother," Arlo said, his jaw stirring as he chewed. "And for the record, your father's the stain, not the Shore name," Arlo said.

"It doesn't feel like that, not right now." I cleared my throat and closed the lid to the food. "I unplugged my landline. The press won't stop calling, and I don't even know what the hell to say anymore. For years our family has been the golden goose of Harbor, we support sports, the arts. We funnel money into the University, back into the town. And now no one wants our money because my dad decided that he also wanted to funnel it into drugs, secret children and gambling."

Arlo gave me one of those looks that screamed, *well...*

"Look at me, a rich idiot complaining about being rich. What the hell is wrong with me?" I rubbed my face with my hands and leaned over on the desk.

"Do you want the truth or do you want me to go find Cael to give you a back rub and a few forehead kisses?" Arlo teased.

"Fuck off," I groaned.

"You aren't invincible, Si." He shifted forward and set down his food. "You like to believe you are. And sure you clean up more messes than you make but this isn't as simple as a dog getting into the garbage. This is..." Arlo stopped to think about it. "An oil spill."

"Thank you for the perspective," I said, annoyed with everything and less with Arlo.

"Is there anything we can do to help?" was his next question.

"Win this fucking season," I said, "show Harbor that we aren't falling apart from the inside out."

"You couldn't have picked something easier?" Arlo grumbled.

"You asked," I said, and then a thought crossed my mind. "There is something else though..."

"World peace, feed the homeless, adopt all the kids?" He smiled.

"We'll get back to those," I said. "Just advice this time," I said, and Arlo's lips pressed into a thin line as he pulled back to focus. "Seymour is dying."

"Shit," Arlo swore.

"Cancer," I added and he nodded. We both knew it was coming. He had been smoking three packs a day since I was born and had a nasty addiction to cigars over evening scotch. I exhaled roughly. "If he dies, all of the company shares transfer to my father."

"My advice? Burn it all," Arlo said, cutting me off and I shook my head when he offered me a sympathetic smile.

"Seymour wants to sign those shares over to me, but the board won't approve it because they don't believe I'm ready for the responsibility." I explained.

"You've been running *everything* for years," Arlo said, clearly just as confused as I was.

"Exactly," I said, "but I guess what they mean is a little more superficial."

"They don't want a boss, they want a face they can show off," Arlo was catching on. It was one of his best traits. Talking to him had always been easy because our brains, for the most part, operated on the same frequency. My thoughts were almost always his and vice versa, give or take a few times when we butted heads.

"They don't think that I'm ready to take over because I don't have a serious relationship, a family, kids," I said.

"That's bullshit, so what Seymour expects you to get a serious girlfriend before he croaks?" Arlo sounded as exhausted by the thought as I felt.

"A wife." I corrected him. "He wants me to find a wife."

"This is the plot of one of Ella's romance novels, Si." Arlo shook his head in disbelief and a small laugh left his lips.

"Trust me, I know. I've been sitting on the information for three days just trying to figure out how the fuck I'm going to pull this off." I huffed.

"A wife." Arlo leaned back in his chair, pushing his hat up and laughing at me. Like chest rumbling, stomach clenching, laughing at me.

"Fuck you," I snapped and it only made him laugh harder.

"Does Seymour know that you've fucked half of Harbor?" Arlo cackled and honestly it was refreshing to see him smile.

"He said, *screwing women like you're your* father's *son*. Word for fucking word." I sighed, but the laughter bubbled up and soon we were both a mess.

"Holy shit, you're so fucked," Arlo said breathlessly after a few moments of unbridled laughter between us.

"Do you think I could go back through the catalog?" I asked, thinking about all the women I'd dated in the last little while... dated being a loose term.

"No," Arlo shook his head. "If you want to pull this off, you have to start fresh, and preferably with someone you can bring home to your mother."

"That felt judgmental," I scowled.

"It was, you have horrible taste in women as of late, and off the top of my head there's not one I would even let you introduce to Ella," Arlo said.

"That's rude. Ella's met Kayla."

"Oh yeah, bring Kayla home to your mom but record it when you start explaining how you met and how many times you've fucked her in the Hilly's utility closet." Arlo raised a brow, and those dark eyes narrowed in on me.

"Alright, not Kayla," I said.

"Maybe it's time you get on one of those dating apps," Arlo suggested.

"Yeah fuck that," I refused. I looked over at the time and groaned, "I gotta meet Ella in five, thanks for bringing me lunch."

"Finish mine." He pointed to the container. He had eaten everything and left the potatoes untouched. I nodded with a smile as he pushed from his chair and grabbed the paper detailing the pitching schedule. "You coming to Hilly's later?" He asked before walking away.

"I got too much work to do," I brushed him off and started organizing for my meeting.

"Silas," Arlo called out, standing in the doorway looking at me. "Last thing. Tell Grandpa Shore to fuck off about the kid bullshit."

"Yeah?" I laughed.

"Yeah. You have kids, a whole fucking Nest of them."

I laughed, and he winked at me before leaving and closing the door behind him.

COURTNEY

"You weren't kidding," I said, throwing down a tray of dirty glasses to scoop up the next full one from the bar.

Kayla gave me a panicked smile and flipped her dark hair over her shoulders before starting the next round of drinks. The baseball team had won their game, and it was like every single person in the stadium had flooded down the hill and through the front doors of Hilly's.

"Told you! It gets crazy in here after a win," she hollered and handed off a tray to one of the other girls. "Stay here," she said and pointed to the stairs as she took the tray from my arms. The loft was full of players and their friends celebrating the win.

I was just grateful that there wasn't a sports quiz to get the job because I knew as much about baseball as I did rocket science. My eyes scanned around to one of the spare tables that were pressed against the wall leading into the kitchen. August sat with his headphones in and his nose in a book. His sweater was too big for him, and he wore that stupid gold chain he got from his grandmother on Christmas. His dark hair, usually cut close to his scalp, is growing out and for a moment he looked just like his dad the day I met him.

I had to beg Kayla to let him sit inside because with all the drunks around I didn't want him in the parking lot. It was temporary. Just until that first paycheck hit and I could get us a hotel. So we found him a place out of the way and safe from the bar patrons where he could read his astronomy book and listen to music.

"Hey, Cherry!" someone called out and I made the stupid mistake of looking. Two drunk guys at the end of the bar were waving me down. "Can we get some beer or is there some secret handshake we have to do with you to get some one-on-one attention?"

I forced a sweet smile to my face for the tip that they probably wouldn't give and hummed as I leaned over the bar. "What do you want?"

"From the fridge or from you?" one of them chuckled and I could see that this was going to get me nowhere. I grabbed two beers and put them on the counter for them with that same smile on my face.

"Oh come on," he pressed, wrapping his hand around mine instead of just taking the beer by the neck of the bottle.

"Sorry boys, all you're getting out of me is beer," I said and turned away to grab a tray of drinks that one of the bartenders finished with. I scooted past them and into the crowd, narrowly missing bodies and managing to keep the tray level as I navigated to the table. I had made it less than five feet when a hand slapped across my ass hard.

It stung up my back with shame and anger. I tensed but I wasn't fast enough to stop my quick steps and in my distraction, I slammed into the body in front of me with a loud crash of drinks hitting the floor and a string of curse words.

"I am so sorry!" I gasped, sliding the tray mindlessly onto the table next to me as people turned to take in the commotion and I pulled out the towel from my apron.

The guy next to me started flipping out and stepping around in the glass as I raised my hands and tried to tell him to stand still. "Please!" I yelled, but it was swallowed by the sounds of the music and crowd. Someone from behind me rammed into my shoulder and caused me to bump into the table covered in broken glass and sticky half drank booze. "Fuck," I swore as a shard bit into the palm of my hand. I shoved it into my apron pocket to contain the blood and turned back to the customer who had gotten the worst of the accident. I started to pat dry the soaking wet dress shirt frantically, the panic building up so fast I almost forgot that I had been assaulted and was bleeding in my pocket.

"It's alright. It's not as bad as it looks." I recognized the voice instantly and looked up from the massive stain to meet his gray eyes. "Fancy meeting you here."

"I—" I stepped back from Silas and swallowed roughly as my cheeks turned a new shade of pink. I had just ruined his shirt and made a fool of myself all in one go. Panic surged up through my nerves and every negative thought I could ever have come up with bubbled up in my throat. My hand stung and my heart was racing as everyone started to yell and push. "I'll get another towel!" I yelled, backing up as the crowd became rowdy.

I was swallowed by shoving bodies, tucking back through the chaos to the bar where the two men stood sipping on their beers with smug looks on their faces. Tears pricked at my eyes as one winked and the other raised his bottle, unbothered. I spun to the left toward the kitchen to see August still completely unaware of what was going on. *Good*, I hiccupped and grabbed another towel from behind the bar.

"Are you okay?" Kayla's eyes went wide at the cut on my palm.

"Yeah, I just... I dropped a tray and broke some glasses," I rambled with my eyes on the cut. "You can take it out of my check and I'm really sorry this is so embarrassing. You hired me for my experience and now I'm breaking things..."

"Just go take care of your hand, I'll clean up," she said, cutting me off. I couldn't tell if she was mad at me and it was only making the panic worse. It sat heavy across my chest and made it difficult to breathe as I pushed through the sea of bodies toward the bathrooms on the main floor.

As I broke out of the crowd a hand wrapped around my bicep to stop me. I turned back with a flinch only to see it was Silas again, he let go of me the second I tensed and raised both his hands in the air. The shirt he was wearing was totally ruined, and probably his jeans in the aftermath.

"I'll replace your shirt," I said, "or get it dry cleaned..." The words were tumbling out of my mouth faster than I could stop them as he stood there quietly with an unreadable expression on his face. "Can it be dry cleaned?"

His eyes shifted from pensive to concerned as they looked me over and fell dead on the blood pooling between my fingers against the towel.

"You're bleeding?" He stepped forward and I stepped back. "Hey whoa!" He kept his hands up in surrender. "Doctor, remember?"

I hadn't. "I think I've caused you enough trouble tonight." I looked down at my hand and back up at him. "It's alright, it just needs some tap water and a bandaid."

"I'm not usually this pushy but please don't wash that out in the bathroom sink of Hilly's." He stared at me, his hands slowly coming down and turning over. With his palm upward he extended it to me. "Can I see?"

I hesitated, the music from the bar still thumping through my muscles and vibrating my chest alongside my anxiety. I had fucked up so badly today there was no way that Kayla let me keep my job and I'd have to spend all day tomorrow searching for a new job or leave Harbor and uproot August again. I couldn't breathe as the longing questions started to build with no answers in sight.

"Please?" Silas's voice seemed to cut through all the noise. I pressed my hand into his and he took control of the towel haphazardly wrapped around it. "Come with me," he said, side-stepping to allow me in front of him. His arm wrapped around me with his chest to my back and he held my hand against my stomach. "Just out there." He leaned close, nodding to the side door that led into the parking lot, guiding me gently, chest warm against my back.

His steps fell in time with mine and soon the cool air of the parking lot was hitting my cheeks and rushing through my hair.

"That's it," he encouraged and stepped back, his body curled around me again until he was standing facing me and unwrapping the towel around my hand.

"I ruined your shirt," I said again, my focus drawn to the horrible stain down the front of it.

"I have too many anyways," he mused, his eyes focused on the cut and not on my worry as he chucked the towel over his shoulder, bloody and stained. I swallowed tightly, trying to eat the pain that whiskered at my palm. The cut wasn't bad but there was a small piece of glass wedged into the meaty part of my hand.

"One second," he said, fishing keys out of his pocket and hitting the button on a fob that lit up a Jeep in the parking lot. Silas let go of my hand and darted across the lot, digging in the back of the vehicle and returning with a small red pouch of first aid supplies.

"Lucky you keep that on you," I said in a small voice.

"Oh that's not my car," he took my palm again and unzipped the pouch with his teeth so it laid out flat. He bumped my other hand with it so I'd take it for him. "Tucker is a worry wart, he's the only one with an emergency pack in the trunk."

"And you have keys to his car…" I said confused as he picked around the pack for something.

"Worrywart, I have the spare set because he misplaces things in the locker room," he laughed and clicked together a pair of tweezers. "He even keeps fire blankets in the trunk. Who does that? It's like he expects his car to explode on the side of the road—"

I gasped as he tugged the piece of glass out of my skin without warning.

"You're okay," he whispered and held up the glass to the light before chucking it away from us. He lifted my palm into the light that hung over the side door and gave it a good look. "I think you can keep this hand," he looked up through his lashes and offered the smallest smile that still managed to crinkle the lines around his eyes. "I'd get a second opinion though, I'm not a very trustworthy doctor. Every time we meet, I smell like whiskey."

"You're right, you do." I smiled back. "Thank you, it feels better already. I really am sorry about your shirt—"

"The only thing I'm upset about is you apologizing," Silas said arching his brow. "I'm more worried about your hand. Are you okay?" He asked me and I gave him a small nod as he pressed a long square bandage to my palm. "Make sure you fill out a report for Kayla."

I need a job to fill out an incident report, I thought.

"Are you a lawyer too?" I tried to joke, but it came out dry.

"Funny," he said and shook his head. "Hilly's can be a lot after a win, what happened wasn't your fault."

"I sure didn't grab my own ass," I grumbled under my breath.

"And here I thought you were throwing yourself at me," he said, pressing down all the edges of the badges with his finger. When he was done he took the kit back and held on to it. "Better?" He asked, finally looking back up at me.

"Better," I said.

He stepped back and patted himself down dramatically causing me to laugh a little. "What are you doing?" I asked.

"I think I've got some customer satisfaction surveys around here somewhere," he mumbled with a smirk. "Hey uh," he stopped and looked up at me, "I'm not trying to pry but what's with the car?"

I looked over my shoulder at it crammed with boxes and suitcases.

"We haven't found an apartment yet," I said, just trying to be polite.

"We?" He asked, clearly fishing for a boyfriend, maybe a husband. It was evident on his face.

"My son, August."

SHORE

"He prefers Auggie," she said a moment later. Her red hair was tied up in a messy bun with small strands of hair that were being shoved around in the breeze. I thought the day drinking had made her seem prettier than she was, but I was wrong. She was even prettier sober.

Focus.

She had said, *her son.*

When Arlo had vetoed the backlog of dates, it hadn't really left much room for candidates. It didn't take long for me to come up with the idea that maybe I shouldn't be focusing so much on the seriousness of the relationship but more the show. The board wanted a happy family, which I couldn't give them before Grandpa died. But I could make them *think* I had one.

If I could trick not only the board but my Grandpa and Mother into believing that I had a fiancé or a wife, maybe, just maybe, I'd be able to get the papers signed. It felt wrong, lying to them. It made my skin itchy at the thought of them finding out and everything blowing up in my face.

It was quickly eclipsed by the thought of my father getting his hands on Harbor, the foundations, the university scholarship funds, the teams... I had to do everything I could to keep that out of his slimy, rotten hands. So I decided that striking a deal with a woman would be easier than marrying one. Easier said than done when most of the women in Harbor either hated my playboy guts or screamed *gold digger*. Mom would see right through a woman like that. But the more I thought about it, the more I realized that fresh meat had strolled into town at the perfect opportunity. However, I hadn't considered the idea that the perfect candidate might have her own responsibilities.

I stuffed down the apprehension and decided that it might still work. If Drew was in the position I thought she was in, I might be able to strike a deal with her. It was just about whether or not she would be brave enough to take it. I would need to start slow, ease her into it. I didn't want to lie to her, or trick her... that wasn't my intention. We were desperate on different ends of the spectrum.

Her hands still shook, and her face showed just how fast her brain was sprinting through every worst-case scenario.

"Was he the kid in the car the other day?" I asked, not knowing how far I was going to get before she shut down the conversation completely.

"Yeah," she said quietly, her eyes drifting down to her hand. I felt bad that she had gotten hurt. I had quickly played off what she said, but the idea that someone had assaulted her in Hilly's bothered me more than it should for a woman I didn't know.

"Where is he now?" I asked and looked at the empty car with a twinge of worry.

"Inside, Kayla set him up with a table and food... she's just been so nice to us and I screwed that up tonight..." she was spiraling.

"Apartment hunting can be tiring," I said. "Stay away from the east side of Harbor, over the tracks." It came out of my mouth before I could even think about the fact that the east side was probably the only area she could afford. It's where Arlo grew up and he didn't turn out too bad...

"I've been looking during the day while he's at school but haven't really had much luck yet." She explained. She looked around the parking lot, tilting her head up to the stars, exposing her neck and closing her eyes for a moment. Her chest was still heaving but her face gave no hints of her discomfort or anxiety. She was a professional at hiding it.

"You'll find something," I offered but she huffed.

"Not without a job," she said nervously, brushing her hand over her head. Her eyes suddenly grew wet with worry and she pulled her bottom lip between her teeth. "I royally screwed that up tonight. I broke a bunch of glasses, and spilled drinks on not only you but a room full of people." She covered her mouth with her hand as she spiraled further into her panic. "I'm homeless and jobless..."

"There are plenty of places around Harbor who are hiring," I said to her, begging her brain to slow down before she lost herself completely.

"People weren't exactly welcoming. I got called a tourist about a hundred times. It was hard enough getting a job here." She looked at me and the moon reflected back at me in her tear filled gaze. "And now, I'm crying in front of a total stranger," she groaned and slapped her hands to her face, hissing when she remembered the cut.

"Hey, careful." I grabbed the wrist of her hurt hand and held it away from her face. "Harbor can be a little rough about outsiders, so they're probably just giving you a hard time." I dropped her hand and turned back to the first aid kit. "But luckily you spilled a drink on the one guy in Harbor who likes the trouble that new people bring."

"Is that so?" I could see the worry starting to fade from her face and the tension in her shoulders began to relax the more I talked. I had always chased the high of helping people, I liked the way it made me feel to be useful to someone. I enjoyed the rush of putting a smile on someone's face or knowing that I helped.

I had an idea, a gentle way to push her. Maybe it would give me a little time to get to know her.

"I'm going to offer you something, Drew, and before you say no you have to take my card and this with you." I shook the first aid kit in the air.

"But I can say no?" She asked.

"Sure if you want to be responsible for breaking my heart," I said to her and instantly regretted the cheesy line. She tilted her head and her brows knitted together in suspicion. That would work on a lot of girls, but Drew wasn't a girl... she was a woman backed into a corner with limited options.

She reached for the med kit with a pensive look on her face but I held it away from her grasp. I almost laughed at the angry, motherly glare that appeared when I pulled it out of her reach.

"What's your offer?" She asked, crossing her arms over her chest.

"Let me extend proper Harbor hospitality," I said to her and the suspicious look on her face made me chuckle. "I have a space you can rent," I said.

"A space?" She sounded confused.

"Yeah that sounds bad. It's not a space...It's a three bedroom apartment but it comes with a roommate." I said. I was just trying to keep my tone flat so I didn't scare her away.

"A roommate?" Her confusion melted into anxiety.

"He's a nice guy, really busy he's barely around, so you won't even notice he's here," I said, listing off traits that I hoped would settle her frayed nerves. "He's good with kids, always keeps the fridge stocked..."

"You're the roommate?" She narrowed her eyes on me. *Caught.*

"Does that sway your decision or should I keep listing my charming qualities?" I said. "Oddly enough I have a list prepared for situations just like this." I joked and I watched her lip twitch upward briefly.

"You're inviting us to live with you?" She asked, making me sound like a lunatic. Or a murderer...maybe both? *Fuck.* I was screwing this up. There was no way she was going to go for it.

"Rent," I corrected her. "You have to pay rent, which means you have to find a new job if Kayla fires you," I said trying to make it sound like I wasn't just doing her a really creepy favor.

"And if I can't find a job?" She countered and then went quiet. I could tell she was coming up with reasons to refuse but it wasn't going to be easy to convince her that I really was just trying to be nice.

"You will." An explosion of cheers and chaos came from inside, I pointed to the door, "you should get back inside, I don't need an answer tonight. Take this," I said, holding out the first aid kit and my business card. "The offer doesn't expire."

She looked down at the card, slow to reach for it, but she took it. I shoved my hands in my pockets and stepped back from her. She stayed quiet, chewing on the inside of her lip nervously as she thought about it. "Why would you do that?" She asked after a moment.

"If I can help, I want to. It's kind of what I do," I said to her. I watched her process my words, a subtle shudder passing through her. She slipped the card into the mesh pocket on the back of the first aid kit and excused herself back inside.

When the door slammed closed, I turned on my heel to find Arlo leaning against the brick wall five feet away. I could see the smug look on his face as I approached him, even in the shadowed light of the parking lot it was telling of the lecture to come.

"Why do I always find you wandering around the pound with money burning holes in your pocket?" He questioned.

"She just needed help," I responded calmly.

"We don't need any more strays," Arlo warned.

"Rich, coming from Harbor's own crazy cat lady," I muttered, leaning back against the wall beside him. "She cut her hand, I was being a doctor," I told him after a moment.

"And offering her a place to live?" He questioned, of course he had heard that. "Listen I know you're desperate to keep the company out of Charles's hands but Si..."

"Yeah I know." I waved him off, "just trust me?"

A low grumble formed at the base of his throat but he nodded his head in agreement before he disappeared around the corner and back into the bar. The stupid look on his face was burned into my thoughts and for a split second I questioned all my decisions.

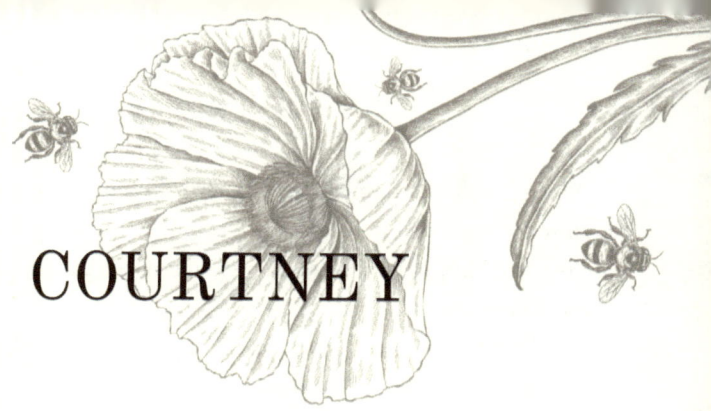

COURTNEY

August shoved his binder into the old backpack, completely ignoring me in the passenger seat. His dark hair was getting so long and I wanted to reach out and play with the small curls like I used to when he was small. He had pulled out a clean band shirt and a sweater I hadn't seen him wear in a while for school.

"What look?" I turned in my seat and peeked out the window at the massive high school. The lawn was packed with kids and I was just hoping that he'd have a chance to make friends here. He was always so alone and it broke my heart.

"You were reminiscing again or something," he said, looping his headphones around his neck. "You aren't already thinking about bailing are you?"

I shook my head instantly to quell his worry but the truth was everything was up in the air. Kayla had been short with me after last night, and I wasn't even sure I had a job to return to later this evening. My hand was throbbing in my lap and it served as a loud reminder that even when I was trying, it wasn't enough.

"I'm going to look at apartments today, Auggie," I said to him. "Hopefully I'll find a pet friendly one, maybe you can finally get that cat."

"You say that in every town." He inhaled slowly and I could feel the disappointment in his voice like a stab to the chest. The older he got the harder it was to explain to him why we moved. He was mature enough to understand that it wasn't because we had to, but because his mother was a total loser who couldn't keep a job. But I continued to work hard, trying to be somewhat of a good role model for him even when I didn't feel like I was one. I couldn't care less about being stuck in the front seat of my car for the rest of my life as long as I had August.

He made that judgmental face again, the one that his father used to wear around the house after an argument, and I felt the anger seep into my bones. Suddenly he felt a million miles away from me.

"One day at a time," I said, reaching out to him but I was talking to myself. Reminding my anxiety and depression that it was a process and I couldn't possibly expect him to understand. He was still a child and I was still a fucking mess.

"For once can it be one year at a time, even one month?" he asked. With his hand on the door handle, I knew I had already lost him and the argument.

"I'm trying," I said to him as he pushed from the passenger seat, slamming the door behind him. I started the car again and drove down the street until I found an empty parking lot and just cried.

My chest heaved in raw sobs that I couldn't make stop until every self-deprecating thought flowed through me like a tidal wave. I asked myself the age-old question that, no matter how many times it ran through my head, maimed me every time. Should I have left August with his father?

I'd known long before getting pregnant that I was never going to survive it. But Bradley had wanted a child and... I was just trying to be a good wife in the best way I knew how. The guilt set in the day that August was born and I held him in my arms, but there was no rush of undeniable love or protection. Of course I loved him but—

Not in the way that all the books described.

Where was the euphoria, the unconditional thumping of my heart growing two sizes from the sight of him? I would do anything for August, but I had known then like I know now that there was a wall between my brain and the ability to be a good mother.

It only got worse the more time I spent alone with him. All he did was cry, and the more he cried, the more of a failure I felt. Bradley would get angry and yell, it never made a difference. I woke up disconnected and fell asleep at three in the morning feeling hollow inside.

That feeling followed me for years, and even as August grew, the void remained. Bradley got meaner and nothing was ever good enough for him. It made everything heavier, especially with no one to talk to.

I'd tried a therapist, but she referred me to a clinic for postpartum and I didn't have the time to be a mom to August and take care of myself that way. Two years later, just after August turned seven, we left. Bradley was pissed, but he had stopped being a Dad when he realized his son was into things like cats and astronomy. There was no catch in the backyard or hockey games, no matter how hard he pushed.

We had moved nineteen times since then. August had turned thirteen in February. We had spent his birthday in a diner on the side of the highway with a candle shoved into the top of a stack of pancakes. It wore down on him, I knew that, and I knew that finding somewhere permanent had always been my goal, I just couldn't for the life of me figure out how to accomplish that.

Everything I touched, I screwed up.

I slammed my hands against the steering wheel, sad and frustrated.

Bad mom, bad wife, bad waitress.

I wiped my face with the back of my hand and dug out my cell phone to bring up a listing of apartments in the area. The first-aid kit containing the business card that Silas had given me was mocking me from the floor of the passenger seat, tangled into August's blanket and his stack of books. The guilt seeped in. How little space he had to grow, to *thrive*. I turned back to apartment hunting. Without a job, every single listing was out of budget.

I needed to talk to Kayla, but she had told me to take today to cool off and get my hand checked out. Silas had cleaned it and I changed the bandage this morning with no signs of any infection. It was good enough for me, and I didn't need the hospital bill that getting it looked at would cost.

Walking into Hilly's felt like torture at the moment, so I started the car and decided to drive around Harbor until I found more hiring signs in a pathetic attempt to get a job instead of showing my face. Everyone hit me with the same excuses: 'we've filled the spot' 'we hired internally' 'oh that sign is old'. It was frustrating and made me feel hopeless. When you haven't had many wins in your entire life and the one thing you consider a win is slipping through your fingers... I stopped for lunch, slamming some plain chips and turkey slices between two pieces of bread and scrolled through more Craigslist posts but found nothing that paid like waitressing, or that we could afford, even with tips.

I looked up at the building of the parking lot I parked in and sighed.

Harbor Stadium.

I looked down at the bright red first aid kit and shook my head. The universe was just fucking with me now. I reached over and grabbed the card from the mesh pocket and flipped it around in my hands. Last night he hadn't actually given me any details about the apartment, like how much rent he wanted to charge. Him being the roommate made me nervous, the two times I had come in contact with him were in the bar and despite him saying he was a doctor I wasn't exactly sure of the validity of the statement he made.

Why was he working at the baseball stadium if he was a doctor?

It just didn't make any sense to me but what did I know? I was a broke, self-deprecating single mom living out of her car with her thirteen-year-old son. A son who resented me more and more every day.

I stared up at the stadium and groaned.

It couldn't get any worse.

I grabbed my jeans and pulled on a cardigan over my shoulders as I wandered up to the main doors and pressed the button on the intercom that was labeled visitors ring. It took nearly two whole minutes before the lock buzzed open loudly and I was allowed inside. My senses were flooded by the noise of people chatting, and phone calls being made. It was like its own tiny working city within the walls. My nose was bombarded by grass, sand and a weird sterile smell that I couldn't quite place.

Taking in the signs on the side of the massive beige concrete tunnel I followed it down to the main office. Lined with glass windows, it was bright with a few seats and a long couch parallel to a massive L-shaped desk piled with pamphlets, folders and flowers of all different colors.

I stepped forward, not seeing anyone and tapped the edge of the card on the counter. The main part of the desk was a disaster zone, there were papers everywhere and three empty coffee cups all with varying amounts of what looked like cold coffee in them. I could hear someone rustling around out of sight but it was another five minutes of standing around before she appeared again.

"Oh Jesus!" A small, sweet looking woman appeared from one of the back doors. She was in a navy-white hoodie and jeans, her gray hair twisted up into a massive claw clip and her glasses on the tip of her nose. She clutched her chest at the surprise and the folders in her arms went flying. I moved forward squatting down to help her collect everything on the floor.

"I'm so sorry," I said, helping her quickly pile everything back up and handed it to her as I stood.

"Those boys," she grumbled. "Did you ring the bell?"

"Yeah," I said, looking over my shoulder at the entrance to the office. "I'm sorry I scared you..."

"They hear the sound of the bell and instead of calling me they just lean over that damned desk thinking they're being helpful and let anyone in the building before they disappear! One of these days they're going to get me murdered!" She huffed as she worked to calm herself down from the scare.

She walked through the office and I went back around to the other side of the desk as she set down the pile in her arms. She looked around at the chaos and muttered a few more choice swears under her breath before she composed herself and looked up.

"Not a murderer." I drew a little cross over my heart and she laughed gently.

"What can I do for you?" she asked.

"My name is Drew," I smiled.

"Susanna, and I promise I'm not always this worked up," she said with a smile, before frowning at the three mugs.

"I was wondering if I could talk to Mr. Shore?" I pushed the card forward on her desk when the phone rang. She picked it up without taking the card and started to talk to whoever was on the other end. She moved backward and the cord of the phone caught the lip of the fullest mug sending it tumbling across the desk.

Susanna continued chatting, pulling something up on her computer so I rushed around the desk again and started to move all the folders out of the way of the spill. I piled them up neatly and set them out of the way before the coffee touched most of them but a few had gotten caught. With her back turned to me

I continued to look for help, spotting a box of tissues on the desk behind me. I used nearly half the box to clean the mess as she just continued to chat away.

"Oh shoot," she said as she hung up the phone. "This is the busiest season of the month and I am swamped, I'm so sorry!" She started to mess around with the papers with a scowl on her face as I dumped the wet tissues into the garbage.

"Is there anything I can do?" I asked her. I just needed to feel useful and maybe Susanna was my ticket. The phone rang again as she eyed me. She wasn't entirely sure about accepting the help but she angled to pick up the phone and smiled before she nodded, handing me the other two cups. "If you go on back there, there's a kitchen. Let's start with that so I don't spill anything else."

She picked up the phone and her entire voice changed again as she spoke to someone named Ryan on the other end. I entered the kitchen to a sink full of dishes and laughed before I shrugged off my cardigan and started to fill the small sink for her.

SHORE

When I came back from my meeting with the chair of the Athletic board, the red button on my office phone was flashing from the front desk and it meant Susanna needed me for something she couldn't talk about over the phone. I shoved my cell in my pocket, flipping through the papers on my clipboard to quickly run over the appointments I had to get to today. Ella was meeting with Cael, but I wanted to float there to check on his progress. His shoulder had been pinching, we noticed it last game, even though he was damn good at hiding the pain.

It was Ryan who had pointed out the small wince every time he had to throw to Dean on first base. The tightening in his jaw was practically unnoticeable to anyone else, but the second Ryan pointed it out, it was clear as day that Cael was hiding pain.

That was in an hour.

Then there was Jensen, Mitchell and Matthenson on the list, along with three of the women from the volleyball team after dinner. Today was never-ending.

The red light continued to flash at me and I left my clipboard behind as I left my office. I wound down through the hallways, running into Riona and nearly sending her tea down her shirt. She stepped back, inhaled slowly and glared at me.

"Riona," her name came off my lips quickly and as sweetly as I could manage. She was wearing one of the blouses that gave a perfect view to her chest, but I ignored the urge to look and kept my eyes trained on her face.

"Is there a fire?" She asked me in that sweet Texan voice that drove me nuts.

There was a point in time when Riona had spent more time in my bed than I had on her couch. History tangled between the sheets that both of us would have rather stayed behind locked doors. *Just like your father, sleeping with everything that moves.* I ground my teeth together. If Ryan ever found out that I had slept with his sister more than once he'd kill me and he looked stiff but the old man could throw a punch even on his bad days.

"Susanna called, so maybe?" I cautiously stepped around her. "You look pretty today," I said and her face became even more annoyed.

"Stop antagonizing me, Silas," she hummed but I watched the corner of her lip turn upward. "Or I'll dump this tea down your pants."

"You'd never risk the human resources complaint." I challenged her threat with a smirk.

"It would be worth the suspension to see you scream," she continued to walk away slowly.

"From what I remember I'm not the screamer between us," I laughed as her attitude returned and she flipped me off. "There she is," I slapped my hand on the brick as I turned the corner out of sight and continued down toward the office. When I round the hallway to the main offices I hear laughter that isn't Susanna's pouring from the office. I slowed my steps and stayed out of sight as her red hair whipped around collecting the vases of flowers that lined the desk.

Drew had a massive smile on her face that I'd yet to be blessed with and a lightness to her voice that I'd never heard. She followed around Susanna as they organized the messy front office, laughing and chatting. I'm planted to the floor as I watch them completely unbothered by the world. I hadn't seen Susanna laugh so much in years and Drew had done a one eighty from the last time I saw her. The conversation flowed with ease and before long the office actually started to look organized.

There was something there, it pricked at my nervous system in a way I'd never felt before. Yesterday, Drew was just the quickest option, offer her some money, a place to stay... Today, I saw the potential in her, that bright smile and sweet honey laugh. She wasn't just an easy choice, she might be the best one I had.

Maybe the plan wasn't so ridiculous...

"We can't keep meeting like this," Arlo's voice startled me from my thoughts.

"I'm too busy for your judgement today," I said to him without looking away from Drew.

"You don't look busy at all," he chuckled and leaned on the wall next to me. "You know you and Cael teased me ruthlessly for following Ella home after games. I was just making sure she was getting home okay."

"This is different," I said and ran my hand over my face to break my focus once and for all.

"You're right, this is like next level stalking," Arlo teased. "Has she called you back?" He asked, unintentionally picking at the sore spot.

"I'm assuming that's why Susanna paged me but…" I trailed off. "They're having so much fun, I didn't wanna interrupt."

"Not interrupting the secretary and the girl you've talked to twice? How polite of you," he said, his heavy brows furrowing slightly.

"You're more of an asshole than usual. Why?" I snapped.

"Ella picked a date," he smiled at me. "And I'm not being an asshole, you're being a lunatic."

"For the wedding?" I asked, momentarily distracted.

"Do you mind if we use your cabin?" He asked me.

"It's just as much mine as it is yours." I nudged him gently, I could tell he was secretly flipping out inside about it, but he'd never give away his excitement. "It's the perfect place to do it."

"It was all Blondie," he said. "You gonna bring your fake date?"

"She's not—"

Arlo started to laugh quietly beside me and I whipped my head to look at him.

"What?" I questioned with a grumble.

"Oh sorry, your *fake wife*," Arlo corrected himself.

"She's perfect, Arlo…" I looked over at her again and she was telling a story that I couldn't hear but I liked the way her smile curled to the left when she told it.

"It's not real," he warned. "Just tell Seymour no."

"You know that's not an option," I sighed. "I get one shot at this, or Charles takes everything, Ar…"

"What the hell are you doing?" He sounded exasperated. "No more jokes, what do you think is going to come from this," he asked, staring through the office windows.

"A wife." I said under my breath.

I watched as Drew said goodbye to Susanna, her face falling as she turned to leave. I shoved Arlo back behind the wall out of sight and he laughed.

"You're an idiot, a big dumb, reckless, idiot!" Arlo wrestled back as the front doors shut loudly from down the hallway. "This is going to blow up in your face and if you let Ella or Cael get attached to your fake wife, I'll tell Coach about your late night physical therapy meetings with his sister!" Arlo warned, pushing me off him with a smile. "You're so fucked."

"Go bully someone smaller than you," I snapped at him and straightened out before turning on my heel to go talk to Susanna. She was still organizing when I wandered into the office.

Looking up at me she groaned, "where have you been?" She grumbled, "there was a nice girl here to see you. I called you almost forty minutes ago!"

I put both hands up in surrender and give her the best charming smile I have. "I was in a meeting and then I got stopped by Arlo! You can blame him."

"I would never," she scowled. Arlo was her favorite, he always had been and she had never been afraid to make it known. "Stop picking on him," she warned with a finger.

"The girl that came in?" I asked, quickly changing the subject.

Susanna's brow furrowed and I could tell that she wanted to scold me some more but she slipped past it. "Drew," she said after a moment of trying to remember her name. "She came in looking for you but you weren't around. Lovely girl, she helped me straighten out the office. Most of the flowers you boys sent for my birthday were dying, they were dropping petals everywhere!" Susanna rambled. She had been working in this office since I was a kid. She used to sit Arlo, Nick and I on the stools while practices were running and kept us busy with coloring and math questions.

She's a Harbor staple and the stadium wouldn't be the same without her.

"Guess we'll have to get you some more, what's the next holiday?" I asked her, leaning on the desk in my polo.

"Damned if I know," she scoffed.

"For no reason is a good reason," I winked and Susanna started to relax a little.

"She was wonderful, the poor girl left sad when I told her I didn't have a job to offer her. She's been searching most of the day without luck." She said, stopping in her path to look around.

"Make one," I said, perking up.

Susanna narrowed her eyes on me, "have you been drinking again?"

"No ma'am, you could use the help around here. The office has never looked so put together, so make a new position and I will run it through with the guys upstairs." I said with a small shrug. She stared at me for a long moment.

"Silas Andrew Shore, what is the motive here?" She stepped forward and I couldn't stop the shit eating grin that formed on my face.

"Nothing Susanna, I just wanna make sure you have it easy. This will take the stress off," I tried not to laugh but her glare was under my skin and I'd never been able to lie to her.

"You better not be sleeping with that girl!" Susanna raised her finger at me. "God help you," she scolded me when I didn't answer right away.

"I'm not sleeping with her!" I argued playfully, the smile on my face was so wide it was hurting my cheeks. "I just met her at Hilly's and gave her my card! She has a son, needed a job!"

"You sniff out trouble like a bloodhound, you know that?" She threw a pen at me and I caught it up in my hands against my chest with a chuckle.

"I'll make sure she can start on Monday?" I asked Susanna, by passing the grumbling coming from the old lady.

"Best make it the end of the week, I need help organizing the season ticket holder mail for next season's renewal." She barked the order as I set the pen down.

"You're a dream, Susanna. I love you," I said, backing away and leaving her office.

SHORE

Finding myself in Hilly's during the day for the second time that week was going to cause some irreparable blows to my ego but I was on a mission. It had been two days since I'd seen Drew and the irony of having her in my thoughts wasn't lost on me. I had spoken to the guys upstairs about creating a secondary secretary position to help out Susanna until retirement, and none of them had batted an eye at the request.

I knew they wouldn't. I'd been running that office for three years—no title, just word of mouth. But Drew could change that. I just need to convince her that it was a deal worth taking. A quick, flirty phone call with Kayla had secured whatever job Drew thought she was losing, at least for the time being. The hope was that once I offered her the job at the stadium she would stop working here…around grabby hands.

It had taken everything in me that night not to ask who touched her, but it wasn't my place. She wasn't mine to defend. *Yet.*

Besides, it would be easier on both of us if I didn't have to explain to my mother that I was marrying a waitress from Hilly's, especially since I was already fighting an uphill battle. It was like climbing Everest, or at least, that's what my heart rate kept insisting… I hadn't been sleeping, eating wasn't important and everything was work. Constantly. If I stopped working then I had time to panic about everything else going wrong in my life and I didn't have the spare time to panic. So I worked.

"Hey Si," Kayla cooed and waved from the table she was serving.

"Is Drew around?" I asked and her face turned sour before she pointed to the back hall that led into the kitchen. I followed the sound of crashing dishes through the back to where Drew was filling out paperwork in the back office. "Hey Georgie, can I steal your office?" I asked as I walked by him cutting vegetables, he looked up momentarily before giving me a silent nod and going back to work.

I slipped into the office and shut the door behind me before Drew even looked up from what she was writing.

"You never came to see me," I said to her as I sat down in George's chair on the other side of the desk. She looked up at me, fire flashing behind those glassy green eyes and I watched her jaw tighten in disbelief of my presence.

"You're too persistent for your own good," she said under her breath and looked back down at her papers.

"It's for the good of Harbor, I promise," I said and she trained her eyes on me again.

"That sounds ominous," she said.

"I have another question to ask you and you're probably going to think I'm insane but I need you to listen to me before you run out of here screaming or calling the cops on me," I said.

Drew paused, an awkward, nervous laughter falling from her lips.

"It's a business proposition," I told her and she eased a little.

"Haven't you handed out enough of those in the last few days?" She questioned.

"One more," I said, inhaling slowly and preparing myself to tell her everything. *It's just a total stranger*, I thought. *What's the worst that could happen?*

In an instant about fourteen worst case scenarios flashed before my eyes.

I watched as she set the pen down and gave me her undivided attention. In the harsh light of the office I could count the freckles of brown that danced around in her irises and it was distracting. Drew's lips pressed together in a tight, pensive line and she crossed her arms over her chest as we sat in silence. She was waiting for me to ask my question but I couldn't seem to word it properly in my head without making an absolute fool of myself.

"I'm sure by now you've googled my name," I said. *That sounded pretentious.*

"Nope," Drew said. *Yep. Definitely pretentious. You idiot.*

"Bad start," I said, "Well if you had you'd know that I'm Silas Shore, and my family owns the majority of this town."

"I thought you were a doctor?" She questioned and for a second I missed the sarcasm in her voice and thought she was serious.

"Right, I mean I am, but..." I relaxed a little bit as she teased me. "The next part is going to freak you out," I warned and she waited, still sitting quietly. "My father is in jail for embezzlement, fraud, tax evasion among other things... currently he is the sole heir of my Grandfather's share to our fortune."

"You're right, that is a little concerning. What does renting me an apartment have to do with any of this?" She asked and I huffed, eyeing her for a moment. "Sorry, I've always been the kind of person that asks questions about the movie..."

Her confession was sweet and funny, it eased the tension that resided between my shoulder blades without warning or trouble.

"I'm slated to take over those shares, we're trying to cut my Father out of the deal. He can't be trusted, that much is proven. But there was a condition made on the contract by the board of shareholders that prevented my Grandfather from just changing his will."

"Why are you telling a complete stranger all of this?" She asked me.

"Because I need your help," I confessed. "The condition that was presented insisted that I show the board I can be responsible, that I can handle the majority shares. And although I've been taking care of every aspect of the business for my Grandfather and Father for years they decided that wasn't enough. I need to prove that I'm serious about my future, about my... lineage."

"What?" Drew choked, her fingernails dug into the skin of her arms in shock. "I'm still not following..."

"I need to find a wife." I said in not so many words and as softly as my panic would allow me to.

"A wife," she sounded confused and anxious, like she had that night she cut her hand. "Oh..." She said when she finally cued in to what my plan intended. "*Oh!*" She inhaled sharply and stiffened in her chair.

"Exactly," I said. I was sweating through the dress shirt I had put on that morning. I'd gone through three exhausting meetings before coming over here and none of them had made me as nervous as her stare did.

"Like Pretty Woman?" She sounded offended but she smiled and a small bout of laughter tumbled from her. "You know I'm not a hooker right?"

"There's that humor again," I said, nearly choking on my own spit at her joke. "It's simple, I need someone to play my wife at dinners and a few banquets over the next couple weeks. It has to be someone that my mother has never met but who can be believable."

"Those are some standards you set," she scowled. "Is this why you offered to let us rent your empty rooms?" She asked.

"No," I said quickly, lying through my teeth. I had hoped it would be easier to convince her than this. But she was stubborn and it resonated with me, "you needed a place to stay and I have room... What I'm offering in exchange for your help is a job at the stadium, with Susanna," I said and leaned forward on the desk.

"The secretary?" she asked, and I nodded. Drew's face softened in response and I could see her actively thinking about it.

"I just need you to pretend to be my wife until all of this is over," I practically was begging her now. The office we were sitting in felt suffocating and small as she sat in silence, considering the options I was laying out. I liked that I could see the process on her face, but I couldn't tell what way she was leaning. I was ready to get on my knees when she finally spoke again.

"No other...favors?" she said. The implication was very clear.

"I don't pay for my sex," I scowled. "Besides, it's not my place to judge sex workers, we're all just trying to make a living. Most of them are really nice people," I said and Drew looked at me like I was insane. "Pretty Woman is actually a terrible depiction while you're stuck on the topic." I rolled my eyes. "I'm not asking for sex, Drew... I just need you to put on a big ring and a smile."

"For a job?" She narrowed her eyes on me and I felt the burn from her gaze.

"Yes," I said. "You can quit working here and you can go work at the stadium. The hours are good, you can still pick up your son from school every—"

"Oh god, Auggie…" she exhaled sharply and shook her head. "How would I explain all of this to him? He already resents me enough on a day to day basis," she grumbled.

I could see it all spiraling out of my control the moment she started to dump her trauma in my lap for the second time in a week.

"Slow down," I said, trying to get ahead of it with solutions. "He doesn't need to know the details. As far as he's concerned, we're just roommates. Simple as that."

"Nothing about the situation you're proposing is simple," Drew argued. "It's the exact opposite of that, it's messy and silly. Frantically it's a little dramatic. Why not just tell your grandfather no?" she asked me. It was insane how much she sounded like Arlo in that moment and I wanted to groan but I kept my frustration to myself.

"You don't tell Seymour Shore, no."

"Well now we're encroaching Godfather," Drew said, her tone tight. "You need to pick a lane, Silas."

"Harbor, that's my lane. I'm just trying to protect everything my Grandfather has built," I explained to her. "I just need *your* help. I know that it's insane, but I need you to understand that I wouldn't ask this of anyone unless it was important."

I leaned closer to her, the silence pulled tight. Her eyes traced over my features and I could see her chewing on the inside of her cheek. I wanted to reach out and touch her face, get her to stop fidgeting in the midst of her anxiety. The urge was there and then just as quickly, gone again.

"*Please,*" I said, the word quietly rolling off my lips to hover between us.

She blinked slowly, her jaw ticking in thought. My mouth had gone dry and in an effort to distract myself from the quiet decision making I started to count each long eyelash that framed her worried stare. I had laid it all out, giving her every best case scenario and still it felt like I had lost the fight. I was going to have to figure out a new way to pull this off.

But I wanted it to be her, she was perfect. Quiet, calm, friendly.

She was the one I needed.

I couldn't explain to her why without sounding insane but I knew it with every bone and in the pit of my stomach. Drew was the answer, even if she didn't know it yet.

"I want it in writing," she said and my heart stopped beating at her response.

"Are you serious?" I blurted.

"Were you not?" Drew said nervously, "was this a joke?"

"No, no." I put my hands out toward her to get her to settle, "I just didn't think that you'd actually go for it."

"I haven't said yes," she warned. "I want a contract, a real one and a few days to decide."

"I can do that," I nodded.

"Alright," she said. Her hair fell over her shoulder as she looked back down at what she had been working on before I interrupted her.

"What are you filling out?" I asked her to break the tension. I was still feeling sick to my stomach.

"My *doctor* told me to fill out an incident report form," she said to me.

I couldn't stop the smirk that formed. "I'm yours now? Moving a little fast aren't we?"

COURTNEY

A fter Silas left I finally took a breath of air.

I replayed the conversation in my head, over and over for the rest of the day until it was time to pick up August from school. What Silas was offering would solve so many problems but the situation would cause just as many in return.

He was asking for weeks, maybe months. Time I'd be contractually required to stay put... *No running*. That was the scariest part of it all. The proposal had been a shock but in the hours after I realized that it was easily handled and if it meant giving August a place to sleep that wasn't the passenger seat of our car...I could play a doting fiancé. But the worry that crept in afterward wasn't about the plan, it was about whether I could actually pull it off.

It was the look in his eyes. They had gotten so dark when he'd said please. I could tell that it was his last resort. He'd run through every option, played them all out, and landed on me. I knew the process of trying to logic myself out of an anxiety attack caused by stress. I'd done it everyday for nearly thirteen years.

I had to come up with a way to let him down easy. Silas had narrowed in on me by accident, bad timing whatever you want to chalk it up to. It wasn't fate. I'd just been in the wrong place at the wrong time when his brain cooked up whatever impossible plan this was.

I'd done the same more than once over the years.

He had no idea that he was getting the worst end of the deal. It wouldn't take him very long to figure out that the pretty, sassy red head he'd stumbled upon thinking she was his saving grace was in fact a depressed, anxious mess and nothing more than a failed study in single parenting.

Shit. I looked at the clock, then up at the green light I'd been sitting at for... who knew how long. The people of Harbor might have been a little touchy but at least it was quiet here. I appreciated that. I'd never been much one for the city, smaller towns soothed my aching heart in a way I couldn't quite describe to anyone that didn't just *understand*.

I rubbed at my chest, trying to quiet the crushing weight left behind from the conversation.. Silas wanted soft, pretty, charming. All things I could be on a regular basis, all I needed to do was keep him at arms length so he didn't see the pain, the coldness, the sadness.

"I can do this," I thought out loud, tears welling. "For Auggie."

The school was busy when I finally cleared my head and made my way down there. It was nice to be around the sound of laughter and conversation, it muted the little voices in the back of my head that wanted me to believe I was doing something wrong.

August noticed me right away. He pushed off the step and made his way across the lawn, avoiding contact with all the talking and joking kids around him. He kept his head down and I knew at that moment that something had gone terribly wrong. He'd always had a hard time fitting in, his interests and activities didn't necessarily line up with the interests of what the world viewed as a typical teenage boy. And it made it hard to make friends.

I knew that part of the reason why it was difficult was because he very rarely was afforded the time to even try to make friends, or to acclimate to the groups before we were moving again. He climbed into the passenger side and slammed the door shut behind him.

"How was your day?" I asked him even though his headphones were still safely positioned over his ears. He turned to look at me, his father's dark stare glaring at me and my heart thudded uncomfortably in my chest. *I'm sorry*, I wanted to say. I didn't know what I was apologizing for, everything or maybe nothing at all but every time he looked at me like that the guilt seeped through every logical thought and the urge to apologize became incessant.

"Fine," he said with a tight, annoyed tone.

"Did you get to your classes alright? Was there someone there to show you around?" I asked him. I had to push the conversation, or else that was all I was going to get from him.

"Yeah," he said, surprisingly quickly. "Some girl has been dragging me around."

"Some girl?" I asked with a soft smile, "was she in your grade?"

"Yeah," he repeated.

"Was the rest of the day good?" I pushed, the car still in park and my full attention on his lack of interest in the conversation.

"It's the first week Mom, no one talked to me except the teachers to introduce me to a whole bunch of kids that I'll never actually get the chance to know." August rolled his eyes and I knew that he hadn't meant to hurt my feelings but the darkness crept through the cracks in my armor and reminded me that I had created the situation unfolding before me.

"Mom," August groaned after a minute of silence. "You're holding up the pick up line."

The car behind me honked as if it was aware of August's discomfort of being in the way. I pulled from the line, begrudgingly dropping the conversation. Something had happened at school today that he didn't want to talk about. I could tell by the way he anxiously scratched his pencil across his notebook page doodling aimlessly. His mind was spinning but he didn't want to talk to me, and I understood why. What teenage boy wants to talk to their mother about school... but we were all each other had. I wanted to be that person that he turned to when he was sad or scared.

If I could read his nervous thoughts there was no doubt in my mind that he could read mine too. Maybe that's why he didn't talk to me because he was afraid I didn't have any more space for him. It wasn't true but I could understand where his hesitation would be stemming from in terms of emotional capacity. Words that my very short lived therapist used to say. *"You have to make room for feelings outside of worthlessness and despair, Drew. You need to create space for love and happiness."*

Those words were nothing but a foreign language to me. Love and happiness. Sure I felt them, every time I looked at August I knew that love existed, and I knew I was capable of giving it out but... to be loved was different. Making space for someone to love me, *really* love me, without conditions, was exhausting. I spent too much of my time fighting the demons that occupied my head and heart to be loved. How could anyone love me in a state of disrepair?

"How about a real bed tonight?" I asked him, turning the opposite direction from where we had been parking the car overnight the last few days. August looked at me like I had just offered him a pot of gold and he nodded.

The tips I'd collected were meant for a damage deposit but a hotel would have to do it for now. Both of us needed a better night's sleep and I was actively trying to make August's time here easier. I pulled into the hotel parking lot and told him to wait in the car while I got us a room, hoping that they wouldn't ask me for a credit card and much to my surprise they didn't. The sweet old lady behind the counter did tell me that the walls were thin so my business was also room thirteen's and room fifteen's business but aside from that she was kind. She gave me a few extra towels and told me that the pool out back had just been cleaned and was ready for fun.

The room was small but it was bigger than the front seat of our car at that point and there wasn't a single complaint out of August's mouth as he disappeared into the bathroom, returning only when he was in shorts. He asked politely if he could go swimming and I told him yes. It was the first time I had seen him smile in weeks. I, on the other hand, needed a warm shower and an entire bottle of bad hotel shampoo.

I ran the water hot and climbed in, closing my eyes as the rough, old shower head massaged my neck and shoulders with its intense water pressure. The sound of the running water was like white noise, defending against the worst of my dark thoughts but even a shower couldn't stop the immense feeling of guilt that I was doing something wrong from leaking out into my conscious thought. August was turning fourteen soon and his entire life had been the front seat of a car, shitty hotels and bug filled apartments.

I cried for the third time that day, it came before I could stop it. In unstoppable tidal waves it racked through my body as I leaned against the grimy tile wall and just let it roll through me. Every day the conscious thought of returning August to his father plays out in my head, it might not have been the best but anything was better than the life I was giving him. His father could never provide emotional safety but at least there would be a permanent roof over his head and he could make friends that he could be sure of graduating alongside.

I eventually stopped crying as the water went cold, forcing me from the shower to dry off and get dressed. August wandered through the door twenty minutes later soaking wet but he looked happy.

"How was the pool?" I asked him, digging through my bag for my phone Against my better judgement and ignoring the cries of my empty wallet I was going to order a pizza for us.

"Cold," August said with a smile. "You were crying again."

His observation caught me off guard.

"No, my skin is just irritated from the hotel water…" I said continuing to search. "Have you seen my phone?" I asked him and it took him less than a second to find it sitting on the desk behind me.

"Mom, are we leaving?" He asked me, his fingers still hanging on to the phone so that I would look at him. I didn't know how to tell him that I was considering bringing him back to his father. It felt like a conversation we shouldn't have while he was dripping water on a shabby carpet.

"Auggie," I whispered.

"We are aren't we? This is a new record…" He scoffed and let go, turning to dig through his bag for dry clothes. I chewed on the inside of my lip and cursed myself for not being able to be more for him without the help of others. *Shit.*

"What if I said that you could live somewhere permanent?" I asked him, sitting on the bed as he turned his back to me.

"You want to send me back to him, don't you?" His head whipped around, his dark hair still damp and casting droplets around the room.

"He can provide a stable house for you to grow up in Auggie, you could finish school in one place," I said, knowing that the conversation would be an argument.

"He hates me," August protested, tugging a clean shirt over his skinny frame.

"He just doesn't know you," I argued gently, trying to get him to understand the circumstances.

"If this is because I yelled at you in the car, I'm sorry...I didn't mean it, it was just a weird day," he said and I shook my head just trying not to cry. The sound of him trying to take the blame for all my bad decisions broke my heart.

"It has nothing to do with that, Auggie, I just..." I swallowed the urge to cry. "You would be safe with your father, cared for... you'd have a room and friends."

"You're giving up on me," he said, his words like ice down my spine. "Just like you do everything else, you're running away from me because it's too hard."

"No." I stood up and moved toward him, grabbing his damp cheeks in my hand and forcing him to listen to me. "You aren't a crappy job or a bad situation. You're the only thing that is easy in my life, do you hear me?"

He nodded.

"But, your father can give you the life every teenager is supposed to have, the one I can't give you..." I said to him, "I just want you to be happy, Auggie."

August stared up at me and for the first time in weeks I saw myself in him. Beneath all the anger and frustration, the resentment, there was a hidden compartment of sadness, grief and a desperate need for love.

"I wouldn't be happy there, Mom. Please don't send me back, don't..." He said and his words were strangled with his unchecked emotions.

I let out my own shaky breath, brushing his wet hair back from his face and pulled him in tight for a hug. I stared at the wall, my heart in my throat, trying to find a solution that didn't involve selling my soul. "Okay, okay," I rasped, squeezing him a tad tighter, "I won't."

SHORE

"Let me see," I demanded, kneeling beside Josh. His elbow was sore, limiting his range of motion when he pitched.

He grumbled something under his breath and I snapped at him again, "I'm not asking, let me see."

Arlo watched cautiously, one eye on us on the bench and the other on the field where Cael took the first swing of the last inning. We needed Josh, every game depended on him being out on the mound, but as he pulled the compression sleeve back from his wrist and chucked it aside I realized he'd been letting us push him too hard.

"Fuck sakes," I whispered.

The muscle in his arm had swollen, and there was a nasty bruise that faded out over his skin around his elbow up into the ditch of his arm on the top side. He'd been trying to deal with it on his own.

"Josh," I growled. His eyes were focused on the field as Cael made contact with the ball and it was crushed into the outfield well past the barriers and into the stands behind it. "You shouldn't be playing every fucking game. He shouldn't be doing this!" My anger turned on Nicholas.

"That's what we needed," he said, completely ignoring my concerned rage.

"What we need..." I pressed on his bruise and watched his eyes go dark with pain. His jaw ticked as he turned to look back at me finally. "...Is a healthy pitcher and this is not it. Why didn't you tell me sooner?"

"Because it's fine. I can get through the next three games, and if we win this series, we get a bye week. You can fuss over it then." Josh reached for the sleeve again but I stopped him.

"Three more games? You've maybe got half an inning left before this turns into something permanent," I warned.

"Drop the big brother bullshit," he scoffed and pushed my hand away.

"This is *'I'm a doctor and you're not'*, bullshit." I growled.

Dean was hovering and laughed at the joke making us both turn to scowl at him causing him to go dead silent. "Sometimes I forget you're brothers and then you do that..." He backed away slowly leaving space for Coach to come in.

"Give me the options," he said as he pulled off his hat and ran his fingers through his hair. "Mitchell, deck!" He hollered before I could say anything.

"He needs a break," I said, as Ella shuffled closer to hear the conversation. "If he keeps playing beyond today, he's going to seriously hurt himself and he'll be done for the season. You're working him too hard!" I snapped at Nick who was speaking in hushed tones with Reyes.

"Piece of shit," I grumbled under my breath and Ella gave me a soft tap on the shoulder.

"Let me tape it, talk to Coach," she offered and I pushed off my knees to give her space to work.

I stepped to the edge of the dugout with him where Arlo stood and Nick joined the conversation. "Did you know it was that bad?" I probed.

"I had no clue," Nick said, "he barely talks and when he does it's about baseball."

"His pitching elbow *is* baseball!" I snapped, trying to curb my anger. Out here Josh was just another player. And he wasn't wrong, Josh would have rather battled through every game than tell me that he was sore and that drove me up the wall for an entirely different reason. I looked over at him, eyes on the game while Ella carefully taped the muscle for some support.

Luckily this game was over, with Cael's grand slam we were up by three and last to bat. But it only put us up by two in the series, meaning we needed two more wins out of the three we had to play.

"You're going to have to prep Reyes. There's no way that Josh plays in these next few games." I looked away from my brother and scowled.

"He's going to fight it. Hard," Nick warned.

"You're the head pitching coach, don't be a pussy," Arlo snapped, his glare sharp. Nick groaned.

"I don't have to put up with this bullshit you know. This fucked up power dynamic, I have a hundred job offers in other cities." Nick's hand shook around the clipboard.

"They'd be lucky to have you," Arlo said, stepping forward, his anger getting the best of him. Coach pressed a hand to Arlo's chest with an icy glare, and Arlo's rage fizzled beneath the surface. They'd been at each other's throats more often lately, and I couldn't figure out why.. Maybe it was because I was failing to be a buffer between them but I just didn't have the time to manage their discontent.

"Enough, focus on the problem," I said, "Josh needs these games, but he'd be better off with the bye week. Can Reyes pull out the next two wins?" I asked.

Coach hesitated, looking at Arlo for answers which only made Nick angrier. I could feel the steam rolling off his shoulders between the four of us.

"He's going to need all the help he can get, but—"

No one pitches like Josh.

That was the unsaid consensus.

"Fine," Coach said. I could see the thoughts spinning behind his eyes. "We make up for the runs in the field. If a ball is hit, a ball is caught. There can't be a single error made." He wasn't really talking to us, more to himself, but we all listened intently to the plan.

I could feel Josh's stare burning a hole in my back.

"Break the news," Arlo snapped at Nick who looked like he wanted to put his fist through his face.

"If you're having an issue with the way I coach my pitchers, Arlo, speak up because throwing a hissy fit about it is incredibly unprofessional," Nick said.

Arlo stiffened. "What's unprofessional is you pushing these kids to a breaking point, like dad did to you and you did to me," he said, holding up his hand. The scars from his surgery had started to heal and fade but his pitching hand would never be the same. "Now you're killing another career, and for what? Revenge because you couldn't make it in the minors?"

The conversation was starting to get louder and as the game ended, players flooded into the dugout surrounding them when they all should have been celebrating the hard win.

"You get more and more like Dad every day," Arlo growled when Nick stepped forward trying to be tough, "Mom would be proud."

That was the snap. Nick flew across the divide and the two of them started to wrestle back and forth in a ball of angry words and violent fists. The dugout exploded with hollering as the brothers tossed each other around, Van shoved through the bodies wrapping himself around Nicholas until he was able to haul him backward off Arlo with one forceful heave.

"Get the fuck off my field!" Coach blocked his path and barked as Arlo stepped forward to attack his brother again. "Cool off," he warned, "we'll have a meeting tomorrow morning."

Ella took to checking over Arlo. "You can check him," she grumbled in passing and looked over my shoulder at Nicholas bleeding from the nose. *Christ.*

Players started moving around like normal after the fight died down and I shifted through the dugout to confirm Nicholas's nose wasn't broken.

"Why do you do that?" I asked him, feeling along the bridge for any abnormalities.

"He started that fight," Nick grunted when I hit a tender spot.

"No *you* did," I sighed, "he's your little brother stop being his number one enemy and have his back now and then, you're supposed to be a team," I said.

"Sorry I forgot you have six months of experience being a brother under your belt and now you're the authority on family dynamics," Nick huffed in anger.

"You're jealous and resentful, and you're acting like Arthur." I snapped my words and his nose back into place.

"He called me a pussy and I'm the resentful one?" Nick shoved me off and gave his sore nose a tiny wiggle.

"That fight wasn't about Josh's pitching schedule and you know it. Talk to him, and be an adult about it because Coach is getting pretty sick of these arguments and you know exactly who his favorite is." I warned as he walked away from me. "And for future reference Nicholas," I said before the dugout door slammed shut, he stopped to look at me once more, "I've always had brothers—Arlo, this team, Josh… and once, even you. So if you ever throw that in my face again I'll make sure you get to call in all those other great job opportunities."

Nick scoffed, a sick annoyed smirk forming on his face and suddenly I wish Arlo had hit him a little harder. He didn't say anything but he stared at me for a moment longer before finally letting the door close and disappearing, scurrying away like the cockroach he was.

When the dugout was finally empty I leaned over the padded banister and looked up at the stadium as everyone started to file out now that the game was finished. With the stadium quiet I finally inhaled, filling my chest with fresh air and slowing it back down to a normal pace.

I didn't even notice him return until he leaned on the bannister beside me.

"Are you okay?" Josh asked, his dark eyes looking up and out at the diamond.

"Yeah, sometimes I like to stand out here after the game in between that time when the laughter and cheering of drunk college students is fading and before the crew start cleaning away the cans and spilled popcorn. It's—"

"Quiet," Josh cut me off and nodded gently in understanding. "I'm screwed aren't I?" He asked after a long bout of silence.

"Not completely, but you're going to have to sit out the next few games and we're going to have to overhaul your therapy during the bye-week," I explained. "It's that or you play on Thursday and never play again. Your choice."

"Do you think it's that bad?" Josh asked. I could hear the concern beneath his typical stoic tone.

"I know it is," I said, finally looking over at him. "Just trust me?"

"I don't know," he smirked arrogantly, "of all the rumors about the Shores, everyone is adamant about never trusting one."

"Shut up," I said, shaking my head with a soft laugh. In moments like these it's nice because it's a small reminder that through all of the drama and all of gossip, I had gained a vital piece of family and repaired a relationship I never thought I would get to have.

I was grateful for Josh and our shared love of silence.

"I promised Dean that I'd help him study so…" Josh cleared his throat.

"Yeah of course, go," I said. "Hey," I called out to him. "When Nick breaks the news to you about Reyes starting, give him hell."

Josh smiled again. "I think I can manage that."

In his absence the stress of holding together our newly stitched together family seeped back in and gripped my bones too tightly to breathe. Drew hadn't called or showed up to the stadium and it was time I started to think of a Plan B of how to get my shares in the company from my Grandfather.

I'd come on too strong and scared her away, trying to fix everything without realizing some things just can't be fixed. I was trying to shove a square peg in a round hole and broke the toy in the process.

I waited a few more minutes, soaking in the quiet before the brooms started to sweep across the concrete and echo down onto the field. I wandered through the busy stadium and collected a few things, and my laptop in my backpack before making my way out to the parking lot. Pushing out in the open air, a chuckle left my lips at the sight of her leaning against her car in a pair of washed out jeans and a zip-up gray hoodie. Her hair was pulled up into a messy bundle at the top of her head and she looked tired but... pretty.

"I was starting to think I scared you off," I said, adjusting the strap on my bag.

"There's still time," Drew answered. The tension stretched between us and for a moment I thought she might still bail. Her body language was timid, closed off—it was clear she was terrified.

"Did you decide?" I asked her. She had to have come to give me an answer, I braced for the worst and waited until she mustered up the courage to speak again.

"Did you get it in writing?" she asked me as I moved closer and I nodded. It was brutal on my nervous system, having so much hope that she might actually be going along with the deal. "Auggie can't know," she repeated it from the day before.

"Our little secret," I said to her, stopping with a foot of space between us.

She stared at me, her massive green eyes a little watery but she stuck her hand out in front of her.

"Husband," she said.

The word rolled off her tongue and for a second I was almost the one to back away from the arrangement. It had taken a lot for her to make the decision. I could see it on her face, the way she squared her shoulders to meet my gaze and how she exhaled a slow, careful breath to steady herself.

I looked down at her hand, taking in how it trembled a little as I closed mine around hers. "Wife."

COURTNEY

August rolled over and cracked one eye open, catching me already staring at him. I was nervous to tell him, and I wasn't exactly sure how. He eyed me suspiciously before sitting up in the squeaky hotel bed.

"Why are you watching me sleep?" He asked me.

"Is a mother not allowed to lovingly watch her son?" I argued.

"Maybe when I was six it was endearing. Now it's kinda Norman Bates-coded," he said, the Psycho reference not lost on me.

Silas had told me that he could be available whenever to help us move into the apartment and he had written the address down in my notes app. He had been insistent about us doing it as soon as possible. Part of me felt bad because there was a good chance he was offering the rush service because he thought we were still sleeping in my car.

He'd written up the contract clearly, and we both signed it after I'd read it over.

We were never to be legally wed, just in show. I wasn't privy to any of his financials but if I needed anything he would provide. He had snuck in a condition that forbade me from paying rent which felt wrong until I remembered that I had a whole fifteen dollars in my wallet.

Lying to my thirteen-year-old made me feel sick, but it was to protect him, to give him a life he deserved and if I could just spend the next few weeks saving money when this was all over I could get us a real apartment and prove to him, to *myself* that I was capable of being a decent mother.

"Do you want to skip school today?" I blurted, sitting up in my own bed and chewing on my lip.

"Why?" He leaned forward, clearly very suspicious of me.

"You're a teenager, you're supposed to be excited to skip school," I said with a nervous laugh but August didn't break his judgmental stare. I didn't necessarily blame him, I had a poor track record for keeping him in school and even worse keeping him in one place. But it wasn't anything bad this time around. "I found us an apartment. We can move in today, if you want."

"Like a real place to stay?" August sat up straighter, suddenly much more interested in the morning conversation. "Permanently?"

"Yeah, Auggie. Permanently. It came with my new job, I'm working for the college baseball team in town." I nodded, and watched him flush with excitement. "I mean...we'll have a roommate for a while but just until I can find us something even better..."

"Anything is better than the car or this hotel. It smells like mold in here," he laughed but a smile formed on his face, one I hadn't seen in a long time. "Thanks Mom," he said softly and the sound of his surprised appreciation was enough to bring tears to my eyes.

"I'm going to shower," I said, my throat tight as I rose from the bed. I refused to cry in front of him, especially when he was so excited. "Get dressed and clean up your things, after breakfast we'll pick up the U-haul." While most of our belongings were in the car, we had managed to collect furniture along the way in hopes that one day we might actually find something more permanent.

"Burritos?" he asked, shuffling from the bed. I nodded before slipping into the bathroom and pressing my back against the door and rubbing my flat palm against my chest to keep my spiraling into a panic attack.

I inhaled slowly, filling my lungs with air on a count of four, holding it and releasing it with the same count. Trying to get a grip before I cried again.

Today wasn't for that, today would be good. It had to be, for August.

I gave him so much hope with such a domestic and mundane decision. Something a good parent would have provided from the start and yet, he was just thankful for a chance at a normal life, even just for a little while.

It broke my heart.

I triple checked the map on my phone as we pulled up to the massive iron gates that blocked the mouth of the driveway.

"Mom, that's not an apartment," August said, peering through the windshield at the massive manor at the top of the small hill. "That's a mansion."

"I'm not even sure this is the correct address," I scowled and flickered back to my note app again, seeing that it was correct. I chewed the inside of my cheek and flipped through my contacts, searching to see where Silas had put his number and called him.

"*Hello?*" he answered and I could hear people talking in the background.

"Shoot, are you at work?" I asked.

"*No, no...*" Silas said, he must have moved somewhere quieter because the chatter died down on his end. "*Are you here?*" he asked.

"I think?" I said, "you said it was an apartment but I'm staring at a massive house that looks like it belongs in a horror movie..."

"*Welcome to the Nest,*" he laughed, but I didn't get the joke and the awkwardness surged between us over the phone. "*I'll open the gate...*" He said after he had stopped nervously laughing.

The iron bars clicked open and swung inward leaving me room to enter, "thanks," I said, hanging up the phone and pulling the car up the driveway with the small U-haul attached to the back. Silas was standing on the porch in a hoodie, looking more casual than I'd ever seen him.

"Who is that?" August asked.

"My new boss," I sighed and cut the engine on the car. "And our new roommate."

"I regret skipping school to get murdered," August muttered, apprehensive.

"Be polite, Auggie. Keep the serial killer jokes to a minimum," I warned and climbed from the car.

"Sorry about the gate, we've had to keep it closed lately, usually it's a free for all..." Silas said, turning to look at August as he rounded the car and leaned against the hood. "You must be August." Silas stepped down off the porch and held out his hand for him.

I cleared my throat when August didn't move to shake it, "I'm sorry it's still pretty early for him…" I apologized with a nervous smile.

"The guys call me Doc, or…" Silas sighed, narrowing his eyes up into the sun, "Grandpa…"

That made August smile in amusement, a tiny echo of laughter tumbling from him. He pulled off his headphones and stared Silas down for another second and stuck his hand out finally, "Auggie," he said.

"I like that," Silas said with a nod. Thankfully one of us was comfortable in the situation because I could feel my skin crawling with the lie that I had told August and it was only making me feel worse.

I took a long quiet breath and forced a bigger smile when they looked over at me. "I know you said that the apartment was furnished but we had some things in the U-Haul and then I can work on finding storage…"

Silas clapped his hands together, "right yeah," he said, turning to look at the open door behind him. "Tour first? Then if you have heavy stuff I can get some of the guys to help."

"Guys?" I asked, I knew that he worked for the University but I hadn't actually dug much into the living situation. My only thought was getting August into a stable situation, not stopping to think that maybe my decision was brash and dangerous.

"Better to show you…" Silas laughed but I didn't find the humor in his surprise. "Follow me," he said.

August looked over at me nervously and I gave him a tiny smile of reassurance before wrapping my arm over his shoulder and leading him into the house.

"Holy crap," August said, audibly as surprised as I was. The house was all dark, polished hardwood and restored Victorian architecture.

"Wow," I gasped and Silas turned back to look at us.

"This is Dansby House," he said with a proud smile. "You'll hear the team call it the Nest, but before you panic, it's not a frat house."

He had taken the words right out of my mouth and I eyed him cautiously, a silent, *you're going to have to prove that statement* quickly passing between us.

"The only parties that happen here are in family birthdays and small celebrations, we don't keep booze in the house, and the guys are all pretty behaved give or take a few." He explained, showing us the massive living room stocked with a few nice couches and a massive television.

"How many players live here?" I asked him.

"Almost all of them," he answered. "But you won't even hear them. Between practice, therapy, classes and games... They keep pretty busy."

"Right," August said, "so we're moving into a dorm?"

"No, no," Silas said quickly, "my great grandfather and grandad had the house built years ago to give the team and staff housing away from the university. A couple of years back I had the basement converted. The apartment is downstairs. It has its own entrance."

"So you guys are rich?" August asked, and I felt my entire body turn to ice in embarrassment, but Silas just laughed.

"The fan favorite term is *stupid rich*," he said, smiling over his shoulder at us. "I just wanted you guys to be familiar with the main house. You're welcome to come up here whenever. The T.V. is bigger and usually Tucker has a stash of ice cream you can get into." He led us into the kitchen which was beautiful and somehow looked brand new but vintage all at once.

"This is the door to the apartment inside the house," he pointed to a door that I had assumed was a closet. "There's a door at the bottom that has a deadbolt so you never have to worry about anyone coming down there. To be honest sometimes I think they forget that I live downstairs..." he said with a smile.

"No we don't." A young blond kid wandered into the kitchen with a smile on his face that screamed trouble. "Cael Cody," he said, holding a hand out to me. "Who's this?" he asked.

"Drew... Courtney, and my son, August," I said, taking his hand. He looked over at August with a softer smile before leaning against the massive marble island in the middle of the kitchen.

"They're renting some of the rooms in the basement," Silas said.

"Strapped for cash, Grandpa?" Cael teased and Silas eyed him with an annoyed look. "I'm going to go find Dean and Josh. We're supposed to help Ella with something for Arlo's birthday tonight but they went missing an hour ago and I'm pretty sure they're—"

Silas cut him off. "Get!"

"Gone." Cael scurried away with a laugh, swiping a rogue hat off the hooks at the back door and disappearing.

"He's funny," August said when the door clicked over and I turned to look at him with a sigh.

"He's a big kid," Silas said, clicking the basement door open. "Come on, I'll show you downstairs before everyone gets home."

We followed him down to the basement and it was like stepping into a different world.

It was bright downstairs, the walls were painted a neutral color and the lights around the apartment were loud and all on. Upon entry there was a long, pristine gray and marble kitchen with running cabinet lighting and a massive steel fridge way too big for one man.

The living room was off to the right of it, with a huge modern but cozy looking sectional, covered in pillows with a television that barely looked smaller than the one on the main floor.

The floor was a lighter gray wood panelling that matched the color of the wall and turned the entire apartment into a stone box.

"Your rooms are back here," he said, leading us past the living room to a hallway, "Auggie, this is you."

"I get my own?" he said, looking at me and I nodded, watching the smile on his face grow with excitement. It had been a while since we could afford an apartment that provided him with his own space. The room was smaller but had a comfortable looking bed and was dressed in dark sheets and a red comforter.

I looked over my shoulder from the door as August made his way inside and set his backpack on the bed. I looked at Silas who was leaning on the wall behind me with a distant, proud look on his face.

"You too," he said, his gaze lingering.

He pointed to the room next to August's.

When I opened the door, it was immediately clear that this room was the master. It was massive and it smelled faintly of the cologne Silas was wearing. I stepped inside, taking in the king size bed and clean white comforter. The row of windows along the back wall looked out to the back of the house. There was a dresser with a small lamp and a fluffy rug that looked like it would tickle the bottom of my feet.

"The dresser is empty, there's a bathroom," he said, and stepped into the doorframe behind me. I inhaled at his proximity, his chest against my back as he leaned over and extended his arm to show me. "Over there."

I moved in the room just to create distance and ran my hand over the bed, the soft fabric so smooth under my fingertips. I turned as he wandered inside.

"I'm just down the hall. You'll barely even notice me."

"Thank you," I said and he nodded.

"Did you put my number in your phone?" he asked me, clearly a little lost in the conversation and feeling nervous about everything. I nodded and he gave me a satisfied hum. "There's a dinner for one of the coaches upstairs this evening. You and Auggie are more than welcome to come get some food."

"Mom!" August appeared in the doorway, his hair messy and his face full of excitement. "There's a projector screen in my room!"

I smiled at August. "That's incredible," I said, looking back to Silas as August returned to his room. "Really?"

"I swear it's always been there," he said. "Two days ago that was my home gym..." He smiled at me.

"You didn't," I sighed. "We could have shared."

"You're paying for two rooms," Silas countered. *I wasn't paying for anything*, I wanted to say but stayed quiet. "Just unpack, get comfortable... if there's anything you or Auggie want that isn't in the fridge there's a little notepad..." he started to back away, giving me some space to breathe, "on the fridge..."

"Got it," I said, with a nod.

"Dinner is at seven," he added, clapping his hand on the doorframe.

"Seven," I repeated back to him.

"If you need any help with the boxes..." he lingered, still staring at me as I shoved my hands into my pockets.

"I'll text," I said quietly. That was enough to finally send him on his way.

TRUE HONEY

I waited until I heard the click of the main door before turning back to the room and looking it over. I hated the sticky feeling of my guilt but as I walked back to check on August it subsided and a smile formed on my face seeing him unpacking his backpack into the side table drawers by his new bed.

One little lie, just to give him a home.

I could do this. If it got too intense, I could always explain to August what was happening, but until then I would let him have a moment of bliss after years of struggle.

SHORE

I set down the massive box on the island. "Did you order enough?" I asked Ella, who was arguing with Cael over how many chocolate chips belonged on the cupcakes as I returned from running a million errands for her.

"The guys are at practice which means they're going to come back here hungry and it's a party," Ella turned to me, tucking a few strands of blonde hair behind her ear. "It's Arlo's birthday…are you complaining right now?"

"Easy, Peachy," Cael teased, "Silas is just grouchy 'cause he's broke." He looked over his shoulder with mischief in those blue eyes.

"Wow, thank you for throwing me under the bus," I snapped at him.

"What does that mean? What's going on?" Ella cleaned her hands off on her cute little apron. I recognized it and my heart clenched a little at the old thing, it was Lorraine's, the leather neckties and heavy jean fabric embroidered with wildflowers. We had bought it for her a few Christmases ago.

"I'm not broke," I said, my eyes lifting to Cael as I helped Ella remove all the takeout containers from the boxes. She had ordered enough Italian food to feed the team twice over.

"Then what's with the pretty redhead roommate and her son?" Cael asked.

"Roommate?" Ella looked up at me, "out with it."

"It's just temporary, she was looking to rent a room and I had one," I shrugged trying to downplay it. Arlo's warning rang like a bell in my head: Don't give the terror twins anything to run with. "It's just a stray cat thing, promise."

My mind wandered to her face when she saw the room. How fast my heart was to betray my rational thoughts as her shoulders relaxed in that moment. Moving all my shit to the secondary guest room was worth the look of relief. I wanted to make sure she was close to her son but I hadn't expected to *feel* the wave of gratitude that poured from her at her realization.

"I don't believe you, but I also don't have the time to press you for more information," Ella said, not stopping as she emptied boxes into pretty bowls and serving dishes.

"Are you going to tell him you made all this?" I questioned, catching on to her plan.

"Yeah, and if you tell him, I'll sick Josh on you," Ella threatened.

"I'm not scared of—"

She silenced me with one sharp look from those fierce brown eyes.

"Secret is safe with me," I said, raising my hands in surrender. "Hey you don't mind if Drew and her son come up for dinner later?"

"Oh, she has a name?" Ella smirked and I rolled my eyes. "Of course they can," she said. "Even if you have them hidden away in your basement apartment."

"They're not hidden," I said, handing her another container. "They're unpacking."

"Where did you find her anyway?" Cael asked, tossing the empty bag of chocolate chips in the garbage under the sink. "She's not a student," he said, lifting his lanky body to the counter. He was wearing a cropped t-shirt that said *'don't bully me I'll cum'* and a pair of jeans that were more holes than fabric.

"Hilly's. She's the newest waitress, but she came in looking for a job with Susanna," I explained, snagging a piece of pasta from the bowl as Ella slid it across the counter.

"And you just happened to know she needed a place to stay?" Cael pushed and it was becoming increasingly hard to avoid getting the two of them involved. Arlo was going to kill me.

"I saw her car packed to the roof one night after Hilly's. It didn't sit right, so I invited her to rent the apartment." I backed away and crossed my arms, leaning against the door frame as the back door swung open and a few players piled in.

"Where do you want this El?" Dean asked, holding up a long piece of paper with the words *You're Old, Arlo* written across it in different colored paint. A Hornet staple.

"Do you guys make those with your eyes closed?" Ella asked, her face scrunching up in a funny way.

"What?" Dean looked down on it as Josh shuffled into the Nest behind him with an amused smile on his face. "I thought it was good... you said it looked good." He turned to Josh for help but my brother couldn't have cared less, he gave Dean a tiny shrug.

"I said it looked good for a toddler," Josh said, moving around the kitchen. He had gotten more comfortable at home, wearing t-shirts and sometimes even tank-tops that showed off the scarring on his arms and chest. I was proud of the progress he was making.

"Hang it up over there," Ella said, pointing to the archway over the dining room. "You—set the table," she told Cael. "And you—living room. Now."

All three boys turned fifteen and a course of ooooh's rang out in the kitchen as she shuffled me away from them. I rubbed my face in my hands and knew I was about to eat whatever Ella was going to tell me. Because that's what we did.

"If you think Arlo didn't tell me everything, *you're wrong.*" Her tone flipped so suddenly I flinched. "What the hell is wrong with you?" She reached out and pinched my arm when I didn't say anything.

"Hey!" I swatted her hand away, "listen," I said, backing away. "It was the only option."

"Making a deal with a stranger to be your wife *isn't* the only option!" Ella was working hard to keep her voice down. And her hands were balled at her sides in frustration. "Are you insane?"

"Do you and Arlo know that you're both playing bad cop?" I asked her with a tiny, exasperated laugh as I backed away and sank into the couch.

"I'm sorry," Ella said, inhaling slowly and wandering over to take the spot beside me. "It's just since I came to Harbor you've always been... you," she said. "You're not supposed to be the messy one. That's for all the other boys. Not *you*."

"I'm not a saint, El," I said. "I'm just a man."

"Exactly, you're a man and right now, with her moving into the basement, you are acting like an impulsive child. Do you really think you're going to fool everyone into thinking she's your fiance?" Ella asked me, her tone gentler than before as she crossed her legs and laid her hands in her lap.

"I only have to fool my mother and grandfather," I said.

"So you're going to tell the boys the truth?" She questioned and I sighed in response, "*exactly*, you know that Cael was already talking about setting up family movie nights for her son? He willingly went into the storage room to find a box of PG-13 DVDs."

"It's been like three hours..."

"He went into the storage room of his *own* accord." She stressed and I heard her loud and clear. Lorraine had died in that room and that fact Cael was willing to go into it after knowing a kid for ten minutes in an effort to make him feel comfortable. "Cael sees himself in that kid and if you let it go too far..."

"I promise to protect him but this is bigger than just the Nest..."

Ella scooted forward, forcing me to look at her, "If you believe this is the right way to protect Harbor from your Dad, then we have your back but I want you to be sure of it before you tangle so many strings because Silas," she swallowed tightly, pausing as the back door clicked open and more players flooded noisily into the house, "you're tying impossible knots."

I waited for a moment after she climbed off the couch, kissing my cheek before she went to wrangling hands to help her finish with decorating. I watched the chaos of the team shuffling around the kitchen, laughing and teasing, knowing deep down what I had to do to protect them, to preserve everything that we had built as a family.

"That's cheating," Cael said as he pushed his arm through Dean's legs to touch the blue circle with his left hand.

"How do you cheat at twister?" Josh asked, perched on the arm of the couch at a distance from the pretzel'd mess in the center of the living room.

"I don't know but I'm convinced Arlo has found a way," Cael whined, nearly losing his balance as Arlo wiggled his foot near Cael's.

I laughed as Ella spun the arrow again and out of the corner of my eye Drew's red hair appeared in the archway of the living room. I excused myself, going the long way around the hall and waving her down into the dining room.

"There's food here and drinks in the fridge," I said, as she approached with August on her tail. He looked to where I pointed and wandered away as Drew stepped into the dining room. "Did you get all settled?"

"There are a few things I need help lifting?" She said, "but other than that, yeah... thank you again for setting everything up for us so nicely. You really didn't have to do that."

"It's no big deal," I said, shaking my head. "Not to be pushy," I said, looking over her shoulder to August still exploring the fridge.

"But you need me to hold up my end of the deal?" She smiled gently, but it didn't reach her eyes.

"Yeah," I said, handing her a clean plate from the pile on the table. "There's dinner next Sunday, with my family... I'd like to introduce you."

She looked over her shoulder at her son and then back at me nervously, "I don't think I should leave him alone right now."

"I promise he'll be okay and if our agreement allowed for it, I would insist you bring him but I'm playing by your rules and unfortunately the timeline doesn't really afford any time for any of us to get comfortable with this situation," I explained as she spooned some pasta onto her plate.

"Do you think Auggie will be okay?" Drew asked with a small wince.

"He'll be fine," I said, "look," I nodded toward the kitchen where Ella and Cael had taken up conversation with August. They were laughing about something Cael had said and suddenly I was very glad that I had forced him to change his shirt before the party. "He's making friends already," I said.

"It would be nice if he made friends his age," Drew said, a smile creeping on her face that wasn't there before.

"Was that a joke?" I asked, leaning on the wall as she spooned pasta onto her plate.

She tossed a scowl over her shoulder at me and I couldn't help but enjoy the way it made all her features look less mousey. "I can ask them to be around on Saturday if it makes you more comfortable?"

"I wouldn't want to put them out..." Drew said.

"Hardly, Cael could honestly use a babysitter," I laughed and pushed off the wall. "Only problem we have is that you can't go to dinner in jeans."

Drew paused, looking down at her outfit and back up at me, "I'm a part time waitress, Silas. All I own are thrifted jeans," she said with an exhausted tone to her voice that she was desperately trying to hide beneath politeness.

"Well, you've got an obnoxiously rich fake fiancé now, so we'll need to upgrade your wardrobe for dinner," I said, lowering my voice and just trying not to hurt her feelings by tucking in the joke. "Mom will never believe it's real unless we prove you're way out of my league."

"Obnoxiously rich?" Drew almost laughed and I could taste the victory of chipping away a piece of her guarded exterior

"Ridiculously," I whispered.

COURTNEY

There was a small knock on the apartment door just after I got back from dropping August off at school. I wasn't scheduled at the stadium until tomorrow and was taking the day to get organized in our new space. I was dumping laundry into the washing machine and paused, not sure of what I was hearing but it came again.

I set the basket on the floor and wandered through the quiet apartment.

Popping the lock I opened the door to find the pretty blonde from the night before standing on the other side with two coffees in her hand and binder in her arms.

"I'm Ella and I'm here to help," she said sweetly, extending the coffee to me. "It's black but–"

"It's perfect, thank you," I stopped her, taking the coffee out of her hand and allowing her to come inside. I didn't have the heart to admit I preferred it with sugar and cream.

I'd drink it black simply because it would make her feel bad if I didn't.

"I've never been in here," she said, looking around curiously.

"Why *are* you here?" I asked nervously, setting the cup down on the long island that separated the kitchen and the living room.

"Oh!" Ella spun, setting her coffee down and holding out the binder to me.

"What's this?" I asked her.

"Everything." She said, sliding onto one of the stools. "To start, Silas told Arlo everything and because Arlo can't keep a secret to save his life. I also know."

"You know?" I raised an eyebrow at her, cautious to lead her into giving me answers because I couldn't be sure how much she knew and I wasn't going to be the one to spill any secrets I shouldn't.

Ella checked her watch. "Auggie doesn't come home for lunch, does he?" she asked and I shook my head. "Good, that gives us lots of time to study."

"I'm sorry, I'm so confused. What do you mean study?" I asked her, letting the binder fall open in my arms. There were at least forty pages, all neatly organized by tabs inside and it looked like a collection of information. On Silas...on everyone.

"Arlo likes to make binders, it's endearing. He put that together for you, and sent me to help." Ella explained and I inhaled sharply. "We know about the deal." She added, sipping on her coffee and making a disgusted face. "Oh, lies. This isn't mine," she switched our cups.

"Why?" I asked her, setting the binder down softly. It was open on a family photo, Silas, two older men and a woman that shared the same icy blue eyes as Silas.

Ella hummed gently before answering, "Silas is kind of important. To all of us, I think Arlo is nervous about the whole fake wife scenario so he's trying to protect his friend in the way he knows how. Which is helping."

I stared at her for a second, clearly underestimating how close Silas was to all these people. The binder was extensive. There were multiple pages on Silas, and one for each person close to him.

"It was his birthday last night?" I asked and she nodded. "And he stayed up doing this for Silas?"

I'd never experienced that kind of friendship.

To be so selfless in their actions for each other was a foreign concept to me.

"You'll figure it out," she smiled at me like I was supposed to understand what that meant. "Start at the beginning, read the page and I'll answer what I can. The hope is that if we can get you fluent in Silas then dinner next Sunday won't be so hard. They'll expect you to know all of this flawlessly. And Silas's mother, Sylwia. She's a wonderful woman, but all of Silas's intelligence came from her DNA. So she'll see right through you if you hesitate on anything." Ella set her coffee back down.

"Silas and Arlo have been friends that long?" I stared at the sheet.

"They're basically brothers," Ella said. "Josh came along after, I don't know the entire story but I know it was bad. Silas stepped up in a big way to get him out of the life that their father dumped him into. Josh has his days now, but Silas saved his life."

"The grumpy one with the curly hair? The one who keeps ten feet away from everyone?"

I asked, flipping the page to find his photo with a nod.

"He's got a bit of a thing about contact. Dean's the only one he really lets in, and even then, some days they argue like they don't love each other," Ella said with a smile.

"So Josh is Silas's half brother, and Dean is Josh's boyfriend?" I asked and she gave me a proud nod.

"Both will likely be around a lot so it's probably best to get to know them, they might be helpful if you ever find yourself cornered by Sylwia or Seymour." Ella laughed.

"Grandpa Shore? Like from the Godfather?" I teased gently, finding humor in it all.

"Exactly. I've only ever met him once at the Gala, but he's a scary old bastard and he means business," she said, flipping to the next page. "He's been around a long time, he's the reason the King family are legacy, he was Arthur King's mentor. And then every single King man followed that path right down to Arlo." She tapped the picture of a group of men arm in arm, smiling brightly. A combination of the Shore family, and the King. "He only wants what's best for Silas."

"By forcing him to get a wife, he doesn't want so he can take over the family business?" I questioned.

"It's not about the business for Silas," Ella said quickly, "it's about what the business does for the rest of Harbor. They have their hands in everything, especially the sports at the college. They don't just fund the baseball team. It's all of the teams. The majority of the money that goes into the Harbor Sports program is Shore money."

"Oh," I looked down at the binder again. All of this information was overwhelming but good to know. At first I thought Silas was just being greedy, thinking over the deal sitting in my bed wondering if I should take it just to help a rich man get richer. But it clearly was never about that, Silas just wanted to protect what he had built. "This is very generous, Ella."

"It's what we do," she responded easily.

"Did Silas really break his hand punching Arlo when they were fifteen?" I gasped at the sheet.

"I learned about that last night and you don't want the details," she said, shaking her head.

By the time we got through the entire book I felt like my brain was screaming for a break. The crash course on the Hornet family was endless. It felt like every page we flipped there were ten more to follow. Over the last two years their lives had drastically changed, mostly for the better but they had all gone through so much.

Ella had me fill out a small sheet to give Silas some insight on my past but I stared at the previous relationship part of her cute highlighted format in terror.

"I...Do I really need to tell him about that?" I chewed my lip and set down the pen. "My last relationship..."

"Why don't you tell me and I'll decide if Silas should know?" Ella offered, "I'm a little better at keeping secrets than Ar," she said with a cute nose scrunch.

"You promise not to judge, I don't know if I can really handle that today," I confessed and she shook her head gently.

"Trust me, if anyone here has a sordid past it's me." Ella leaned forward on the counter and tapped it with her finger nervously. "We talked about Cael, but the reason he and I got so close was because I'm also a recovering addict. A few years ago there was an accident, it killed my twin brother and my parents leaving me a guilt ridden orphan."

"Guilt ridden?" I asked.

"I was driving," Ella said and my heart broke for her.

"I'm sorry," I said, reaching out to tap her hand with the back of mine.

"I'm working on forgiving myself, so there's that. Now, what's so upsetting that you're afraid to tell him? Did you accidentally kill your last husband?" she asked, raising her eyebrow with a smile. "Did you kill him on purpose?"

"No, no," I chuckled softly, "nothing like that." Ella waited patiently for me to find my voice. "August's early years were difficult. I got diagnosed with postpartum depression and... my husband at the time wasn't equipped to deal with it. I barely was."

"You make it sound like he was a zookeeper, and you were an ornery lion." Ella stared at me, her brown eyes narrowing slightly. "Is that the worst of it? He never..."

"No, it was never physical like that. It was more... mental warfare," I sighed, rubbing my chest.

"I do that too," Ella noted, "it's hard when the one person who is supposed to be in your corner falters. But maybe give Silas a chance?"

"It's fake Ella, I don't have to give him anything. I just don't think it's relevant to *this*." I explained and she sighed, but nodded in understanding.

"I hear you," she said, "Silas isn't going to though." She shifted on her stool, standing like she was getting ready to leave. "He's a fixer, and a watcher. He'll figure it out before you can tell him—and sometimes fixing something without all the facts just makes it worse.. So when he eventually makes a mess of it, don't be too hard on him."

COURTNEY

"There's leftover pasta and some fruit in there," I said as he shoved the paper bag into his backpack. I tried to be one of those moms who left cute sticky note messages, but always chickened out last minute.

For the first time in a while August looked like he'd actually slept. He'd showered too, his hair was brushed back off his handsome face and he wasn't blocking me out with his music. I hadn't slept, I just couldn't find a comfortable spot in the bed so I'd gotten up and done laundry and unpacked the only box I kept of my own belongings.

"I'll be okay Mom," he said with a small smile.

"Have a better day," I said and he nodded before climbing from the car.

I was halfway to Hilly's for the day shift when my phone rang and the screen lit up with Silas's name.

"Hello," I said, shoving it between my shoulder and ear as I pulled over onto the side of the road.

"*Hey, can you meet me at the stadium?*" He asked, I could hear the chaos on the other end of the receiver as he shuffled around.

"I have work at Hilly's today." I put the car in park and waited.

"*I thought you quit that job?*" He asked, his voice muffled as the phone slipped.

"No…" I said quietly, I was secretly hoping to hang on to it. Since Kayla hadn't fired me and the tips were decent, given most of the town was University students. And if I screwed up with Silas who knows how long the part time gig with the stadium would last. I needed a back up.

"*Quit,*" he said. He wasn't exactly making it easy to take Ella's advice and trust that he'd do what was best for both of us.

"I need those hours," I said to him, knowing that his head was half in our conversation, half in another. I heard him mumble under his breath something about convincing me later before a door slammed in the background and the noise died out.

"*Call in sick today,*" he said, "*I wouldn't ask if it wasn't important that we go into the city and today is the best day for me to get away from the stadium.*"

I opened my mouth and then shut it again, it was part of the deal... I needed to be willing to help him out with his family stuff to keep the apartment space. I could see August's rested face and relaxed demeanor that morning and chewed on my lip. I couldn't screw this up, I needed to make it work for August.

"I'll be there soon," I said, hanging up the phone to call Kayla with my best fake cough.

She didn't seem too impressed but lately she was pretty over me, between breaking a plate of glasses, cutting myself and having the world's worst schedule. She couldn't be bothered in making my experience at Hilly's fun and I didn't blame her. I was a wet blanket even when I bothered to show up and do my job.

When I arrived at the stadium, Silas was in the parking lot pacing with his concentration on a very loud conversation he was having with someone. He wore a gray dress shirt, buttoned to the top, soaked down the back from the sun. But the moment he spotted me, his demeanor changed, a bright smile was pushed on his face and he shoved the phone into his pocket.

"Hey," he said as I climbed from my car.

"Everything alright?" I asked, trying to force myself into the Drew he had met that day at the bar. Funny, intelligent, sassy Drew with a hint of defiance. I had read about masking on my phone during the nights when I spent more time scrolling on my phone than sleeping. Realizing very quickly that it was something I had become good at without even trying to be.

"Yeah, fine...I'm just going to change and then we can go," he said, pointing to his bike.

Silas started to unbutton the shirt and hauled it over his shoulders. I tried to look somewhere else but he gave me very little time to try as he exposed the flexed muscles of his arms and torso. I hadn't given much thought to what was under all those dress shirts, but it definitely wasn't supposed to be all that toned muscle and sun-kissed skin.

For a doctor he sure got a lot of sun.

His eyes met mine and he let go of a tiny chuckle as a smirk formed on his lips and I could feel the heat rising up the back of my neck. He had caught me staring and I looked like a total idiot. He tossed the shirt over the seat of his bike and pulled a clean t-shirt out of the bag at his feet, pulling it down over his head before he quickly fixed his hair with his hands.

"Come on," he said, reaching around his bike and extending a helmet to me.

"Oh, you want me to get on that?" I pointed to the bike and shook my head. "Not a chance."

"I promise it's safe, I've been riding it my entire life," Silas said. I could see the assurance in his eyes but it still felt like a questionable decision.

"We can take my car," I suggested.

"No offence but your car looks more like a death trap than my bike," he said, his grin widening.

"Don't insult my car," I said quietly, tucking down into my hoodie and he laughed, putting both hands in the air.

"I'll admit it's because I'm not very good at being a passenger," he said.

"You a control freak? *No...*" I teased, not even sure where the statement had bubbled from but trying to hold on to the confidence that came with it.

"Unfortunately," he said, wetting his bottom lip.

"Those things terrify me," I confessed.

He stepped forward, a small smile on his face and nodded, "I think that's the first honest thing you've told me about yourself other than your name."

"Does it get me out of riding your death rocket?" I asked, swallowing tightly as he approached.

"No," he laughed. "Everyone is scared at first," he said, holding out the sleek black helmet in his hands. "But then the rush hits," his tone dropped an octave as he brushed the hair back off my shoulders gently tucking it back so it wouldn't get caught.

I was focusing too hard on holding my breath to protest.

"We have to be back by three so I can get Auggie," I warned.

"I promise I'll be safe and will return you to Harbor before three in one piece," he said before he helped me into the helmet.

I peered up at him through the open visor and tried to seem a little more relaxed but the reality was my heart was racing a million miles an hour and I was so scared I could feel the fear in the back of my throat.

Silas tapped my helmet with his hand and smiled knowing he had gotten his way. "One second," he laughed, backing away and scooping his backpack off the ground. He tossed it lazily into the window of a nearby mustang, reaching in to pop the trunk. He dug around in it for a second before finding a second helmet with a little grunt of pride and returned to throw his leg over the shiny black bike with ease.

Holding his hand out to me, I swallowed down the bile that rose in the back of my throat and climbed onto the back of the bike as he pulled on his own helmet.

"Make sure you lean with me, follow my body," he said.

"Now there are instructions?" I said nervously, trying to stop my hands from shaking.

"You have to hang on," he called over his shoulder, lifting his elbow and letting his fingers dangle, calling out to mine. "I don't bite, Drew," he added, sensing my hesitation.

I reached forward and he hooked his fingers into mine pulling me closer against his back and tucking my hand flat to his stomach. I mimicked the motion with the other hand and interlocked them as the bike rumbled to life.

"Hold on," he said over the sound of the engine. "*Tighter.*" He warned.

He didn't have to worry about that, the second the bike jolted forward my grip tightened around him and I pressed my helmet between his shoulder blades, screwing my eyes shut in fear. I could feel the soft laughter that shook his stomach. The wind whipped around us, filling the helmet with loud, white noise that was almost calming after I got over the initial stomach churning panic.

When I finally found the courage to lift my head we were coming down through the rush hour traffic that led into Lorette. The vibrations of the bike between my legs masked the shaking in my hands and I could feel myself relaxing enough to enjoy the drive. Silas was quick, but he was cautious and it showed in how smoothly he rode between cars.

Once we broke from the grid locked traffic he parked the bike and killed the engine. He slid off, pulling off his helmet and setting it on the seat in front of me.

"Give yourself a second. First rides can make your legs feel like rubber," he said, fixing the rogue pieces of hair that were messed up by the helmet.

I slowly got off, feeling the ground beneath my feet but he was right, my legs were still racked with the after vibrations and it took me a moment to get myself together enough to pull my helmet off.

Silas laughed as my hair came out even worse than his.

"Here," he said, stepping forward to take the helmet as I tried to comb out the helmet hair.

Once I got it to lay flat, I readjusted in my sweater and tried to calm down from the exciting start to the morning. The store he had parked in front of wasn't a clothing store but a jewellery store.

"No, we can tell people that it's getting sized," I stepped back from him.

"Absolutely not," he said, his jaw ticking. "You're going to go pick one out and we're going to tell *everyone* that will listen that I just know you so well that it was exactly what you wanted."

"That's a big lie, Silas. Weren't we trying to keep things simple?"

I said, trying not to hyperventilate from the added pressure. *If you lose a ring like that...* "What if I lose it?"

"You're not going to lose it," he said without hesitation. "And after this is done you can pawn it if you want, keep the cash."

That made me scowl.

"Or don't," he said, "I'm just trying to show you that the ring, the money, doesn't matter. I'm willing to sacrifice everything to make this work," he lowered his voice. "I *need* this to work."

"Fine," I said but only because the desperation in his voice was evident and it had an effortless way of sliding through the gaps in the wall that I had built around myself.

He looked elated that I had agreed to the ridiculous notion of a ring and he backed up toward the store. "This first, then shopping," he said, too excited about it for his own good.

The store was smaller and smelled overwhelming of polish. There was an older gentleman behind the counter who looked suspiciously happy to see Silas as he pulled out a box of rings from behind the counter.

"Mr. Shore," he said as we approached the counter and I shot Silas a nervous glare. He had planned this right down to having the man pick out a few rings I might like. There were three rows that contained five rings each ranging from large to larger and on to so ridiculous that I had to contain my overwhelmed laughter just seeing them.

"These are all too big," I whispered, turning my head into his shoulder so as not to offend the clerk. "What about something small, simple..."

Unexpectedly, Silas agreed and asked the gentleman to collect some other choices. When he disappeared down the glass display Silas turned his chin down to meet my eyes.

"Pick the one that suits you," he said gently. I opened my mouth to protest. "Do not pick one because you think it's cheap or costs less because it's small." His tone was stern but low and encouraging all at once. "I'll know."

When the man returned the rings he brought were much more reasonable in size. I stepped away from Silas who hadn't moved despite my sudden closeness and pressed against the glass display case.

The top row featured gold bands with simple, variously cut diamonds that were all similar in size but there was one in the center row that caught my eye. It was smaller than the rest in its row, a teardrop shape and shiny against the golden band. But it had two small diamonds inlaid resting against the thinner end of the teardrop. A trio of diamonds, perfectly welded together.

"That one," I said to Silas and he smiled, picking up the ring and holding it in his palm, probably just happy that I had chosen one that actually had some weight to it. Silas lifted it to my hand and slipped it over my finger while I desperately fought against the nauseous feeling in the pit of my stomach.

"What are the chances?" He asked when the ring fit perfectly. His eyes trained on my hand as I wiggled my finger around to test if it was loose but much to my surprise it wasn't.

Silas looked up at me and didn't say anything but I could feel him wanting to confirm that I was sure about my choice. *It's just a lie Drew, everything is constructed for show... A business deal.* If this was just business, why was my throat dry and my heart trying to break free from my chest?

I nodded and Silas took that as confirmation, leaving the ring on my finger, he turned and convinced the clerk to sell him the show piece instead of waiting two weeks for a brand new one. I couldn't tell the difference, it looked perfect to me.

I flexed my left hand and inhaled slowly, trying to steady my thoughts.

If you screw this up... I cleared my throat and shoved down the bile coming back into myself as Silas paid, not only for the ring but what sounded like other expensive pieces of jewelry I didn't need. He thanked the clerk and wrote down instructions of where to send the purchases before shuffling me back into the sun.

COURTNEY

"Are you alright?" he asked, his hand wrapping gently around my bicep.

"Yeah," I lied, my eyes still on the ring.

"Are you sure, we can take a break...shop later..." He started to pivot the plans we had set out and I stopped him.

"We have to be back in Harbor—"

"I didn't forget. That was just a lot and I'm checking to make sure that you're ready to handle more," he said to me.

I took a second to steady myself, breathing in and out trying to convince myself with each breath that I could pull this off, if not for me but for August. For our future. It was just shopping, with a rich doctor who'd probably never done a single thing wrong in his entire perfect life...

"I'm ready," I nodded.

He eyed me for a second, and in a pathetic attempt to distract myself I let my eyes wander over him as the sun highlighted the peppering of gray in his dark hair. The small scar on the right side of his forehead and the two patterns of freckles that danced across his jaw. I hadn't really noticed how attractive he was until I was knee-deep and overwhelmed by every little noise around me. It was like everything was muted outside the tight bubble that wrapped around us.

"Before we do this, two rules," he said, standing in front of me with his arms down at his sides and a serious look on his face. "One, you see something you like, you buy it. No arguments," he said and I opened my mouth to argue. "Don't immediately break rule one," he laughed, the lines around his eyes crinkling in response.

"It's just a lot to remember," I said, finding my voice even if it was quiet.

Silas's laughter faded into a smirk, "rule two, if you don't like something that they bring you, or suggest, don't take it just to make anyone feel better."

"Shouldn't I be looking for things your mother will like?" I asked him.

"No." Silas shook his head. I was slightly confused on what he wanted me to do, if impressing his mother was the answer to his problems then wouldn't he want me to dress for her? "My mother will see right through us if we pander to her, she's too smart for that. We have to elevate your voice, so pick what you want."

Ella's words echoed: *Silas gets all his intelligence from her.*

What if I didn't know what I wanted? What I liked? I thought, staring up at the massive glimmering store front. I wore jeans and old t-shirts every single day, the last time I had bought something off the rack was before I was pregnant with August. I'd lost whatever sense of style I had in the last thirteen years of mentally abusing myself and my body.

"Follow me," he said, reaching for the door and swinging it open for me. He led me inside, his hand warm and steady against my lower back as I navigated each shaky step. The store inside was just as expected, high ceilings and wooden beams all connected to give it a sleek yet warm aesthetic that should have been welcome. If not for the two women behind the counter, their expressions souring the moment they saw me.

A low groan left Silas and his hand left mine to dig into his jean pockets, he pulled out his wallet. Whipping it open as he wandered toward the staring women he pressed something to the counter loudly, making them both turn their heads.

"I'll get a drink," he said to them, looking back at me before he turned on them again, "and some manners," Silas added with a polite smile.

"Of course, Mr. Shore," the blonde said, scooping up what he set down on the counter before starting to boss the other woman around.

"You know they never stare at me for wearing jeans in here," he whispered with a funny look on his face as he returned to me. "Why are you still standing around, you have free reign." He circled me until his chest was against my back. "Champagne?" he asked with a grin.

I went to shake my head but stopped, looking up at him over my shoulder and shrugged. "Sure."

"On a school day? My little rebel," he laughed, the lines around his gray eyes crinkling. "Start looking, I'll be right back."

Silas left me standing in the middle of the store and I felt so overwhelmed for a moment that I could cry before one of the women appeared to my left.

"Are you shopping for an event?" She asked.

"A few I guess?" I said and her brow furrowed as her eyes darted to the heavy ring on my finger, drawing attention to the lie we were stringing. "I'm in town for the month meeting my fiancé's family before the wedding and the airline misplaced my entire suitcase."

"Oh that's the worst!" It was like her mood had flipped completely and suddenly she was sympathetic to my ratty jeans and faded hoodie. "Well let's get you out of these old things and find you some staple pieces before we get fancy with dresses..." she started to mumble as she walked away in a hurry. Lying to her was as easy as flirting for tips, muscle memory by now. *I could do this.*

"Everything good?" Silas returned, handing me a skinny glass filled with bubbles that tickled my nose when I brought up to my lips.

"Yeah she went to pull me stuff," I said, looking over at him. He looked impressed by my initiative and I couldn't help but feel a little more confident about myself as his stare softened and his lips curled into a smile.

She returned a little while later and led us to a private changing area with couches and change rooms with thick curtains and dimmer lighting. She had hung way too many clothes on the hook for me and took my glass from me before I could even finish, shutting the curtains in my face so I could start.

I stared at the hanging clothes not sure where to start and still in my jeans when Silas cleared his throat.

"You didn't die in there, did you? You got quiet," he said from just outside the curtain as his shoes appeared underneath it.

"Alive." The single word made him laugh but I was still terrified of everything in front of me and I could feel the panic starting to set in. *What if even after all these fancy clothes I'm still not good enough to convince his family?* I held my hand up in the small warm light and stared at the ring that weighed heavy on my finger.

"Are you dressed?" He asked, interrupting my anxiety attack.

"Yes."

The curtain flung open and he looked me up and down before his eyes raked over the hanging clothes.

"What's wrong?" he asked, and leaned against the frame of the dressing room.

I thought about lying to him but swallowed the fear and confessed.

"I'm overwhelmed," I said, and even though the words rolled off my tongue slowly and left a bad aftertaste in my mouth it felt good to say them out loud.

"Okay," he said, his eyes darting back and forth as he straightened out. "So, less options?" he asked, starting to rifle through the clothes. "Start slow..." he mumbled, taking most of them into his arms and backing away to drop them on the love seat. "Try those." He pointed to the clothes left hanging. Two pants and two blouses. "Better?"

I felt my pulse slow down, and my breathing returned to normal as I nodded at him. I wanted to say *thank you for helping* but all that came out was, "better."

He watched me for a moment longer, as if he didn't believe me, before finally sinking back onto the couch and letting me close the curtain again. In private I took a second to prepare myself before I stripped out of my clothes and pulled on the pants. They fit my hips like a glove and hung in a loose drape that pooled at the floor without shoes on. The first shirt was a glittery silver tank top that fit too loose around my neckline and made my skin look pale.

"Drew?" Silas's voice floated over the curtain and made me pause, "everything okay?"

I reached out to the curtain, thinking about drawing it back and stopped.

"I don't think I like this," I said, peeking out around the curtain instead. Silas leaned forward on his knees sipping on whatever was in his glass with a tight jaw. I don't even know why I told him that but something about Silas had turned me into something August would describe as a 'trauma dumping weirdo' and wasn't really a fan of it.

He set the glass down and looked at me with such a serious expression I could feel his encouragement from across the room. What I hadn't expected was for him to ask a question so simple that made me feel so complicated. "What don't you like about it?"

"Uh," I paused, looking down at the shirt and thought a little harder about it.

"There has to be something," Silas said as he rose from the couch, "and if it's the price tag..."

"I know, I know," I said, finally finding the courage to pull back the curtain the entire way.

"Oh," his lips parted as he took me in.

"It's bad," I sighed, wanting to cover up. To cross my arms over my exposed neckline, or to retreat back into my hoodie and never be seen again.

"Only because it's making you uncomfortable," he said, still rooted in place. "Not because you don't look amazing."

"It's too silver and there's not enough of it," I said, looking down at the way it wrapped around my stomach and clung weirdly in all the most exposing spots. "I feel like a busted-up can of sardines."

I wasn't used to being on such a display. I used bigger sizes to hide the body that I couldn't stand to look at anymore and now every single rigid curve of it was on display.

Silas chuckled.

"It's not funny," I said quietly and his smile dropped. He swiveled, looking at the piles of clothing he had laid on the love seat and started to shuffle things out of it. "What are you doing?"

"Removing anything silver or designed for someone half your age," he said, concentrating on the clothing inside of it. "What about this one?" He asked, holding up a dark blouse with cap sleeves and pretty shiny detailing around the collar.

"Yeah," I said, reaching out for it. His fingers brushed against mine as I took it and I could feel his eyes on my back as I retreated to the fitting room.

"For what it's worth, you'd put all the other tin cans to shame in that," he said as I closed the curtain.

I laughed under my breath as I slipped from the ugly tank top.

"I heard that laugh," he said, his voice muffled behind the curtain.

The new shirt fit better and covered more areas of my chest that I was uncomfortable with, so did all of the other shirts he continued to hand me. Eventually we weeded out anything that I didn't feel comfortable in and even found a few pieces that I genuinely liked including a few dresses that Silas insisted upon for the fancier events.

Once he'd set up the delivery he ushered me from the store, getting me something to eat quickly before promising to have me home to August by the time school was out.

He helped me with my helmet again, staring at me with a soft expression that didn't leave space for me to feel anything but seen. "You did really well today," he said with a smile before he shut the visor on his own helmet and climbed onto the bike.

I glanced at the ring again and nodded. Maybe I could pull this off. For August.

And maybe even for myself.

SHORE

I felt strangled by my own tie as I opened Drew's door and helped her out. Arlo had given me the mustang for the evening so that I didn't have to put her on the back of the bike in dress clothes. I didn't really see an issue with it, I rode the bike in a suit all the time...

Don't make her ride that bike in nice clothes, Silas. He'd warned me that if I so much as started the engine, he'd know, and then gave me the hundredth rendition of the Arlo King Mustang Monologue.

Drew looked up at the house, her green eyes wide with what could have been mistaken for wonder but was definitely terror. Her hair was pulled into a soft bun, a touch of makeup making her lashes impossibly long. The new clothes she had picked out had been delivered at the end of the week and she had picked a simple long sleeve black dress that hugged to her hips in the most distracting way.

I was going to tell her how wonderful she looked but Dean's Jeep rumbled over the gravel in the driveway and stole the sound from my lips. Josh climbed out of the passenger side in a sweater and his hair brushed back neatly off his face. He looked like he wanted to puke.

That made two of us.

Dean blazed over in a blue dress shirt barely containing his shoulders, his goofy grin as loud as his arrival.

"We haven't been properly introduced, I'm Dean," he said to Drew, knocking her from her trance. She smiled at him politely and shook his hand.

"Drew," she said.

Josh looked us both over before introducing himself and extending his hand to her. "I didn't know you were bringing anyone to dinner," he said, his eyes drifting down to the ring on Drew's hand. She'd taken it off the second we'd returned to Harbor, putting it away in a safe space until she was forced to wear it again.

"Didn't he say family only?" Josh questioned.

"You brought Dean," I said, quickly defending myself.

Josh's jaw ticked, his eyes darkening; he didn't have to say a word. He was violently protective of the safe space he had created and willing to ruin tonight early over it.

I didn't want to lie to him, not after all we had been through to get to a place where I could be honest but I also didn't expect him to lie *for me.*

"Okay, tough guy, grill him later," Dean said to Josh, his eyes trailing up to the living room window. My grandfather was standing in the window with a drink in hand and a scowl on his face. "I don't remember Seymour being so scary," was the last thing he said as the four of us climbed the stairs into the house.

Drew curled her hand into mine without asking, her smile sweet and eyes softening with each step. Logically I understood that she was putting on the show I had asked of her but the feeling of her hand in mine brought a small comfort as we wandered into the lion's den. Dinner tonight was going to be a shit show but at least I had her to keep me distracted. The stress of upholding a lie of that magnitude consumed all my thoughts and made it easier to focus on the current problem in front of me.

Getting the board to approve Grandpa's move to sign the shares over to me was all that mattered. The phone call I'd had with Dad earlier that day had proven every dark suspicion I'd had about his motives.

"I heard he's sick," Dad said from the other end of the shoddy phone call.

"Who told you?" I asked, mostly because I needed to know if there was someone leaking information.

"He did," Dad practically snarled, "just because I'm stuck in this concrete box doesn't mean my entire family has shunned me, Silas. He wants what's best for everyone."

What was best for everyone, was not best for my father. But for some reason he held on to the narrative that he was the victim in all of this. I had seen Josh's scars, there was only one victim here and if I could prevent more damage at the hand of my father I'd do anything.

"I'll be out in a few weeks and ready to take my position on the board. I'll need you to start running some interference with the press, force their hands and flip the story back on my side. We can say this was all a misunderstanding, that there was a disgruntled lower level employee who pinned it all on me. We have work to do with Harbor, it's time our town sparkles again," he was rambling as my heart raced in my chest angrily. "I've been speaking with a developer about getting a new stadium up, one with the capacity for a casino. We could be making so much more money on that team if we ran the gambling that flowed in and out of Harbor."

He wanted to...what? I swallowed tightly.

"You aren't getting those shares," I said bluntly, "and you aren't getting out of prison."

"Those shares are already mine, kiddo and there's not a damn thing you can do about it so if you want to keep living your cushy life as a second rate doctor at the University that I funded to hire you, then you're going to start following orders and get me the hell out of here." He threatened, his voice low and promising.

"You don't feel remorse for a single thing you did, do you?" I asked him, my mind wandering back to the images of Josh's apartment that were burned into my memory. The smell of his mother, the garbage... the locks on his bedroom door. The shame and guilt my mother felt every time she had to leave the house only to be hounded by the press about her adulterous husband. The way no one could enjoy anything anymore without it being tarnished by Charles Shore.

"I didn't do anything."

I hadn't even realized I stopped walking before we even got into the house, Drew paused beside me watching my face cautiously as I ran through the conversation again. Tonight was the most important step toward protecting everything we had built.

"Are you okay?" Drew asked me and it took me a moment but I nodded at her, another lie to add the mountain that was forming. She squeezed her hand in mine and I forced a weak smile to my face. I went to step inside the house but she stopped me, angling her small body in front of mine and letting go of my hand.

Her fingers fidgeted with my tie. She hesitated, clearly debating whether to say anything, then looked up at me and spoke.

"Two rules," she whispered just for me and I met her gaze. "Rule one, if you want to leave at any point tonight, we go. No questions asked," she said and I couldn't help the smile that curled on my lips.

"What if?" I said and she shook her head.

"Don't immediately break rule one," she mocked my voice and I chuckled, letting her continue. "Rule two, no more being mean to your brother to make yourself feel better. He's nervous too, his hands are shaking."

I wanted to tell her that it wasn't from nerves, but from touching her, but I wasn't about to dump ten years of trauma into her lap ten minutes before dinner.

"Seems someone has been doing their research," I said to her as she fixed the tension on my tie. The ring on her left hand glinted in the sunlight and reminded me what we were going through hell for.

"Ella is a very sweet girl and made me a study sheet," Drew said, "we spent a lovely morning together going over everything. I'm ready."

"She won't say a word," I said quickly, trying to head off whatever worry flickered behind her eyes.

"Is that better?" She asked me, ignoring the statement.

"*Better*," I said.

It was odd how quickly our anxieties mirrored each other and how the roles were reversed. I didn't feel like I was being strangled alive anymore so yeah, it was much better. I continuously forgot how observant she was, she had spotted me that day at Hilly's with such eloquence I should have been prepared for how smooth she could be when she actually got to know me.

"Are you ready?" she asked me, stepping back to admire her handiwork.

I took her hand again and led her inside the massive house, her eyes widened in shock as I took her through each room, showing her the history of a family that would soon be hers.

No, not hers. Not for real.

Josh was already being bored to death by business conversation that he wanted no part of but Seymour didn't give a shit what anyone wanted. He just liked to talk. Dean looked uncomfortable sitting on the sofa in the lounge holding two glasses of whiskey. I wandered over and took one off his hands.

"Seymour poured it for Josh even after he told him no," Dean said quietly, lifting his cup to his lips. It was no different than the last few dinners that Josh had joined me for, Seymour didn't believe anyone could be an alcoholic, let alone be a recovering one.

"Can you believe that I was gifted two grandsons and neither of them give two shits about the business?" He held up two shaky fingers with a scowl on his face as he exclaimed in dramatic fashion. "Are you going to introduce me, Silas?" he snapped at me and I turned to Drew who was all smiles for the old man.

"Seymour Shore." He held a hand out for her and Drew stepped into it, leaving me alone and feeling her absence like a tidal wave.

"Drew Courtney," she said sweetly, holding out her left hand for him. *Clever.* Grandfather's eyes flickered up from the ring to me and back to Drew.

"How much is he paying you?" he asked her.

"Seymour," Mother sounded appalled as she strutted into the lounge with a drink in her hand. "Where are your manners?"

"I'm dying," he said, like it was a reasonable excuse to be rude.

"Dying men can have manners," she scolded him.

Mom walked around the room, coming to me first, "Happy birthday, love." She wrapped her hands around my face and kissed my cheek. "You look nice, are you sleeping better?" She asked and I nodded.

I could see the surprise on Drew's face as Mom backed away. *It's your birthday?* It was written all over her face but she shook it off just as smoothly.

"Sylwia Shore." She offered Drew a hand. Technically she was in the progress of reclaiming her maiden name, Kott, but she had given me a speech about how it was easier to continue with her current introduction. It was less confusing, she said, but I could see the hurt on her face every time she was forced to use it.

"Drew," she said again. My mother held onto her hand, her eyes casting over to me in the same way my Grandfather's did.

"Interesting," she hummed, "it's beautiful."

"Silas deserves all the credit," Drew recovered quickly, straightening her shoulders and holding my mothers intense stare.

"I'm sure he does," Mother cooed with a knowing smile before turning to Josh. "You look handsome today," she said to him, and Josh nodded a quick thank you.

Their relationship was still weird, tense at moments but both were doing their best to adjust while working through their own issues caused by the same man. A rapture in our family that no one really knew how to handle.

"Dean," she said hello to him, her hand brushing his shoulder in passing. "Dinner is ready," she added.

Grandfather disappeared through the archway after her, leaving the four of us in limbo. Josh cut me a sharp look, his eyes demanding answers.

"Later," I said to him and the denial of any information in the moment infuriated him.

"This family loves secrets more than an alcoholic loves a brewery," Josh said, shaking his head angrily before starting to walk away from me but Dean stopped him with a flat palm to the chest and whispered something in his ear that made Josh's shoulders relax and his jaw unclench.

When the two of them disappeared into the dinning room without another word, I leaned my head back and dumped the remainder of the old whiskey down my throat in a single gulp. It warmed my chest and stomach but did nothing to help the anxiety that was coursing through my bloodstream.

I'd known going into tonight that it was going to be bumpy but I hadn't expected everyone to question my decision that loudly. Drew watched me, her hands folded together in front of her like she was trying to become smaller to give me space to be angry.

"I'm sorry," I apologized to her quickly, not wanting her to feel unsafe or uncomfortable just because I did.

"You didn't tell me it was your birthday. It wasn't in the binder," she murmured.

The hurt was evident.

"I'm not really big on it," I said, "we don't really do birthdays in my family."

"Everyone should do birthdays," she said softly, relaxing just slightly into the moment. She looked around me at the entrance to the dining room at the sound of Grandfather laughing loudly at something.

"When you want for nothing, birthdays are irrelevant, what do you get a man who has everything?" I said, mocking my father but feeling the serious implications behind his words. It had never been about not knowing what gift to buy, it had been about not wanting to put the effort into spending time with me. "Enough birthday talk," I said, forcing a smile to dodge the raw spot my childhood had left behind.

"Alright," she said, "we should go in before they notice we're whispering in the other room." It surprised me when she stepped forward and tucked her hands into the lapels of the jacket I was wearing, her face closer to mine in a strangely intimate way that made the breath catch in my throat. "Put your arms around me, Silas," she instructed. I listened, pressing the palms of my hands up her back and resting on her shoulder blades.

I could feel the heave of her breathing and in the momentary silence of everything, it slowed my heart rate as I mimicked her breaths and calmed down. I opened my mouth to thank her for being so kind but was cut off.

"Are you two joining us or?" Josh snapped from the archway and I looked over my shoulder with a nod. She had been putting on a show for him without a second thought.

It stung as she pulled away and left my mind screaming for her comfort.

It was just situational, I reminded myself.. If we were having the same conversation in the kitchen of the Nest none of the secondary stuff would have happened. I'd begged her to play the part, and she was nailing it, so well, in fact, she was starting to fool even me.

COURTNEY

D inner was an absolute shitshow.

Seymour spent the majority of it talking and ranting about business issues no one at the table truly understood and my mind was stuck on how sad Silas had looked talking about his birthday.

Birthdays are irrelevant, that's what he'd said. I didn't believe it. Birthday's should be celebrated, enjoyed. It's about surviving the year behind you and opening up the possibilities for the next year of life. Parties and presents were symbolic of wealth and happiness to come. Silas looked devastated, sitting at the end of the table with a solemn look on his face and when dessert was nothing more than a banana pudding I couldn't stop the feeling of sympathy that bubbled up.

During the brief moments where Seymour wasn't talking, Sylwia filled the space with questions about my life. How we met, how long we'd known each other, did I like baseball, where I'd been born? Each question got more personal than the last. She was digging, trying to catch me in a lie but it was buried so deep in my chest that she would never find it.

In the car on the ride home Silas turned to me, "tonight went terribly," he laughed, losing the tie around his neck.

"If anything, it tells me that we need to have an actual conversation," I said to him and his brows scrunched. "I don't know anything personal about you. The binder had everything except that. What if she'd asked your favorite color?" I said.

"Red," he answered quickly. "But don't tell anyone because they all think it's Harbor blue," he said, with a laugh. "Also what binder?"

"I'm serious," I said as he pulled the mustang into the garage, completely avoiding telling him that Ella and Arlo had given me a treasure chest of cheat codes. Cael was asleep on the couch when we wandered into the house and Ella was sitting at the island with a book.

"Hey you two, how did the night go?" she asked and Silas grimaced as he chucked his jacket on the island. "Well, we took Auggie for dinner and then to the stadium and he wore Cael out, both of them fell asleep a little while ago on the couch but we got Auggie to bed."

"You carried him down those stairs?" I said in surprise. I hadn't been able to carry August in years and he hadn't slept deep enough to even try. I smiled, picturing him happy.

"That would have been me." An enormous man with a shaggy brunet mullet that may or may have not been cut in the dark wandered through the kitchen. "Van Mitchell."

He held out his hand for me and I almost gave him my left before tucking it behind my back. I felt Silas slip the ring from my finger, shoving it in his pants pocket as I shook Van's hand.

"Is that short for anything?" I asked him.

"No," he chuckled, grabbing a bottle of water from the fridge. "Pretty sure my dad just named us by playing name association games. My sisters are Cosy and Guthrie, who my Dad lovingly calls *Gut*."

I giggled at the names, one being very girly and the other being very strange and Van shrugged, "I can't say anything, my son's name is Auggie."

"Weird names are cooler anyways," Van said. "He slept like a rock, I don't think I've seen Cael run that much in his entire career…"

"Trust me it's as much of a surprise that Auggie was participating in any type of exercise, he's more of a 'stars and music' kid," I said, it was nice to engage in a conversation that didn't feel like there were stakes involved. They were just genuinely curious about everything.

"He's cool," Van said, leaning over to kiss Ella on the head before excusing himself.

"I should get Cael upstairs, if we leave him on the couch, Jensen will have his hand in a bowl of hot water and we just got the pee smell out of the fabric from the last time that happened..." Ella said and at first I thought she was joking but Silas offered to help and I realized that it was an actual worry.

I kicked off my shoes as they left the kitchen and made my way downstairs and into my room to change. My mind was still processing everything that had gone on that evening, from the easy dismissal of his birthday to his family being less of family and more of a company. It felt cold and wrong. I tugged my hair out of the rigid bun it was wrapped into and let it fall over my shoulders before slipping into a tank top and pajama pants. I cleaned my face off, lingering on how sad Silas had looked and had a brilliant idea.

In the kitchen I found everything I needed to make pancakes and started to quietly put them together when Silas appeared in the doorway.

"What are you doing?" he asked me.

"Showing you how birthdays are done in our family," I said, whisking the batter.

He eyed me for a second before disappearing through the apartment to his room, when he returned twenty minutes later his hair was damp and he was wearing a t-shirt and shorts looking more casual then I'd seen him before.

"Can I help?" He asked, standing on the other side of the island.

"Pour us a drink?" I asked, it had been a while since I had one with an actual adult and I was so nervous at dinner that it wasn't even on my mind.

"Whiskey okay?" Silas asked, and sauntered over to the cabinet, unlocking it and grabbing a bottle.

"Perfect," I said. I set the plate of pancakes on the island between us and he poured two glasses.

"Does whiskey go with pancakes?" he asked me, sliding onto his elbow as he lifted the cup to his lips.

"Whiskey goes with everything," I argued gently. "Hold on," I said, leaving the kitchen to get something from my room. The pack of candles that had been in my purse for years was still going strong and I pulled one out before bringing it back to the kitchen. "Red," I said, shoving the candle into the stack of pancakes.

He stared at the candle as I lit it, his expression softening as his lips formed a tight line.

"Happy birthday, Silas," I said to him, raising my glass to him but his eyes were fixated on the flame. "Blow it out, make a wish."

I could see the gears turning in the back of his mind as the wax started to melt, he had too much on his mind and for once we were on the same page. Eventually he blew it out and gave me a soft smile.

"What did you wish for?" I asked him.

"If I tell you, it won't come true," he said, grabbing a fork from the island.

"I didn't think you were actually superstitious," I said, following his movements and taking a piece of pancake. They were perfect, fluffy and warm.

"A man has to believe in something." He chased his pancake with whiskey. "You know... it kind of works," he said, surprised, then laughed.

"Told you," I said.

"I don't think I've ever met anyone that celebrates with pancakes," he said to me, eating more. His gray eyes watched me as I sank lower onto the island across from him and sighed.

"Wherever we were, there was always a shitty diner about a mile away and over time, pancakes became our birthday cake..." I said, remembering all the birthdays we'd spent in different colored booths on the side of the highway laughing and singing together.

It was the fondest memory I had of our relationship. It was the one time I never felt like I wasn't doing enough, because as long as August had a song and pancakes, he felt loved.

"I think the last time we celebrated my birthday I was eleven and Dad took all of us to a baseball game..." Silas said, clearly remembering details about the day that weren't as fond as the ones I'd recalled. "It was a Lorette game," he scoffed, his jaw tightening. "He disappeared half way through and never came back. The Longhorns won that game."

"How young was Josh?" I asked him and he flinched.

"Can I see the notes that Ella gave you?" he asked me instead of answering. I pushed away from the islands to grab them for him. "This isn't notes, this is a textbook!" He took the binder and squinted at it for a second before cursing under his breath.

"Do not laugh at me," he warned, reaching for something in his backpack on the floor. When he returned he was wearing a slim pair of dark reading glasses that highlighted the blue in his gray eyes and made his face look sharper.

I choked back a laugh, and he narrowed his eyes.

"Sorry," I said, raising my hands in surrender. "I know why they call you Grandpa now," I teased and he shook his head at me.

"None of them know about these," he said. "It would only be worse if they did."

"You look cute," I offered him the compliment, "very... studious."

"Cute?" Silas scoffed, "great now I'm blind and *cute*. Oh how the mighty have fallen."

"You're a year older too. Blind, cute, and officially old," I whispered and he dropped the paper completely baffled by my teasing.

"Kick a man while he's down, why don't you?" He joked, reading the paper over, his expression turned sour, "she gave you the polite SparkNotes, which I appreciate but—"

"But?" I waited.

"First of all, Arlo wrote these. The part about Josh is correct but he left out most of the details," Silas said. "Our father is in jail for a handful of pretty shitty crimes."

"Same Dad?" I asked. It would explain how uncomfortable his Mother had been at dinner, sitting next to her husband's love child couldn't have been the easiest thing to do in the world. But they all seemed friendly enough, so it must have been a work in progress.

"Josh's mom passed in the spring, but my dad kept them a secret until recently. I had no idea I had a brother living half an hour from me my entire life," Silas explained and the room went cold.

"I'm sorry," I said instinctually, reaching across the island to touch his hand.

"I gained a brother," he said like it was the only fact that mattered in the moment. And maybe he was right to feel that way. From the sounds of it their father was at home in jail and for the better of everyone.

"You're very much a glass half full person, aren't you?" I asked him.

"Maybe," he poured more whiskey for us. "Maybe I just firmly believe that everything has a solution and every bad day has a matching good one."

I thought on that for a moment, the idea that bad days weren't lonely, just separated from their good days. "Like soulmates?"

"Sure," he said, "not everyone can be everything all the time, everyone needs help during the lowest times. Bad days just need a good day." He downed the next glass of whiskey faster than the first and sighed.

"Do you have anyone?" he asked quietly.

"August," I said.

"What about his dad?" Silas asked and I should have expected it but it surfaced those feelings I constantly tried to repress.

"I haven't really spoken to him since Auggie was ten, we have conversations here and there," I confessed. "*If* he calls, it's for his son."

Silas's jaw tightened but he nodded his head. A man who was working through his own father's troubles could see the harm in near and far phone calls. It didn't bother me that August's father was like that, when he did call he only ever made August feel inferior or weird about his interests. It was always a harsh conversation about what August should be doing and never about what he enjoyed doing.

Sometimes when he would call, I'd ignore it on purpose just to save August the soul sucking disappointment of remembering his father was a misogynistic asshole.

"Are you in legal trouble is that why—"

"No," I cut him off before he could say anything else. "It's nothing like that, we were just better off without a man like that in our lives even if it meant moving around and living in a car."

"Well you're out of the car now," Silas said.

"For now," I corrected him. "But now it won't be so difficult to save up for a proper place for us. So," I paused, not meaning the conversation to get so tender, "thank you."

"You're welcome," he said, pouring me more whiskey. "I guess if you have a study sheet about me, I should have one about you?"

"What do you want to know?" I said, standing up straight and waiting for his first ask. I'd rather answer myself then look at the sheet Ella had me fill out anyways.

"You know my favorite color," he said.

"You mentioned something about Harbor blue," I said and his lips curled at the corners of his mouth making the lines around his eyes crinkle. I could tell he wasn't entirely comfortable in his glasses but they highlighted all the most handsome features of his face.

Maybe it was the whiskey, or just the quiet ease of the moment, the first of which neither of us were trying to convince the other of something. But I took notice now. In the way his top lip was a perfect, muted pink cupid's bow, hidden beneath an old shave and his cheekbones were sculpted high but rounded in pleasure when he smiled. Sun spots and freckles showed his age worse than the glasses but he had a handsome, kind face that made it easy to get comfortable around. And that wasn't something I took lightly.

I took the empty plate and set it in the sink with all the other dirty dishes, giving myself a chance to cool down and allowing my cheeks to return to their normal pale color.

"Green," I said, turning around and leaning against the counter.

Silas was standing up straight and removed his glasses, setting them on the counter. "Like your eyes?" He said, sparking something that had long died inside of me and the collection of the whiskey in the pit of my stomach started a fire.

"Like Granny Smith apples," I corrected him and he nodded.

"Are they your favorite food?" He asked, circling the counter and grabbing the bottle of whiskey by the neck, pouring more into my empty cup.

"Pickles," I said, almost embarrassed to admit it.

"Pickles?" Silas laughed, he didn't move away after pouring my drink and I could smell the whiskey and syrup on his breath.

"Plain, garlic, baby, fried..." I said, my lips curling up into a smile. "I'd eat pickles three meals a day and be perfectly happy."

"Very classy," he said, taking another drink before setting the bottle on the counter next to me.

"Alright, my turn. You take care of athletes, you seem to have a soft spot for the ones upstairs, but did you play baseball too?" I asked him, taking another sip. The whiskey went down better than hours spent studying.

"I've been playing since I could run," Silas said. "Our family has interests and investments all over Harbor but my Grandfather only has one love and it's the Hornets. I played five years with them, had the opportunity to go professional out of high school, but as nerdy as I sound, I wanted education."

"Playing baseball your entire life left you stuck under your family's thumb," I said with a nod. I didn't understand the pressure he was under but I could sympathize with the feelings of letting someone down. I had been on that pedestal before, the fall sucks.

"I watched baseball tear the King family apart, I never wanted that life. I wanted to be able to fix stuff, hold people together, and create spaces where they felt safe." Silas explained and I was slowly starting to understand him a little more. "What did you do before August was born?" He asked.

I hadn't been asked that in a long time, and for a split second I almost couldn't remember and then it came back in a strange, emotional wave that threatened to wash away all the walls that kept the darkness at bay.

"I taught art at an elementary school," I said. "Easily the worst age group to teach art to."

Silas chuckled. "Do you ever think about doing that again?"

I shook my head. "They've got more requirements for teachers now, my education wouldn't get me hired. I never really wanted to do that, it was just a way to gain some independence in my life."

His cautious approach to asking questions was twisting all my coherent thoughts and I knew that the whiskey was partially to blame, but I didn't want him to stop.

COURTNEY

"Do you like music?" He asked as I was focusing on the drying strands of dark hair and the tingling sensation in my fingertips. "You must get through a lot in the car," Silas said.

I shook my head gently. "Podcasts. We like crime podcasts. Well *I* do. If August had his way he'd be buried with his headphones. He likes it loud," I said.

"When I was his age," Silas smiled, wetting his bottom lip as he leaned in, "I did too. It was the only thing that got me through studying. That and the lemon potatoes from the university cafeteria."

"Is that your favorite food?" I asked him, squeezing my glass to keep my hands from shaking. It had been a while since I'd drank and I was quickly being reminded of my tolerance. I felt flirty and unburdened by my anxiety for the first time in years. It helped that Silas smelled like mint and sunshine, a mix of outdoors and something fresh.

It tickled my nose and made my head fuzzier than it already was.

"I think it was what kept the twenty-year-old me alive for about ten years…" Silas's chest vibrated with a soft laugh. "If I had to pick it would be sour straws."

"That is the favorite food of a child," I said, lifting the glass to my lips.

"Hey, I didn't judge your pickles," he feigned offence.

"Pickles have nutrients," I argued, my brows coming together in the center and my jaw tightening.

Silas inhaled, his chest rising slowly as he lifted his finger to rub the space between my brows to smooth out the frown lines. He stopped when his eyes met mine and retreated with a soft sorry from his lips.

"Can I blame the whiskey?" He asked, but he didn't move away.

"Do you want to?" I countered.

"Do you always answer a question with a question?" He asked, reaching for the whiskey again. He had forgone the glass and was just sipping from the bottle, his lips damp as he pulled it away.

"Only when that question has serious implications and goes against our business agreement," I giggled and a small hiccup of whiskey rose in my throat faster than I could get my hand over my mouth. "Sorry."

"Is this alright?" Was his next question.

"The game of twenty questions?" I asked quietly, never breaking eye contact with him.

"The flirting?" He corrected, his jaw tightening as his eyes flickered across my face leaving a trail of heat from his gaze.

"Are we flirting?" I asked him.

He offered me a tiny huff, his eyes gleaming with genuine interest, "the whiskey isn't doing me any favors but I could have sworn you were flirting with me."

"Oh it was definitely the whiskey," I said and lifted what was left in my glass to my lips.

Silas watched me down the last of my whiskey, his Adam's apple bobbing as he swallowed, a slow smile spreading across his face. "Mm, so it was just liquid courage?" He stepped forward, his leg resting between my thighs. "No actual interest in this old man?"

That made me giggle. "It was the glasses," I teased. "Total turn off." I looked around the apartment, feeling too warm under his gaze.

"Right," Silas chuckled and it caused the muscle in his stomach to tighten with laughter. When he caught me staring, his smile only grew more smug. "So no chance you'd find an attractive, successful, charming, recently turned thirty-five, old man appealing?"

I shook my head slowly, the lie seeping out of me in the form of a smirk that gave away how quickly I was becoming wrapped around his finger. How a simple birthday gesture had blurred lines so quickly. It was only half a bottle of whiskey... I turned my head down between us to hide the blush creeping to my cheeks.

Silas towered over me, reaching out and gently tilted my chin up with his index finger, forcing me to meet his intense gaze. "Liar," he said softly, his thumb brushing over my bottom lip.

I opened my mouth to stop him but accidentally ended up leaning further into his touch. It had been a long time since I felt at peace enough for a man to touch me. And sure it was the whiskey making the world hazy and my decisions easy but Silas was right there, begging me to at least try.

His eyes softened, catching the flicker of vulnerability I hadn't meant to show.

He leaned in and lowered his voice when he asked, "how long has it been?"

His thumb continued to gently bug my bottom lip, his touch both comforting and electrifying. I wanted more and knew I shouldn't all at the same time.

"Since what?" I asked, inhaling a slow, steady breath.

"Since someone touched you like this?" he asked. "Gently. *Intentionally.*"

So much for that steady breath, it caught in my throat, sticky and hot as his hand moved to my waist. He left space for me to pull away if that's what I wanted but his fingers grazed the top of my pants and seared a wanting impression on my skin.

"You can blame your honesty on the whiskey," he urged when I didn't answer right away.

How long had it been exactly, there had only been August's father, before and after but...

"Since before Auggie was born," I whispered, the idea of having not been touched in nearly twelve years sinking in and spreading across my chest like a rash. Between taking care of my son and my own crumbling mental health, I hadn't slowed down enough to have a moment like the one Silas and I were sharing.

His eyes widened slightly, taken aback by the admission. I can see him doing the math in his head, quickly coming to the same conclusion I had. It had been over a decade since I'd been intimate with anyone. Silas's hand tightened on my hip, wrapping his other hand around my waist. There was no escaping anymore.

"No one? Not even a kiss?" He asked.

"Maybe a few misplaced ones from my ex-husband," I huffed, "but nothing of substance or importance," I said, the last word lingering on my lips as I worked to hide my shame over the matter. A grown woman who hadn't been kissed in that decade, with three drinks in her and ready to make another string of mistakes.

Silas's expression became unusually tender, almost protective in nature as his lips pressed into a line and his fingers traced my jawline. "Here I am an idiot who never thinks twice about physical touch." He chuckled. "If the whiskey is being honest... I get whiny after a week, but you..." He paused, his words coming softer, slower. "You're starved for it."

"You're making me sound pathetic," I said quietly, wrapping my hand around his wrist to stop his trailing touch. It was too warm and made me feel too many emotions that I couldn't control.

Silas shook his head, his eyes never leaving mine. "Not pathetic. *Neglected*. There's a difference." He paused, his thumb tracing small circles on my jaw. "While we're blurring lines, I'm going to say this and whether or not you remember it or choose to acknowledge it is fine, you won't hurt my feelings. I know what this is between us, but Drew," he sighed. "You deserve to be touched, to be wanted. It's nothing to be ashamed of."

I was still stuck on *neglected*. The word echoed around in my head, dancing with the hazy lines of amber and warm glimmering lust that clouded my judgement. *By my ex, by myself.* He had unintentionally hit the nail on the head and I didn't know how to respond.

"Now I know for sure the whiskey is talking," I said instead, shoving away the absolute despair over unresolved trauma.

Silas leaned in closer, his forehead almost touching mine. His breath was warm against my already hot face as he spoke softly, "maybe the whiskey is wise then. Because sometimes it takes being a little tipsy to speak the truth we soberly ignore. And in the spirit of drunk words and sober thoughts, I've been ignoring a certain string of ideas since the day I met you."

"A doctor and a philosopher," I whispered, the teasing tone dying from my voice the closer he got.

"Just a man," Silas lowered his voice to a husky purr, pulling his hand back to tangle with mine as his eyes locked on me. "One who wants to touch you, Drew, even though I know I shouldn't. Not like this, not when you're drunk and vulnerable."

"I'm hardly drunk," I said, even though I could feel the heat from the whiskey coursing through my veins, *just enough to do something stupid.*

His eyes flickered to my lips, his self-control visibly wavering. "Tipsy enough to do something you might regret tomorrow?" He challenged softly like he could read my mind, his thumb returning to my lip. "Or tipsy enough to finally give in to something you've been denying yourself for too long."

"Let's pretend it's the first and you stop asking dumb questions?" I whispered under my breath.

My heart was racing but I didn't give a second thought to what it might mean come morning. Heat pooled between my thighs and my mind was consumed by the idea of his perfect, charming mouth touching me there.

Silas's breath caught sharply, clearly ready for either answer. The last thread of his restraint snapped.

"Fuck it," he muttered before his lip crashed against mine in a searing kiss. His hands framed my face as he kissed me, turning it deep and pouring hours of pent up desire into that one moment.

I wrapped my arms around his neck, lifting into him and tying my legs around his waist. The kiss was warm and frantic—tasting like whiskey and bad decisions, but feeling like flying. Every other bad thought faded to black as he carried me through the apartment to his room.

He kicked the bedroom shut behind us, his lips never breaking from mine. Silas's hands gripped my hips tightly as he walked us backward towards the bed, his body pressing against mine. He only broke the kiss to trail hot, open mounted kissed down my neck, his stubble rough against my sensitive skin.

I swallowed tightly, ignoring the thoughts of being incapable of feeling so wanted after so long. I shoved away the sadness and self doubt of never being enough. It was easier that way to banish my past to the confines of the locked doors within my shattered confidence. Away from anywhere that they could destroy the good that had recently flooded into the cracks.

I reached down, playing at the hem of his shirt before I pulled it over his torso.

Silas hummed as my fingers traced the lines of his abs, helping me lift his shirt off completely. He was in insane shape, years of baseball training clearly evident on his lean, toned body. His eyes darkened as he watched me drag my bottom lip between my teeth, tipsy with desire.

I wiggled back on the bed and leaned up on my elbows to watch him. His pants were low on his hips and showed off the hard lines that led beneath. Silas slowly hooked his fingers into the waistband of his pants, dragging them down inch by inch, revealing his toned stomach and v-shaped muscles that lead lower. My eyes trailed over him, admiring the large, dark raven tattoo that stained his muscular thigh. My mouth went dry as his fingers curled into his boxers.

"You can still say no, you know, there's nothing wrong with a drunk make out and stopping before we go too far," he said, gently pushing his boxers down slowly. His length popped free, long and thick, curving slightly upward. Silas watched my every reaction, his voice lowering, "Drew," he breathed. "Tell me what you want."

"I want you to cross some lines," I whispered, arching off the bed, my hips raising toward him.

A low groan escaped him at the request, his pupils dilating with lust. Without hesitation he crawled over me, getting between my parted thighs. His hands slid under my shirt, pushing it up and exposing my stomach. I was grateful for the darkness of his room, I wasn't sure how he would react to a body that had never once been taken care of. But those were the thoughts of a terrified woman who hadn't been touched since her body was stretched and misshapen by pregnancy and life.

The woman in his bed, writhing from his touch was confident and brazen, she was fueled by whiskey and want. I inhaled a shaky breath as his lips brushed against my skin.

"So responsive." The words tumbled out of him like a chuckle against my stomach as his hands spread out on my sides and he painted open-mouthed kisses up my torso. He paused at the bottom of my bra, looking up at me through his lashes and smiled. "Lift up for me?"

I listened, lifting my hips from the bed to give him room to slide the waistband of my pants over my hips along with my underwear. He tossed them aside, leaving me bared to him in just my messed shirt and bra. I lifted from the bed, pulling off my shirt with haste as Silas spread my thighs wider, settling between them as he hooked his fingers into the strap of my bra and pushing it down over my shoulder. He revealed my breast little by little, his hand roaming my ribcage possessively as he lowered further exposing the swell.

Silas paused again, looking up at me with intense eyes.

"I just need to get it out of my system," I whispered to him, pushing my hand into his hair, begging him to stop looking at me like that. "I need to let go."

His expression softened from my words, understanding flickering in them as he leaned down and captured my exposed nipple between his lips. His fingers dug into my side as he sucked firmly, dragging a loud gasp from my lips. Silas growled approvingly against my breast as my hips ground against him. The friction was exquisite torture and it took everything in me not to let him know just how tortuous. His hands slid around to grip my ass, pulling me harder against his straining erection as he released my nipple with a wet pop.

In seconds, he reached for the bedside drawer and a small foil package is between his teeth ripping it open and sliding the condom over his shaft with the precision of a man that's done it a hundred times. I had to shove away the twang of jealousy that bubbled up at the thought of other women in his bed, this was temporary... just a release.

Silas's eyes met mine with wild, lust blown pupils. A devilish grin spread across his face as he shifted his weight, positioning himself more firmly between my thighs. He reached down between us, dragging his knuckle against my hot skin before guiding himself toward my entrance.

I could see the hesitation on his face, "no more thinking," I said as he paused in thought. "No more talking," I demanded, rolling up against him, desperate for more. Needing it to chase away the shadows.

With a shuddering curse Silas broke free of the last threads of his restraint at the needy rolling of my hips against his. He gripped my hips tightly and slid himself inside me with one powerful thrust. A guttural moan tore from his throat at the connection and I pressed myself deeper into the mattress as he rubbed against every wall.

My whole body shuddered from the intrusion, pulsing around him as I melted away from the world and into the euphoria of how it felt to be adored.

Silas began to move, setting a fast pace that made the bedframe shake beneath us. His hand roamed my body possessively, squeezing my breast and gripping my thighs. His fingertips were rough and dangerously warm against my skin, they'd leave marks in their wake and I didn't give a shit. It felt so fucking good.

His movements became more frenzied, lost in the sensation he finally let himself go. He leaned down to capture my lips in a hot kiss, swallowing the pathetic cries that split from them. Silas's hand slipped between our bodies, finding my swollen clit and rubbing in tight circles, determined to push me over the edge.

I let him take me, it felt good and for once nothing could touch me.

It was just him and me, tangled together as the world became numb and my body exploded with fireworks lighting up the space between us in the form of moans and panting breath. It was like he could feel me letting go completely, my body tensing and then releasing waves around his shaft. It was too much, too good. His teeth were on my skin, stifling his own moans as he chased his own release over the edge.

I met him halfway, raking my nails down his back, melting into every relentless thrust, as the orgasm wracked through my body like a tidal wave. My orgasm set off his, and he buried his face in my neck, groaning loudly as he followed me into the abyss.

Silas collapsed against me, wrapping his arms around my back and pulling me into him as his mouth left a trail of warm kisses over my sweaty skin. I closed my eyes to block out the way the room was spinning. I wasn't that drunk, but the mixture of the mind blowing orgasm and the whiskey, I wasn't even sure I could figure out which way was up.

I don't even know if I cared which way was up.

Just a man.

Silas was more than just a man.

I bit down on my lip as a tiny shudder rippled through me and I fought to control my racing heart. Traitorous and loud, it demanded more. I barely noticed Silas slip from between my legs and disappear across the room. He returned wearing a clean pair of boxers and handed me a t-shirt that wasn't my own. I took it from him with a shaky hand wiggling it over my head and shoulders without much movement.

"Dizzy?" Silas asked, kneeling on the bed beside me. He leaned over and kissed me again, slower that time and it pushed a strange feeling around in my chest as I followed his retreat and took another without asking. "Stay here until you get your legs," he chuckled.

He got comfy in the bed next to me, his sheets smelling just like him.

"Just until I'm not dizzy," I said, the whiskey swirling around my thoughts.

His lips found my ear, his scruffy jaw tickling my sensitive skin as I curled against him and tried to come down from my tipsy high. I closed my eyes again, ignoring how good it felt to be held as his hands roamed my back beneath the sheets.

It was only in the silence that the realization dawned on me.

What the hell had we just done?

SHORE

It was rare that the sun woke me up but I had slept through all of my alarms and rolled over in the bed expecting to have contact with Drew but she was gone. I could still smell her on my sheets, feel her on my fingertips, and it was infuriating.

I understood why she slipped away, August couldn't know and he was too old to hide things from. We had been stupid last night but I couldn't help myself, she just... she took the time to recognize what I needed and it cracked something inside of my brain.

I was the helper, I didn't need help.

But she didn't make it feel like that, she just was there.

I was choosing to blame the whiskey and the pancakes, pushing aside the fact that I couldn't get the taste of her out of my mouth. And I had brushed my teeth twice that morning.

Fuck me.

I made my way out into the apartment and Drew was leaning over the counter in a pair of jeans that highlighted the perfect curves of her ass. I took a deep breath in, adjusting myself in my pants before clearing my throat and wandering over to the fridge.

Drew looked up from the page she was reading and offered me a small smile. I wanted to kiss the way it softly curved to the left but shook out the feeling and grabbed a protein shake from the back shelf.

"Do you know algebra?" she asked. The question caught me off guard as I approached her. Her gentle scent hit my nose and flashes of the night before blurred across my vision as the smell of orange blossoms engulfed me.

TRUE HONEY

My eyes flickered to a small hickey on her collarbone, barely exposed beneath her sweater. I reached out and pulled the sweater over her chest and she looked down, zipping it up further with a nervous chuckle.

The tingling sensation of seeing it made it hard not to tell her how much I liked it.

I rolled back my shoulders, hiding the immense emotional frustration coursing through my body that she was just pretending like it didn't happen. We had both felt how real it was. I knew how much she enjoyed it, the sounds of her doing so were burned into my mind.

I sighed, letting the feeling pass.

"A little why?" I said, instead of telling her how I felt. Setting the drink down and angling myself to look at the paper, when I got too close she pushed the paper across to me. It shouldn't have stung, but it did.

"Auggie is failing it," she said, "and I don't know how to help."

There was a hint of despair in her voice, one I hadn't heard since the night at the bar. I watched her carefully trying to read her expression past the hardened one she liked to use around me. The guilt flickered in her eyes and I realized then, she was blaming herself for it.

"Algebra is hard. I barely passed it in school and I'm a genius." I smiled at her, trying to calm her down a little without giving away just how much I had figured out. "Luckily for Auggie you two gained more than one roommate," I said.

"What exactly does that mean?" Drew asked, her hair falling over her shoulder.

I pulled out my phone and dialed a number, looking over at her as it rang, "Tonight we have some fancy dinner party to attend, if you can swing it…"

"That's the deal isn't it?" she said, brushing over the fact that somewhere between the question and last night I had forgotten that our domestication wasn't real. *Shit.*

"Yeah, I can get Cael to hang out with Auggie, if he's okay with that?" I asked.

"Of course," she said, straightening out.

"Hey, can you come here?" I asked over the phone, waiting a few seconds before getting an answer and then hanging up.

"Do you have a secret math genius living under your roof that I should have known about?" Drew asked, her eyes lighting up and leaving behind the sadness as Auggie's door clicked open and he joined us in the kitchen.

At the same time the basement door opened and Dean walked through. He was clearly getting ready to go down to the stadium when I'd called him, his duffle bag hanging over his shoulder.

"You needed me?" he said in a sleepy voice. "Hey Drew," he added, realizing we weren't alone.

"Drew, and her son August. They were at Arlo's birthday," I said.

"Right, Auggie?" Dean said, eyeing me weirdly. Thankfully he didn't say anything about the dinner last night. "I heard he went to the stadium with them the other night... he's quick, Cael slept like a rock that night. We couldn't even get him off the couch." Drew laughed and looked over at August who nodded at him in approval before quietly padding around the intrusion and rummaging through the cupboards. He retreated with a chocolate Pop Tart and joined his mom at the island.

"Auggie needs a tutor in Algebra. Do you think you have time to get him caught up?" I asked. Dean yawned, shaking off his sleep and held out his hand for the worksheet.

"Is this really how your teacher explained this to you?" He looked up from the sheet to August. "No wonder you're confused. If Auggie doesn't mind learning while I cook dinner, I can help. It's my week on meals," he explained, brushing his hand through his messy blond hair.

"I'm good with that," August said with a shrug and shoved a piece of Pop Tart in his mouth. "That teacher's been on my case all week." He spoke with his mouth full.

"Auggie," Drew scowled with a tiny laugh, the sound was like honey.

Dean was staring at me with a shit eating grin on his face when I broke the gaze I'd held on Drew and I just shook my head.

"Get out of my house," I said to him.

"Ask nicely," Dean replied, but when I shot him a dirty look he backed down like he always did and made his way back to the front door. "I'll be home by six, meet me upstairs and bring a notebook," he called to August before leaving.

"I have to get to the stadium for a meeting," I said, "I'll see you guys later."

Drew watched me as I collected my things and August talked in her ear, her eyes thankful and soft. I gave her a wink, knowing the implication behind it, and snuck out of the house, weirdly regretful about leaving them behind. I would text her details later and even the thought of talking to her made me excited like a fucking school boy.

I threw my crap into my backpack in the garage and pulled my helmet over my head just praying that the vibrations from the bike and the fresh air in my lungs would clear my thoughts and give me a second to think rationally about all of this.

I just had to survive the day without tripping over my own feet, or running into Ella or Arlo. They'd be able to smell the sex on me and if that happened, I'd be screwed. Ella would make me talk about how my dick made a decision for me and now I was tangling in Drew and her innocent son in some sick game.

Arlo would remind me that I could get sex from anyone and that the fact that I had slipped so easily into Drew's arms only meant that I was letting myself catch feelings for a woman I barely knew.

I didn't need their speeches to know that I was acting like my father and screwing this entire fucking thing up because I couldn't control myself. But I closed my eyes as the bike rumbled to life and a flash of her red hair crossed my mind, coupled with the sound of her giggles and moans.

Maybe I wanted to lose control with her.

"Fuck," I swore and pulled from the garage to start my day.

By the time I got home Auggie was shoving homemade quesadillas in his mouth at the kitchen table while Dean and Van argued over the notes spread out across it. I watched them for a moment, almost choking up as I remembered when that used to be Arlo and I trying to help Cael with his schoolwork.

I slipped out and downstairs to get changed before the dinner party just hoping that I wasn't going to have to convince Drew that we were strictly business partners and last night hadn't ruined anything. Except for maybe every ounce of my resolve surrounding her and that guarded heart.

But I didn't have to convince her of anything.

She was standing in the kitchen pushing earrings into her ears, her hair cascading down the back of one of the dark blue dresses she had chosen. It showed off her back, cutting low on her spine to reveal her perfect skin. She turned to look at me and scowled.

"Why aren't you changed?" She asked.

"Going, going!" I raised my hands in the air and shuffled past her, pausing briefly to get my fix of her smell and to admire the high halter satin neckline that covered the hickey I had given her.

"It was the only one I picked that covered it other than the black one, but I wore that to dinner last time..." she started to explain and I stopped her.

"You're beautiful," I said and watched the pale complexion on her cheek turn rosy.

"We're going to be late," she whispered when I stopped moving, looking over my dirty hornets polo and pants. "Shower," she added, "you stink."

"Trust me where we're going tonight they won't notice how I smell." I laughed before jogging back to my room to get changed. I pulled on a clean black suit with a black shirt buttoning it to the top and shrugging into a matching jacket.

I pushed my hair back, freshened up my cologne and rejoined Drew in the living room. Her legs had been elongated by the dark heels she'd slipped on and my breath caught in my throat as she looked over her bare shoulder at me.

"Better?" I asked her.

"Better," she practically purred.

"What did you tell Auggie?" I asked her.

"I just told him that I started doing assistant work at the stadium and it requires me to join you at events for the team," she explained. "No tie?"

"Not tonight," I said, reaching my hand out to her. She eyed it for a moment before stepping forward when I rolled the diamond ring between my fingers. I slipped it onto her hand, lingering a little too long and giving her reason to pull back with a scowl on her pretty face. "You're going to be pissed though," I said to her.

"Why?" Drew cocked her head to the side, exposing the length of her neck and I fought to keep myself in place when what I really wanted to do was put my lips on her throat.

"We have to take the bike."

"You're seriously making me ride that death trap..." she looked down at herself, "in this?"

"We're not going far," I assured her.

In reality, Arlo had offered me the keys to the fast back, but I selfishly wanted Drew wrapped around me, even for ten minutes. I needed it.

"Fine," she agreed, collecting her things and following me out to the garage. I helped her with the helmet, tucking her hair behind her ears before sliding it over her head. Fighting the urge to be a mindless idiot with every glance and touch.

The ride over was exactly as expected, a balm to my frayed nerves with her arms wrapped around me and her body pressed to my back. I handed the keys over to the valet as she straightened herself out.

"Still beautiful," I whispered, wrapping my arm around her waist and pulling her close as we ascended the stairs into the museum. It had been rented out for the evening so we could host a collection of shareholders and investors from across the country.

I had given Drew basic details but kept the pressure of everything going exactly right off her shoulders. Tonight was about convincing those men that I was responsible and had my life on track for a wife, a future. That I could be the stable and trustworthy primary shareholder they were looking for.

Everything had to go perfectly tonight and I knew that Drew wouldn't be the issue.

It was me they were watching.

"Silas." My Grandfather's voice boomed across the marble floors and I felt Drew turn it on beside me. A bright smile pulled against her cheeks and she tucked herself against me, small, unthreatening, perfectly poised.

I hated every second of it.

"Seymour," Drew said, holding out her hand to him. He was already into the scotch and the overwhelming cigar smell seeped out of his clothing and into the air.

"You look lovely tonight," he said to her, his demeanor very different in public. He looked over at me and I could feel his icy, judgemental gaze. He was going to make tonight hell. "Come, I want to introduce you to some people."

"I'll go get us drinks," I said to her, not quite ready to release my grip around her but knowing I had to. She could handle my grandfather on her own, I knew she could. She had spent the week handling me and I had far more issues sober than he did drunk.

"Whiskey?" I asked her and she offered a small, polite chuckle that was filled with annoyance before nodding and allowing my grandfather to pull her from my grasp. My side was cold without her and I watched them disappear across the room to a group of men I recognized. The Harbor Six. Every single one of them were legends in their own right, business men now but once they were all elite athletes that had gone through school at Harbor and came home to watch the town flourish.

Evan Poly was the most notable of them all. Harbor's most prolific hockey player in the last fifty years. The only person that's ever come close to his statistics was Kenji Carter. He held investments all over town but the majority of his riches came from real estate holdings. The man to his left was a concerning addition, Darby William, who had been a heavy hitter for the Hornets in the sixties. He was a racist, homophobic asshole who treated everyone worse than the dirt beneath his feet.

I watched from the bar, my hand finding the highball glass without taking my eyes off Drew as she was led like a lamb to the slaughter. She introduced herself and stayed close to my grandfather, but I could tell by her body language that she was uncomfortable beneath all that show.

COURTNEY

"I'm a teacher," I said when asked what I did for a living. I wasn't going to tell them I was a waitress no matter how long ago it was that I stepped inside of a school.

"Raising our youth!" Mr. Poly praised. "That's not an easy job," he said, "I was an asshole in school and I sure know Darcy was too!"

"Teachers are glorified babysitters, Evan. There's a reason we have to go to university to be taught by professors," he sneered, his fat hands gripping an empty scotch glass.

"I can't possibly speak for all of them but I'm sure most teachers would have to disagree with you, Mr. William," I said, trying to hold my own but I could feel the nausea churning over in the pit of my stomach.

Seymour Shore's hand felt hot on my lower back and there was no way to control the panic that spread across my chest from speaking up. Mr. William scowled at me, clearly not accustomed to women speaking in his vicinity and it only worsened the anxious monster that awakened inside of me.

I fought to keep it together.

"How about we have this conversation when you have kids of your own Ms. Courtney and you're in need of daycare. Women these days, they get ahead of themselves and don't understand how the world works." Mr. William shot back and it took everything in me not to correct him.

"I look forward to that conversation, until then we can agree to disagree," I said instead, holding steady and actively forcing myself to be polite. These men were not fooling around, and neither had Silas. He wasn't wrong when he said that impressing them wouldn't be easy. It also made sense why they had put stipulations on his shares. They were hyper focused on their sons and their money. Everything with these men was about passing on a legacy and preserving the family name.

"Leave it to Silas to find the most headstrong woman in Harbor," Mr. Poly said next and I held my tongue, grinding my teeth together to keep quiet. I was led to believe that it was somewhat of a compliment, but I could see the true meaning behind his statement. It was absolutely an insult.

"Mouthy is the word you're looking for Evan," Mr. William said and the lot of them laughed around me like it was the funniest joke they'd ever heard, leaving me standing there stiff and subject to their ridicule.

"At least it's a pretty mouth." I heard one of them say, and it was like I could feel their grubby hands all over my skin. It was worse than any night shift spent fending off grabby drunks. Here I couldn't make a scene, I couldn't stop them. I had to pretend that I was none the wiser to their sick comments and belittling.

I could feel the tears stinging at the corners of my eyes but I refused to give them the satisfaction of reducing me to that and took a long, quiet deep breath to steady myself. Not even tempted to search the room for Silas in need of help I just smiled like an idiot, playing the part of stupid, doting fiance the way I was supposed to.

"Like father like son," Mr. Poly added with a sick smile.

My first two shifts with Susanna had gone well and it had taken me less than ten minutes with the woman to realize she was a gossip. I'd learned just about everything about everyone in the two shifts. Including every single thing she knew about the situation with the Shore family.

Charles Shore was a piece of work.

Josh Logan was a sweet kid despite what the papers liked to say. *"He's incredibly polite and never has a grumpy day. He's all smiles in this office."*

Mrs. Shore was a kind woman, with an intense family history but she was spoken about in the highest regard, by just about everyone.

Silas was her favorite topic, her *favorite boy*, she called him. The most notable of compliments she threw in his direction, was that he was the one person who would drop anything to help someone else.

That spoke volumes about him and told me that he was nothing like his father.

"How is Charles?" Mr. William said, "I heard that the drug addict killed herself," he added.

"Taking the easy way out," Mr. Poly added.

Seymour was notably quiet. I couldn't tell if it was because he condemned what his son was doing or if he just had nothing to add but there was a bright, playful smile stretched across his old face.

"She was disposable," one of the other said, "Charles should know better than to fuck whores without protection. Now he has that bastard running around that could ruin your entire fortune."

"Joshua has no interest in such a thing," Seymour finally said, bringing his glass to his lips.

"You say that now but you should be nipping that in the butt," Mr. Poly said with caution, "it takes one argument, one instance of you denying him something for him to change his tune and slap you with a lawsuit."

"And to think all that stress over a bastard because Charles couldn't keep his dick in Sylwia." Someone hissed.

I hated how they were talking, especially in front of me. I didn't want to be hearing any of this.

"You better keep your door unlocked and your legs on a hinge, Ms. Courtney. The Shore men are known to wander. Wouldn't want you to have to share your inheritance with some mistress," Mr. Poly teased me but I found no humor in the statement.

"If half of us had the balls that Charles had, we'd be happier men," Mr. William said and I checked out of the conversation, glossing over until a broad chest pressed tightly to my back.

"If you'll excuse us," Silas said tightly, his voice low and commanding across the group. Most of them gave nods, allowing Silas to pull me back away from them and into the crowd. As soon as we were free from their scrutiny I could breathe again.

"Are you alright?" He asked me, handing me a glass filled with whiskey that even smelled too expensive for me to drink.

"Fine," I said, taking back the whiskey in a controlled sip.

Silas stared across the ballroom, his eyes a cold, distant gray. I could read every thought flickering across his face. I had screwed that up back there and ruined his chances of making this work. I would be the sole reason that he never got his hands on those shares. All because I couldn't play nice with some drunk old men for more than ten minutes.

"I'm sorry," I said after a prolonged beat of silence. The anxiety was all consuming and spread across my chest like wildfire, unstoppable and burning every logical thought in its path.

"What?" He looked down at me finally, his brows crumpling together and his jaw tensing with a visible tick. His gaze lingered and I couldn't tell if he was angry or not but it caused my heart to race.

"I could have handled that—"

"We're leaving," he said, his hand wrapping around my arm gently.

"We just got here, Silas." I looked up at him, begging for him to clarify what the hell was going on inside of his head. He couldn't be serious? We hadn't even eaten and there had to be more people he needed to introduce me to for the sake of the will.

"And I'm done," Silas sighed and moved around me to shuffle me out the door. We took the stairs back to the street but instead of getting the valet to bring his bike around Silas called for one of the drivers that was parked in the street. "Go home, Drew."

Silas opened the door for me and waited for me to get inside.

"I thought you were coming?" I asked, holding on to the window instead of getting into the car.

"I needed to get you out here, I *have* to stay."

To clean up the mess I made, no doubt. I nodded, not saying anything else before I climbed in and let him shut the door behind me. I had screwed everything up for him and now he was going to have to manage the fallout and come to terms with the fact that he might never get what he wanted.

The car ride home was silent. I wanted to text him, to ask if I'd done something to deserve that cold goodbye, but I already knew. I knew what I had done and there wasn't anything I could say to fix the problem. I shouldn't have slept with him but it hadn't dawned on me until after I had found my head and come down from the high that Silas's touch seemed to bring me.

Sleeping together had created a hundred more problems.

I'd been an idiot about all of this.

The house was empty when I got back, August nowhere to be found but there was a note on the counter about going to Hilly's for dinner because Dean burnt whatever he was making. I was grateful that the apartment was empty, all I wanted to do was cry.

But like a bad omen my phone vibrated in my purse. I set it on the counter, pulling it out and answering the call before I even registered the area code. *Shit.*

"Drew?" A voice came from the other end. "Don't hang up on me Drew, I can hear you breathing!"

"Bradley," I acknowledged him. "What do you want?"

"I want to know why my son just sent me to voicemail!" Bradley's voice was loud and dominating as I tried to collect my thoughts.

"He's thirteen, Bradley. He isn't always going to answer when you call, he's not a dog." I tried to curb my tone to avoid a fight.

"Don't patronize me, Drew. What lies have you been spewing at him? The last time we talked he wouldn't even give me your address for birthday presents," Bradley snapped.

That's because there was no address... I tried to stifle the groan that rumbled deep in my chest.

"Do you have a pen?" I asked him slowly, as I turned to look for the stack of mail that Silas left laying around. On the top was a letter addressed to him from the prison and it made me sad staring at it, knowing it probably came from his father.

"You're in Rhode Island?" He hissed the moment I gave him the zip code.

"There was a job opportunity, so I took it," I said.

"A job opportunity? Are you teaching again?" He asked me.

"I'm working with a college baseball team," I said instead, deflecting the fact that I worked under the lowest paid person in the building as her assistant.

"Right," Bradley only found that unbelievable because never once had I shown interest in sports and I still wouldn't, but the pay was good and Silas...

I inhaled slowly, almost grateful for the bombarding from Bradley giving me time to forget how badly tonight went. The look on Silas's face when he sent me away.

"You have the address, is there something else you wanted?" I asked Bradley to fill the silence.

"To speak to my son," Bradley reiterated.

"Try his cell phone again," I said calmly despite wanting to tear my own hair out.

"Good to know you're useless as always Drew, have a good night," he snapped before the line went dead.

I set the phone on the counter, closed my eyes to breathe, and peeled off the dress, leaving it crumpled on the floor. Then I stepped into the shower and let the hot water drown out the noise in my head. Closing my eyes I let the sound of the high pressured stream wash over me and create a veil of white noise that cut off the world entirely.

I pressed my forehead against the cool tile wall and tried to breathe through the violent panic that filled me. I'd fucked up bad tonight it was only a matter of time before Silas got sick of me and August as charity cases. I couldn't do a single thing right for him.

I could feel the disappointment in my bones, heavy like cement in my veins. And there was nothing I could do to stop it. August's heart would be broken. My head was so foggy that I hadn't noticed the temperature change, freezing against my hot skin. I stood there as long as I could before I finally submitted and turned the water off, wrapping myself in a towel to find some pajamas.

I wandered back into my room to find a box on my bed that wasn't there before. I looked over at the door, still locked and wondered if I had missed it when I came in but the dress I had left on the floor was also gone.

The note on the top was signed *'Mom sent over a few things as a welcome to Harbor gift. Silas',* but looking inside the box it was clear that he had gone out of his way to pick all of its contents.

There were two new sets of dark silk pajamas, a brush, two bottles of shampoo that probably cost more than three tanks of gas, new makeup brushes and makeup, along with tons of snacks I'd never seen before.

With tears streaming down my cheek I rubbed the fabric between my fingers, unsure how I felt about the gifts when I hadn't done a single thing to deserve them.

SHORE

The wrench slipped and pinched my skin hard enough to make me swear and hurl it across the garage, earning me a dirty look from Arlo.

"What is wrong with you?" He grumbled from behind the hood of Josh's car.

The one thing that usually calms me down was only pissing me off and I can't get the look of disappointment and fear on Drew's face out of my head.

"Nothing."

Arlo leaned out around the hood further and narrowed his eyes on me. He was covered in grease up to the forearms from working all morning to get the damn thing running again.

"I told you I'd just buy him a new one," I said to him with a sigh.

"Did you tell him that?" Arlo chuckled and continued to work. The thing needed just about new everything and by the time we were done working on it, it would basically be brand new anyways. But it was slow moving because Josh was determined to pay for every part on his own. "It's fine, I like being out here."

"Yeah me too," I said, continuing to hammer on the bike.

We'd spent countless hours here over the last fifteen years. It was the only place where nothing was expected from us. We could work in silence or spill our guts and neither of us bore any harsh judgement toward the other. The garage had heard every little secret and every difficult conversation we had ever had. It was a sanctuary.

"Alright, *stop*," Arlo said, coming around the car. "You're going to break something yanking on it like that," he warned. "I know something's wrong because you're never reckless with that bike. You drive that thing like someone's grandma. What's going on?" He demanded, cleaning his fingers on the rag, his dark eyes watching me carefully for any twitch that might give me away.

Don't think about Drew. I pressed my tongue to the roof of my mouth, but her laughter was already echoing in my skull. I remembered how soft her skin was and how good she smelled tangled in my sheets, tipsy off whiskey. The ghost of her laughter and moans were making it hard to keep it together.

He started to laugh, a knowing smile pressing across his hard face slowly.

"You like her."

"Who?"

"Don't play dumb," he warned. "You know who."

I shrugged and Arlo lunged at me with his fist in the air. He playfully shoved me sideways making me lose my balance and tip back into the concrete, "stop fucking around, you like the red head don't you?"

"Drew?" I played dumb, laying back against the floor and inhaled one long deep breath as a smile formed on my face.

"No, it's not like that," I said, pushing up onto my elbows to face him.

"You're so full of shit," Arlo snapped, crouching down in front of me.

"It's a business arrangement, Ar," I muttered, forcing myself to meet his eyes. I knew the second I let my eyes leave his he would figure it out. It was such a stupid mistake.

"You fucking *slept* with her," he accused and it took everything in me not to flinch. "You did, didn't you?!"

"Keep your voice down," I said, kicking my foot out and catching his shin hard enough to make him lose his balance.

"Why? Afraid the entire Nest will know about your slutty side activities?" Arlo laughed but his eyes were vicious and locked on mine. "Si, you're too smart to be that fucking dumb," he said with a shake of his head and sat back on the ground to stare at me.

"It was just once, and she pretended it didn't happen the next morning. We're fine," I said, mostly trying to convince myself.

Arlo stared at me like I was losing my mind and maybe I was.

"You're an idiot," he responded. "You have a pool of women that would jump at the chance to spend one night with you. Why the hell did you sleep with the one that you have a contract with?"

"It just happened, it was my birthday and we were drunk..." I led off.

"You were drunk?" Arlo scoffed. "Even better, you had drunk sex with the single mom who you're parading around like your fiancé."

"Alright hey, enough of the judgement please," I said, waving a dirty rag in surrender before chucking it at him.

"Do you like her?" He asked and I opened my mouth to deny it. "Don't fucking lie to me, asshole, or I'll go get Ella and you can deal with her judgement."

"Mercy," I sighed, "I can't take another scolding from her this week," I said.

Arlo smirked, "I warned you not to involve them."

"I tried not to, but you know them..." I felt cornered and frustrated, so far from my usual confidence. "Besides, I know about your little binder. You prick."

"This family needs a new hobby," Arlo said with a laugh. "If we collect any more strays we *will* be the Brady Bunch and Josh will never let anyone live it down."

"I'm not collecting strays, and neither is Ella. Drew is just—"

"Yeah, that's what I said... what Cael said... what Dean said..." Arlo's list would be endless.

"Okay, okay, I hear you but I'm positive. It's not serious, it was just a one-time thing," I said to him.

Arlo tipped his head back and a throaty, wild laugh exploded from his chest, "shut the fuck up Silas," he said after he calmed down.

"I'm over you, go get me Ella. At least she'll call me handsome when she insults me," I groaned.

"If she calls you handsome, I'm making her get her eyes checked..." Arlo teased. "It is serious and you're trying to pretend it's not to spare yourself the shame if it blows up."

"What's that supposed to mean?" I asked.

"It means you're an idiot," Arlo said again.

"Stop calling me that," I warned and he raised an eyebrow at me.

"Stop acting like one," he countered. "I once had a man tell me to take a chance on something that I thought was ridiculous. A feeling that I was dismissing because I was afraid to make a fool of myself."

"There's more at stake in this situation than just being rejected for a Gala date, Ar." I scratched my fingers into my beard and sighed.

"Do you ever listen to yourself?" Arlo asked. "You walk around here like you're the only person that can save Harbor. It doesn't need saving Silas, this town will survive without one ultra rich asshole running it."

"You know that's not true. We have hands on everything in this town, in the university… If that money goes to my father, we have nothing," I said but I could hear the bullshit coming out of my mouth.

Arlo cocked his head. "Since when did your father's money mean more than our family?" he asked, a final blow to the argument I was never going to win.

"Without that money we don't have a home, Arlo… A team, a stadium."

"I don't need any of that shit and neither do you," he shrugged like none of it mattered and maybe it didn't but it felt too big and too important. "So tell me what you do need," he said, softer than before. "And if it's the redhead then we make a game plan and you stop being a pussy."

"Fuck, Arlo, you're mean today," I grumbled. "You're asking me to make a choice between what I know I should do and what my dick wants… the answer seems kind of obvious."

"Your dick, or your heart?" He poked me in the check with two fingers. "You have one of those, I know you do… it even works sometimes." Arlo offered me a sympathetic smile.

"Either way, I have to be responsible."

"You can have both," he said after a beat. "You really can."

"It feels selfish," I confessed.

"That's because you're the most selfless person I know, brushing your teeth before saving the world probably feels selfish…" Arlo laughed. "You also don't know when to ask for help…"

"I'm slightly over this garage therapy session, I'm not going to lie," I said.

"Why not? You're lying about everything else…" Arlo said. "Do you like her, Si?" He asked me, the conversation somehow getting even more serious.

Did I?

Her smile flashed across my mind and her laughter filled my chest thinking about that night we had, drenched in whiskey and how easy it had been to talk to her. I could talk to her... I looked up from my greasy covered hand and met Arlo's glare.

I didn't have to answer him out loud, he already knew.

"So ask her out," he said.

"You want me to ask out my fake fiancé on a date..." I scoffed, I never realized just how stupid it all sounded until it rolled off my own lips.

"Take time to get to know her properly, not because of some business arrangement." Arlo pushed off the ground back to his feet and held out his hand to me.

"Wow, sage advice." I took his hand and brushed myself off.

"Try; I'm sorry I'm a stuck up ass, please rip up that idiotic paper contract and..." Arlo smiled. "I think you're really *fucking* pretty."

"I mean if it worked on Ella," I laughed.

"It didn't, I never said that to her because I have tact and know how to flirt." Arlo walked away from me before I could argue and left me alone with my thoughts.

"You gave her a fancy book and lurked around for a month."

"Yeah," he scowled at me like I was fucking clueless, "*flirting.*"

Ask her out.

Easier said than done.

COURTNEY

"Morning, thank you for calling the Harbor Stadium, you're speaking to Drew. How can I help you?" The hours blurred as people called nonstop, all of them angry about the rising cost of season tickets.

Susanna had warned me that it was one of the busiest times of the year, we didn't deal with the customers, but transferring nine out of every ten calls upstairs felt tedious and it made the day drag on. I had a shift at Hilly's later that night and my feet were already killing me but now that I was putting an extra paycheck into my account at the end of the month kept me standing.

That and the hollow, devastated look on Silas' face when he'd sent me home.

He hadn't spoken to me since.

No doubt trying to figure out how to get rid of me without causing a mess but as soon as I had enough for first and last month's rent I would get August and I out of his hair.

I pushed myself out of bed that morning on the pretense that I had to take August to school and nothing else. If my brain had its way I would have never left. My bones felt like lead and I was so cold that I moved a little slower, like there was ice coating all my muscles. I just needed one more week of work.

I'd just add it to the long list of mistakes I'd made over the last fifteen years.

I talked to August about his dad and received the expected answer. He didn't want to speak to him and had sent his last four calls to voicemail. Moments like that made it harder and harder not to bad-mouth Bradley in front of our son. But it wasn't up to me to decide how August felt about his father, all I could do was stand by and reassure him when things inevitably went wrong between the two of them again.

"Yes sir, one moment please." I said through the receiver and transferred the angry customer upstairs to sales. I hung up the phone and before I could even take a breath it rang again. The same conversation happened about a hundred times in the next two hours. 'No sir there's nothing I can do, you can speak with sales.' 'This is the front office, you're looking for a sales representative.' 'Please give me one moment to find you someone who can help.'

It felt endless.

The next caller was a particularly snippy woman with a shrill tone in her voice and a preconceived notion that I was an idiot.

"I don't want to spend my afternoon being handed off between a bunch of morons on the phone, you're going to tell me right now why my season ticket price went up nearly two hundred dollars." She spat through the receiver and I could feel my chest tighten.

The thing about trauma was that it never gave warning for when or how it might show up. With my mind still swirling around the topic of Bradley, it snuck past my defenses and suddenly I was back in the living room being screamed at for a crying baby that I couldn't soothe. I tried to clear my throat and get a word in against her, trying desperately to slow her down just long enough to transfer her upstairs. But she was relentless, the stream of irritation and rage licked words flowed from her without remorse.

All over tickets to a baseball game.

It felt foolish, *I felt foolish.*

"How hard is it to be a mother, Drew? You sit at home all day with him and the one thing you're supposed to do you can't even manage that. What's wrong with him?" Bradley asked, raking his anger across my cheek. *"What's wrong with you!? Answer me!"*

A surge of pent up anxiety rattled through me and stung at the corners of my eyes and as she continued to berate me over the phone. I tried to catch a full breath of air but my throat was sticky and dry all while her voice melted into the memories of Bradley.

It was a tangle designed to wound.

"You're useless to me and him if you can't figure yourself out Drew. You wanted a baby, you begged me for this and now you've let yourself and this house go. It's

all in your head, you can make the decision to get up and be better." He snapped, throwing his glass in the sink so hard it shattered against the bottom. "Clean that up and get dressed, we're going for dinner."

"Are you even listening to me?" The woman's voice whined through the phone.

"I'm sorry, Ma'am, you're looking for the sales offices. One moment please," I said not giving her a chance to get a word in otherwise. I hung up the phone and excused myself from the desk, Susanna just offering me a distracted smile as she continued to work.

I couldn't breathe, but I pinned my shoulders back and looked both ways down the hall before turning left and just walking. Eventually finding an unlocked door I slipped inside and luckily found the storage closet empty. It was packed floor to ceiling with equipment, helmets, bats.

I slumped against the concrete wall thankful for the silence as the tears finally poured from me in private. Over the years I had gotten pretty good at hiding my sadness from others, from August. I knew I wasn't perfect at it, that sometimes I let it slip and he was the first to be hurt by it. But it was never meant for him, sometimes it just got to be too much and I had nowhere to run and hide it from him.

I rubbed my thumb down the palm of my hand, trying to ground myself in touch but the old emotional wounds seemed to split open like they'd never healed. I gasped for air through the tears, only working myself up worse.

Glass smashed, it shattered across my memories and the sound of slamming doors and a crying infant flooded in and filled every space in my mind like a collapsed dam. Tucking my head between my knees I forced my body to inhale, forced my lungs to fill with air before I could drown completely in my emotions.

"Figure yourself out Drew."

It repeated in the back of my head like if I said it to myself enough times that maybe I would miraculously just figure it all out.

The door popped open and I flinched, scrambling back against the wall to my feet and rubbing the tears off my face with the back of my hands. Silas's brother, Josh, stood in the entrance. His dark eyes moved over me before he stepped inside and closed the door behind him.

"I'm sorry, I just came in here for some quiet," I rambled.

"It's alright, I don't mind sharing my panic attack closet," he said, a delicate curve to his lips, that might have been a smile, formed.

I chuckled through the last sob and stared at him in wonder.

"Are you okay?" he asked after a moment. I assumed he was dressed for warmups before the game and must have been coming down here to grab something before heading out to the field. He was wearing cleats and a pair of athletic shorts with a dark compression long sleeve and Hornets Athletics shirt.

"Yeah, fine." I said, sniffling.

What he did next surprised me. Instead of grabbing what he needed and leaving, he slid against the door and found a spot on the floor. He stared up at me, waiting for me to mirror him and when I finally did he pulled off his hat and hung it between his knees, picking at the frayed edges with his fingers.

"Dean likes that word too," he said after a moment. "I'm fine, it's fine..." he grumbled. "I hate that, when is anything ever fine?" He asked.

"Dean is your boyfriend right?" I questioned and he nodded.

"It's funny how it sounds coming out of someone else's mouth, scares me a little," Josh sighed. "You're Silas's-"

"Fiancée," I finished quietly. *For now.*

"Around here that makes you family you know," he said to fill the silence that flooded in. "They're really loose about the term," he grumbled. "And it can be great to have them but sometimes..."

"It's nice to have quiet?" I asked him and he nodded.

"Silence is my favorite sound," Josh admitted. "And the Hornets are loud."

"Very," I smiled at him, I could feel the anxiety retreating and I was grateful for the conversation he had so generously provided.

"Do you like the silence too or are you crying in the storage closet for another reason?" He asked eventually. Every time someone walked by the door I flinched nervously, thinking they might try to come in here or might be looking for us. But Josh never moved, his body like stone against the floor, his brown eyes so cautious of everything around him.

He was nothing like Silas, not in a bad way, just... the opposite. Silas seemed to be the type to give and give until he had nothing left, his generosity being his downfall. Josh was guarded, careful with his words and slow to give his trust to someone. It was clear that he had questions he wanted to ask me, perhaps for the sake of his family...for his brother but he didn't. He continued to let me be sad until the last tear dried up and I finally started to feel like myself again.

"This job can be a little overwhelming," I confessed, unsure where the honestly had come from.

"You're working in the office with Susanna?" He asked.

"I know it's just a secretary job—"

"I was going to say she might be the hardest-working person in the whole building.

Josh cut me off. "I couldn't answer phones all day, I'd go insane."

"A week ago I would have sold her job short but today I'm learning that she does in fact do more than anyone else," I chuckled under my breath, still trying to compose myself.

"That's usually the case," he said.

"Can I ask you something?"

He scratched the back of his neck and pulled his hat back over his messy hair with a nod.

"Is Silas really the guy everyone makes him out to be?" I asked and Josh's serious expression softened. "They all tell stories about him like he's the best of them."

"I wouldn't really know," he said, the honesty in his voice was refreshing. "We didn't grow up together, so I don't have the stories or the memories. I have..." he paused, "*had*, a lot of resentment and anger toward him for a long time."

"Because of your father?" I asked, knowing I was probably wading into dangerous territory. Worst case scenario, he didn't answer.

"It's easy to assume a person is like their father through rumors and gossip, I didn't know a lot about Silas for a long time." Josh inhaled slowly, "What I do know," he said, wetting his bottom lip. "Is that Silas has never let me down. Even when I bit the hand that fed me, even when I didn't deserve his kindness. He just kept trying."

"Thank you," I said to him, knowing exactly what he meant and finally understanding Silas a little better. "Sorry for invading your panic attack closet."

"I don't mind sharing," he said with a small smirk. "You're family, remember?"

SHORE

I had made up my mind. I was going to follow Arlo's terrible advice and be selfish for once. Incredibly selfish. All I could think about was her and she'd been avoiding me like the plague since the last dinner disaster. Sending her home in a car to put distance between her and all of the horrible things coming out of those idiot's mouths had seemed smart at the time.

Until I realized that I had sent her home alone.

She thought she did something wrong and now I was paying for my stupidity.

I shrugged into my favorite hoodie and a pair of shorts before wandering out into the kitchen hoping to catch her before I needed to be at the stadium for the Harbor VS. The Hornets game. Cael had organized it to raise money for local animal shelters; it had turned into more of a Willy Wonka situation when he proposed a lottery for kids to get to make up the opposing team.

Families could buy chocolate bars at games and if your kid unwrapped a bar with foil, they got a place on the team. It was ambitious, but it was working, from chocolate sales alone Cael had raised over a hundred grand and the games ticket sales would raise even more.

August was at the counter alone in the kitchen and I looked around for Drew, trying to dampen my disappointment that she wasn't awake yet.

"Morning," I said to him and he grumbled something under his breath. It took me another five minutes to ask him where she was.

"She had to work," August said without looking up from his papers.

"Work?" I said. My confusion was palpable because August finally acknowledged my presence.

"Yeah she went in to help I guess and picked up a shift at Hilly's for later," he explained.

Why would she do that? I chewed on the inside of my mouth and considered the fact that she was preparing to leave. She was trying to make more money so she didn't have to rely on the income from me and the stadium.

"And she just left you here?" I asked him.

"I'm thirteen not three," August glared at me. "And you're here." The kid reminded me of a young Cael, all bones and skin, no muscle or desire to have any. He was lanky. But the attitude that ran from his toes to his nose, that was all Josh. I set down my protein shake on the counter and leaned against it.

I could tell he wanted to say more.

"She only gets nervous leaving me alone at night, during the day she can call to check on me..." he explained in a less combative voice. "I'll walk over there for dinner later."

I stared at him for a moment, his fingers finding the half-eaten bagel beside him as he focused on his homework. I couldn't be frustrated with his push back, if it was me I'd be the same way about some guy moving in on my mom. Even the idea of it made my skin crawl but I knew that if I wanted to make it work with Drew, August was the way I got my foot in the door.

He was the guiding missile in her heart, what he wanted he got and only because Drew worked her ass off to make sure he had it. It was the reason she had taken the deal in the first place.

August.

"Get dressed," I said to him and he scowled looking up from his homework.

"What?" He said.

"Get dressed," I repeated, "sneakers, shorts... whatever. But we need to be at the stadium in twenty so..." I tapped the counter and collected my drink, popping the cap on it and pounding it back as August slowly got off his stool. "And here," I said walking over to the closest, I tugged out a box of old hornet hats and tossed one at him. "Put this on, I don't need you getting a sunburn."

I sounded like my mother.

"Or whatever," I added as he eyed me with caution.

It was another ten minutes before he appeared again in a pair of shorts and a t-shirt that looked somewhat clean. His hat was pushed down over his hair and without the dark shaggy mop in his eyes he looked so much like Drew it was scary. It was like all his features softened and everything she gave to him was able to shine through the surface.

I cursed under my breath realizing that we couldn't take the bike and we were going to be late anyways. We were going to have to walk down because Arlo would have left the house already and I wasn't putting August in a car with anyone I didn't trust with my life.

"Come on," I said to him and we started to make our way down. It was clear when August took control on the path that he had been taken down this way before and that they had taken it upon themselves to bring him in like he was just another family member. I wasn't sure why I was ever nervous about it.

"What's going on today?" he asked when we popped out from the path into the parking lot of the stadium and it was full of cars. "I don't really like baseball..." August said, looking over at me.

"It's a charity game, you can hang out in the dug out and throw garbage at Cael all game if you want," I said, swiping my card on the door and letting him slip inside in front of me. The stadium was alive with energy, Susanna was fielding phone calls and people crowded around the desk as we passed through the tunnel and into the main part of the offices.

The locker room was bustling with players and members of Harbor who had won special privileges for the day. Each member of the team had been assigned a child that they would cart around the stadium for hours until the big game. Cael had a small ginger child dangling by the ankles and it reminded me to double-check all the waiver forms before the game started.

"Cael, put him down!" Dean snapped, wandering across the locker room in a jersey that looked a size too small on his giant frame with a little girl following close behind her hand tucked into his as he tried to get control over the room.

"What the hell is going on in here?" August asked from behind me and I turned to look at him with a scowl.

"Don't swear," I said.

"Do I have to remind you I'm thirteen, *hell*, isn't a swear." His eyes narrowed on me and Van wandered over with an exhausted look on his face.

"No one said we'd be babysitting," he said. "Cael gave us no information about what we were doing before the game and not a single one of us is qualified to juggle twenty kids... Can you like... do something?" he asked, whipping around to holler at one of the boys who was chucking cleats across the locker room.

"What makes you think I'm qualified?" I scoffed.

"I don't know, you've been wrangling all of us for years..." Van said as he tried to stop the kid from causing any damage. "You kept Cael alive, that instantly makes you more experienced than all of us."

"Barely," I ground out through my teeth.

I looked around at the carnage happening and stuck my fingers between my lips before whistling loudly. It was like someone had hit pause on a remote the way everybody turned to look at me and froze in place.

"We've got ten minutes until the game starts, I want Hornet's players in a line here," I pointed to my left, "and Harbor Guests, here..." I said pointing to my right. "Make sure that you're with your designated Hornet."

Cael stared at me like I was intruding on his perfect day and scowled, dropping his child to the ground with a soft thump before moving him into line with the rest of the kids. "Take them out for warm-ups as the stadium fills up and run off their energy..." I said to him,

"What's up Auggie?" He fist bumped him gently and completely ignored what I said. "Hey, I have someone I want you to meet," he said, throwing his arm around August's shoulders and walking him over to the opposite end of the locker room to where Riona's daughter stood with her arms crossed and her earphones in.

Usually I would protest, but the combination was oddly well met and Cael knew it too because Daisy smiled the second he introduced them and I hadn't ever seen her do that in all the years of knowing her. Cael wiggled his eyebrows at me as Daisy showed August her phone and handed him an earbud, forcing him to slide off the headphones he was always wearing.

With him busy I was able to get the rest of the team on the field without any hiccups. Once the game started the guys and the children were all too busy to cause trouble. Cosy Mitchell was the captain of the Harbor team, representing all the shelters in need around the city. It was weird to see her on the field, in comparison to Van she was a little shorter, a little curvier and alot less sunshine than her brother. But she was in a good mood and it showed with each inning that they played.

I was proud of Cael, beyond comprehension for putting the entire game together. Riona was standing in the dugout with Ryan as the game started, her hair pulled back into a ponytail and dark sunglasses over her eyes.

"He's doing a really good job," she said to her brother as they watched Cael run across the field. In the time since the exhibition game Cael had switched around some of his classes, leaning more into public relations work and event planning. At the time Ryan had found about fifteen issues with it until he saw how great Cael was at planning parties.

"Silas holds his hand through all of it," Ryan grumbled, but I could hear the pride in his voice.

"Not this time," I said. "He did this one all on his own."

Riona smiled out at her nephew who was correcting August's swing in the batter's box against Josh.

"You aren't supposed to be helping the enemy, Cody!" Josh hollered, gloving the ball.

"Grow a heart, Josh," he said back, returning his concentration to August.

Josh glared at him but a grin cracked through his usual grumpiness and it warmed the corners of my heart to see him so at ease. August managed to crack the next ball he was thrown to the outfield and with everyone cheering him on he scored the last run of the game pointing at Daisy with a goofy grin on his face.

"Did that kid just point at my kid?" Riona dropped her glasses, two piercing eyes staring at me as I tried to slip out of her line of sight.

"Teach her young, baseball players are in a league of their own," Ryan said without taking his eyes off the field, but a suspicious smile played at the corner of his lips.

"Oh no," Riona said, shaking her head. "Keep your sneaky little egotistical baseball players away from my daughter."

Ryan hissed, swatting away his little sister's hand as she tugged on the baby hairs around his neck with a growl. "Pull Shore's hair, that's his egotistical baseball player," Ryan sold me out.

I put both hands in the air and back far away from Riona's reach, "he's just living in my basement with his mom. He doesn't even like baseball..." I tried to excuse the behavior. "They're teenagers and Cael, you know your nephew that you love so much," I laughed as she stepped across the dugout at me. "No, no," I stuttered, "he introduced them!" I blurted as she reached for a bat.

After the game, I found August sitting in the medical offices with Ella, Cosy and some of the boys after the game, the two of them going back and forth in conversation as I filed some things away.

"What are the really big ones?" He asked Cosy.

"Maine Coons," she said, brushing a piece of her hair behind her ear.

"They're cool," he said with a nod, "or the naked ones," he chuckled. "That would be fun to have."

"You could dress them up in little sweaters," Ella added, her eyes lifting to him and smiling. "Or a Hornet jersey... I wonder if they make pet ones?"

August shrugged, "One time I found a kitten in a dumpster but she died a couple days later. She was just really little," he said, not sounding bothered by any of it but his smile dropped. It was clear the kid was just in search of a friendship that wasn't contingent on location, something that would always be there in the face of inconsistency.

"It happens more than you think," Cosy said, sipping on water. "But for every kitten that doesn't make it, so many more do. That's important to remember," she smiled at him and August nodded. "The life they did live was perfect because you made sure of that." She reassured him.

"I had a cat growing up named Sassy, she was this gray tabby cat we got from the shelter and I had this rag rug in my bedroom she used to love to sleep on. Every day after school I found her there, on that stupid rug." Ella told her story with a smile as her pen worked across a report.

"Mom never let me have a cat," August said after a few minutes. "I guess we can't really have them because we move around so much."

"Do you want one?" I looked up from the filing cabinet as I clicked it close.

"What?" August's gaze moved from Ella to me, shocked and confused.

"Do you want a cat?" I asked him again.

"Mom says—"

"Auggie," I cut him off, "do *you* want a cat?"

Ella stared at me like I was out of control but I was enjoying the tiny adrenaline rush I was getting from doing something I knew would probably blow up in my face later. A cat was permanent, it was what August wanted, maybe what he needed and I was in the position to give it to him. Was I crossing the lines of the contract between Drew and I? Maybe, but in that exact moment, the look of pure excitement on her son's face. *I didn't give a shit.*

Cosy looked between us, "I can unlock the shelter. We have a few cats that could be a good fit..." She said quietly.

"It's up to Auggie," I said, never breaking eye contact with him.

"You have to tell Mom," he said, "she's going to hate this."

"We can take the truck," Van said and Zoey squealed with excitement, collecting her bag.

"Can I come?" Dean asked and Cosy shrugged.

The six of us made our way down to the closed shelter, it was quiet inside aside from the occasional mewl and bark. Cosy popped the lights on and let us all into the back behind the employee door where the kennels were.

"There's three kittens in there, and the rest of the upper kennels are all adult cats..." she waved to the back, "the dogs are—"

She started but the rest of the group were already gone on their way for cuddles leaving August and myself to look at the cats. He walked up and down the line, completely bypassing the kennel full of tiny fluffy kittens to some of the older cats.

"This one looks friendly," I said, hooking my finger inside and wiggling it toward the skinny orange cat who looked completely uninterested in my advances. I continued down the row, each cat similar in size but all had different stories and backgrounds. I went to call him over to look at the tabby cat in front of me but August was long gone, his eyes wide at the last kennel in the row and a gentle smile on his face.

"This one," August said quietly.

I wandered up beside him and looked inside the kennel to find the mangiest cat I'd ever seen with my own eyes. It's head snapped in my direction with a loud hiss that made me take a step back from the door.

"Auggie, dude. He looks like he has his own brand of fleas," I sighed.

"He's been bathed," Cosy interrupted, "I have the wounds to prove it. We found him in a dumpster, I've been calling him Oscar."

The cat was mostly white, with splotches of orange and dark brown fur that patterned around his ears and ears, spreading out into larger stains along his spine and back legs. His eyes looked old like he had seen some horrors in his long life in Harbor.

"He's a little grumpy but I think it's just because he's been on his own for so long," Cosy said standing behind August.

I looked at the cat again and oddly enough could see my brother in him. I hated how easily I was swayed by my emotions in situations that had nothing to do with Josh. But at every turn in my life I wanted to do better by him, making things right in the universe that I hadn't even wronged. And the look on August's face told me that there was no way we were leaving the shelter without that cat.

"Alright, get me the papers."

It was a struggle to even get the cat into the travel kennel, that I had to purchase on top of the adoption fees, the toys, the bed, the food... August just kept putting things on the counter and Cosy just kept ringing through.

Arlo was at the island with Josh and Cael when we came in the back door with the cat and a happy August. His eyes narrowed on the kennel and then back to me. *Leave it alone.* I thought, not saying a word but his lips pursed together and he gave me a tiny shrug.

"Oh shit!" Cael exclaimed, leaning down to peer in the kennel. "What's this handsome dude's name?" He stuck a finger in the kennel and the cat purred, leaning against the door and welcoming the touch. *Of course it likes Cael.*

"Red," August said.

Josh looked around at all of us with the funniest smile on his face, knowing how much they all hated the color.

"Why Red?" Arlo asked, his brows coming together in the center.

"After the Cincinnati Reds."

"Wow," I swore under my breath. He had picked the name because he overheard me talking to the press about cheering for the Pittsburgh Pirates. He was too smart and too quick for his age. August unlocked the cage and Red sauntered out over the counter, eyeing me carefully before it flopped down and rolled straight into the outstretched arms of Arlo.

I tried reaching out again only for Red to swat at me for even trying to get close to him. The cat fucking loved everyone *but* me. I had let the kid adopt a grumpy old cat and now I could only hope that Red liked Drew enough to convince her that what I did wasn't a violation of our agreement.

"Man he hates you," August chuckled. "It's kind of hilarious."

"I like this kid," Arlo mumbled, too busy scratching Red's belly to notice Cael messing around on his phone.

"What are you doing?" I asked him.

"Changing your name from Gramps to Cat Daddy in the group chat," Cael laughed, not looking up from his phone. I sighed and left the four of them to fuck around with our newest family member, I needed a cold shower and a game plan.

SHORE

"A cat?" Drew looked from Red, curled up in a ball in August's arms to me with a terrified expression on her face. "You got him a cat?"

"He wanted a cat," I said, deciding that honesty was the best policy.

"So you just...got him a cat?" Drew asked, her shock still rampant. "How old is that thing?" She gaped at it.

"Cosy says it's eleven, roughly..." I cleared my throat as Drew moved toward her son and gave the cat a chance to smell her before curling her fingers into the hair between his ears. *Right, why wouldn't the evil cat love her? Why do you hate me?* I glared at the mangy thing.

"You bought my son a senior cat without talking to me?" Drew's voice sounded a little less strained that time, like she was coming around and no longer mad at me... hopefully. "Why?"

"We were at the stadium yesterday-"

"You were at the stadium yesterday?" She looked at August who just shrugged. I could hear the concern in her voice over the fact that I was parading around her son without her knowledge and behind her back.

"He was home alone, said you were working at Hilly's..." I raised an eyebrow at her, *you were supposed to quit*. "Him and Van's sister were talking about cats, one thing led to another. If it's any consolation, I tried to get him to go with a kitten but he wanted that...thing."

Red's entire body vibrated with a low growl.

"Is it rabid?" Drew asked after the interaction.

"No, Red just hates him," August teased, a string of light hearted laughter falling from him.

Drew snorted, and it was the first I'd heard that laughter in days. I leaned into the sound, my heart rate slowing from the light tone in her voice. Her bright green eyes met mine and I held my breath, the sparkle was bright and a defeated smirk formed on her face.

I adored the way she looked at me and even worse I enjoyed how warm my apartment felt with them in it, in my life. It was the most reckless chance I'd ever taken but one so worth it that I couldn't remember how it felt to be alone.

I would do anything to make her see that.

That much was decided.

Smiling with pride I took her in, leaning over her son and the cat. She was wearing the pajama's I bought her, and I could smell the body wash from her shower rolling off her skin. It was all making it very hard to control myself. I wanted a repeat of my birthday, a hundred repeats.

Drew Courtney was under my skin and I liked the way she rested there.

"I can't believe you got him a cat," she sighed under her breath but I could tell that August being happy did the same thing for her. She rubbed her hand into the back of his unruly hair and watched him faun over the cat gently.

"What are your plans for the day?" I asked, changing the conversation as I wandered to the fridge.

"I have a day off," she smiled at me, "probably laundry."

"Screw laundry," I said, "I have tickets to the game this afternoon. It's a playoff game, it should be really good."

Drew looked apprehensive, "I don't know anything about baseball, it would be a waste of a ticket."

"You don't have to know the rules to enjoy the sunshine," I said, the meaning behind my words doubled. I just wanted to enjoy her sunshine, rules be damned.

"I don't know," she chewed her lip.

"I'm down," August piped up. "Will Daisy be there?" he asked, unknowingly walking me into another *oops* conversation with his mother.

"Maybe," I said, I wasn't sure.

"Who's Daisy?" Drew asked, her tone sweet but her eyes locked on mine.

"One of the daughters of a woman that works at the stadium, she was at the game yesterday..." I said, glaring at August for being a snitch but he only smirked at me and retreated to his room.

The minute his door closed Drew glared at me. "You got Auggie a cat? What is wrong with you?!" She said it like it was meant to be serious but her little smile and the way she swatted the air in front of me was so adorable there wasn't a chance in hell I was taking her seriously.

"I got *us* a cat," I said, and she froze. "There's no point in arguing it. Red hates me and even I want him here. It makes Auggie happy."

That stopped whatever argument she wanted to make and she gave me a small nod. "Okay," she conceded. "It was ridiculous though, and probably expensive," she added.

"*Yeah*, the shelter cat really put me out." I grinned at her. "Do you think you can cover my rent this month?" I teased her and she sighed, but a smile cracked on her lips. "Go get ready."

When they reappeared I chucked a jersey at August who held it with a confused look on his face, "Cody?" he said.

"Trust me, it'll earn you some brownie points." I handed another to Drew, who was wearing jeans and a tank top that showed off her pale skin, covered in freckles I didn't get to admire in the darkness of that night. I stepped closer, unable to help myself as my eyes ran over her skin, taking in each bundle of beauty. "Here," I said. "That's a relic, don't get mustard on it."

"Shore," she said, holding it up to show off the massive seventeen on the back. "Go grab your hat from upstairs, you left it on the island," Drew said, her tone shifting into mother and away from her own. August slipped into his jersey and bounded from the apartment into the main part of the Nest. "I can't wear this to the stadium if I'm going with Auggie," she held out the ring and I nodded, taking it in my hand and hooking it onto the ring that held my keys.

I opened my mouth to say something and closed it again. Not wanting to ruin how well the morning had been going but needing to say it to her. I knew that if it was eating at me after a long week, it was surely tearing her apart.

"Hey, I need you to know you did nothing wrong that night," I said, the words roughly bucking from my throat.

"Then why send me home, alone?" She asked and I expected her to.

"Because I didn't want to subject you to that type of conversation any longer, I didn't bring you there to be a pin cushion for a bunch of rich old men who still haven't figured out how to buy manners," I said. "You did nothing wrong." I repeated, driving home each word.

I watched the words hit her like a ton of bricks, unable to tell if they helped or only made things worse but she forced a smile to her face. I just wanted her to tell me what the hell was going on in her head but every time I thought I was getting somewhere with her, she shut the door in my face.

She's worth it.

Drew slipped into the jersey and I stepped forward, taking the chance that she would let me help and when her hands dropped to her side so I could do the buttons my heart seized. Maybe we were making progress after all.

"Beautiful," I whispered and the color flushed to her cheeks.

"Say those in front of an audience, otherwise I might start believing you mean them," she said to me as I finished the last one. I wanted to tell her they weren't for anyone but her but I kept it to myself and offered her a soft laugh in place of a confession.

"Today isn't about work, it's about you having a fun day with Auggie. We should probably go before he hot wires one of the cars in the garage to see his new crush," I teased and the light returned to her darkening eyes.

"A cat *and* a girlfriend," she grumbled. "You're a bad influence."

"God, I hope so." I looked at her over my shoulder and winked.

The stadium was packed by the time we got there and I led them to their seats. They were sitting in the front row behind the cage next to Cosy and some of her friends. I waved to them before making sure Drew was comfortable and handing August twenty dollars for snacks.

"I'll meet you in the front office after the game, okay?" I asked them both and Drew nodded with a smile.

The dugout was alive with playoff energy and the longer I stood in it the less I focused on her. Arlo kept giving me side eyes like he wanted to have a heart to heart about my stupidity but I kept three players apart from him at all times.

I didn't want to have a conversation, I wanted to be left alone to be stupid about all of my decisions. Especially the ones that involved the pretty redhead, laughing in the stands with her son as he tried to shove a whole hot dog in his mouth.

I was too far gone and I liked the way it felt to be lost.

Lorette was pushing the pace for the game and if Logan didn't start throwing outs Ryan was going to lose his shit by the end of the next inning. The boys were doing okay with runs, in fact it was the only thing keeping them alive. I watched as Cael stepped to the box, digging his toe into the clay and looking up to the sky before he steadied his breathing and readied his bat for the pitch.

His jaw twitched from the movement. Something was wrong.

I stepped forward and with me Ella moved, she saw the same flicker of pain in his eyes. He was hiding an injury. I wanted to call it out, to tell Ryan to pull him off the field but I opened my mouth too late and Cael swung.

It was like watching the muscle tear in slow motion. Arlo held his breath beside me as the bat connected with the ball and soared over the infield wide of center and past the barriers. The team erupted loudly but the three of us didn't move an inch, knowing exactly what he had just done.

A home run but at the worst cost.

Shit.

"Silas," Ella's voice broke as Cael's entire left side went limp.

"I know, don't move, let him do his circle," I said quietly, putting my hand up and wrapping it around the bannister as we all watched Cael run the bases without contest and a huge smile on his face. He was putting on a show. "Get the bag, we're going to have to force him out of the dugout," I whispered to Ella as the team cheered loudly for their shortstop.

"Arlo, manage Ryan's expectations just for the next two innings. Do not let him on to how bad this might be," I said and he nodded tightly, his hand clenched at his sides. My heart was hammering in my chest uncontrollably waiting for his face to fall as he came into the dugout but he took each high five without giving them a clue what happened.

Ryan eyed him and his eyes flickered to mine before returning to his son's.

"Locker room now," he said and Cael was in the process of arguing when Arlo blocked his path into the dugout further, his hard glare looking at the door to the tunnel. Dean appeared beside me, wanting to know what was going on.

"Do not lose this game," I warned him. Leaving out the fact that if they didn't it would all be in vain.

Dean tapped his fingers to his chest and started to rally the boys as I pushed my way around them. Ella was standing on the other side of the door with the medical bag slung over her shoulder and a devastated look on her face.

"I'm alright, Peachy—"

Cael didn't make it a step before the pain took over every muscle in his body and he crumpled against the wall with a shocking thump. Ella gasped her brows pulling together as I bent at the knees scooping up his body by the waist. She darted ahead of us, opening the doors so we could pass through. My grip was tight around him, carrying the majority of his weight just trying to keep him upright long enough to get him into the medical wing.

"Something isn't right," Cael groaned, as he rolled onto the nearest bed. "I can't feel my arm but the pain in my shoulder is—" his words trailed off and his body tightened again.

"We can't fix this here," I said to Ella and she instantly whipped her phone out calling for an ambulance. "Cael listen to me," I said but he was lost in whatever wave of pain had hit again. "Cael come on," I tapped the side of his face and he forced his eyes open. "There you are, they're going to have to assess you but there's a good chance you just tore the muscles in your rotator cuff...*again*."

"You and—" he screwed his eyes shut through the surge of pain. "Peachy said that if it happened again—"

"It would be the last time you played, that's right Cael," I reminded him with a soft tone in my voice as he fought back a string of frustrated tears. "You should have told us it was sore."

"I just wanted to play," he groaned, "I didn't want to let dad down again."

I cursed the words that tumbled out of him as Ella returned.

"What do you need from me?" She asked, her brown eyes filled with worry.

"Go back to the game," I said and before she could argue, I cut her off again, "one of us needs to be here in case something else goes wrong and Josh needs to be watched like a hawk. We can't lose them both. I have all of Cael's medical information and can handle the doctors at the hospital," I explained and Ella nodded, understanding without any more arguments. "Go, do not tell Ryan a single thing outside that Cael just needed some ice, wait until the game is over."

Ella disappeared from the office and eventually the paramedics were brought back through the stadium quietly. They stabilized his shoulder as he barked at them not to give him any drugs. I calmed him back down, with a simple promise to keep an eye on what they were giving him. He stared at me, more terrified of the drugs to ease his pain than the agony of his shoulder being torn to shreds and that broke my heart all over again. Meanwhile, the crowd had no idea they'd just watched what might be his last game ever. I ran my hands through my hair and climbed into the back of the ambulance with them, telling them to leave the lights and sirens off.

The nurses at the hospital wasted no time getting him a bed and there had been more than one doctor in and out of his temporary room in the emergency room. He needed more scans but it was pretty obvious that he had just caused irreparable damage to his body. It wasn't until we were admitted to a bed and Cael was finally asleep that I caught my breath long enough to remember that I promised Drew and August I would meet them in the office.

I texted her quickly, letting her know that I wouldn't be home for a while feeling shitty on top of guilt for accidentally forgetting about them in all the chaos. I had let Cael's injury slip through the cracks and found out first hand what it looked like when I failed my team and got distracted. I pressed the heels of my palms into my eyes and did my best not to lose my shit as the distant beeping grew incessant.

"Is he okay?" Ryan's voice broke as he stepped into the room. His hair was a mess, his hat crumpled in his hand and a distant look on his face.

I nodded, "he will be... Ryan—"

"He's done, isn't he? He won't be able to play after this?" He asked me, slowly approaching the bed and his sleeping son.

"Chances he'll be back on the field are low," I confirmed and Ryan's hand roughly curled around the handle of the bed. "I don't know how I missed it," I said.

Ryan glared at me and without words, I could feel all of his accusations. I pulled the medical chart from the base of the bed and read through everything explaining what it all meant in simple terms. The more I read, the more devastated Ryan looked. Walking the line between Coach and Father was harder than it looked and today Ryan was battling against the expectations of both.

"Go home, Shore." He didn't look up from Cael's face, his voice tight with anger, "you've done enough today. I'll call you with updates."

I couldn't help but feel like a scolded little kid leaving the hospital but I called a cab and by the time I made it back to the Nest my entire body was exhausted with guilt. I fielded whatever questions the boys had before wandering downstairs in search of my bed but when I pushed open the apartment door the smell of dinner hit my nose.

Drew and August were setting the table with dishes I had never used. I pulled at the collar of my shirt just trying to get my head in the right space as the door clicked shut and Drew's eyes found mine.

"We thought you might be hungry," she said, and the sweet tone to her voice was enough to have the glass walls built around my heart splintering and threatening to shatter.

"It smells amazing," I said, inhaling my words.

"Enchiladas," August said.

"Don't those take hours to make?" I questioned, kicking the shoes off my sore feet and walking over to the fridge.

"Silas it's nearly midnight," Drew said, her eyes drifting to the clock on the stove, 11:49.

Had I really been at the hospital that long? It had felt like all the time was jumbled up into a few minutes not six hours. "Thank you for dinner," I said, trying to maintain myself until I collapsed in bed. "It's late, you guys didn't have to stay up waiting for me."

"You shouldn't eat alone," her voice was patient with me, more patient than I probably deserved after I forgot them waiting at the stadium. Drew made a plate for me as I grabbed a cup from the upper cabinets and filled it with water. "How is he?" She asked.

He's a recovering drug addict laying in bed suffering through a career ending shoulder injury without a lick of pain medication. "He's been better."

I didn't notice the shake in my hands until the glass slipped, shattering against the corner of the island, the pieces skittering across the kitchen floor. "Shit," I swore, turning to clean it up and watched as Drew moved faster, scooping up the bigger pieces of glass with her bare hands. "I can do it," I said but she didn't listen, she just kept moving. "You're gonna cut yourself," I murmured as she moved around me.

I popped open the cupboard that held the broom but by the time I turned around she had already collected most of the glass. I was getting frustrated by the silence and she wasn't taking a minute to just let me help. It was my fucking fault the glass was broken. My head is fuzzy and I'm bared down by guilt so badly that I can feel it like lead in my bloodstream. I was so flustered that I didn't even realize that I was raising my voice until I barked, "stop!"

Drew froze by the garbage can, inhaling slowly before she turned around and excused herself from the kitchen leaving August and me standing there without explanation of what just happened.

"What was that?" I asked August as her door shut, the floor still covered in water.

"Oh she just does that sometimes, it's not your fault," he said to me, wandering toward the bathroom he returned with a towel just in time for me to fully process what he said.

"What do you mean she just does that?" I asked, "hey no, give me that." I said, my voice going soft as I took it from him and making him step back just in case there's more glass.

"Uh—" August backed away, his nervousness palpable as he chewed on the inside of his lip. I could tell that it was a conversation he wasn't sure if he was allowed to have but I stared at him for a moment longer and eventually he folded. "My dad does that."

"Does what? Auggie?" I said, my heart rate picking up as I cleaned up the last of the water. I stood up and chucked the towel in the sink, pausing to pry the answer out of him again before sweeping the broom over the floor. "Yells?" I asked.

"No," August said and stopped, "well yeah." He corrected begrudgingly, "but he breaks a lot of dishes."

What? The way he said it flooded my body with an unfamiliar heat, one that I had felt the day I found out that Josh was attacked by Ian. The kind that made me want to spend all my stupid rich resources to make a wrong, *right*.

I ran a shaky hand through my already stress-tugged hair and inhaled slowly before I spoke again. "Did he ever hit you or your mom?" I asked, carefully watching the way August answered.

"He never hit me," August said.

"What about your mom?" I asked, and waited, my heart in my throat. *Please say no*. If August even hinted at it... I ground my teeth together trying to control my expression so I didn't scare him out of being honest.

"I don't remember," he answered, clearly uncomfortable with sharing too much without his mother around. I understood, I'd stop digging.

"He was never really nice to Mom, still isn't. He's not even really nice to me. I think that's why we move around so much. She gets nervous when she messes up and then gets in her own head." He was talking from experience

I yelled at her, that's why she took off. In a moment of frantic distraction and exhaustion I had done the one thing unknowingly that might have set us back another ten steps.

"It's okay August, I shouldn't be prying." I patted the island. "Hey did you get to talk to Daisy?" I asked, changing the subject and letting him distract me with his crush news as my eyes stayed focused on the door that separated Drew and I.

Later that night I was laying in bed staring at the ceiling, contemplating every wrong step I took that ended up with Cael in a hospital bed, when there was a soft knock on the door. The handle turned before I could say anything and Drew stood in the cracked doorway, illuminated by the bathroom light she left on for August.

I stared at her for a long second before nodding gently, letting her know I was awake. She padded across the room in her pajamas and slipped into bed, her body curling against mine.

"You should be sleeping," she said, her voice muffled.

"So should you." I whispered back, nuzzling my face into her hair. I didn't care why she was awake, only that she had come back to me.

SHORE

Sunday morning came quick but I was determined to set everything back on the proper path. I woke up early and got August set up with the boys as they went down into the city for the annual Harbor U walk for Cancer. They weren't going to go, they were all too wound up about Cael. And I didn't blame them but they needed the distraction and Cael had organized their appearance with the town. He'd be upset if they didn't show.

Knowing the hospital was the final stop helped; they could show up for the town and visit Cael if he felt up for it. If anyone, Cael would want Dean's company for a moment. I was unable to sleep at all, waiting for news from Ryan but he was too pissed off to speak to me. When my phone rang at four am, I fully expected an earful, but it was Riona. Her soft voice as she told me that Cael was going to need more than one surgery nearly broke my heart but at least someone had called. So I got up, my bed empty of Drew and cold. She had left after I fell asleep and it stung. But I would focus on what I could control. First getting the boys out the door to the walk and then I spent the next two hours in the gym sweating out the guilt before getting breakfast made and knocking on Drew's door.

"Auggie?" She called out, her voice sleepy.

"No, Silas." I braced for her to tell me to fuck off, but instead there was a long silence, a little shuffling and then the door creaked open. "Breakfast, coffee?"

"Oh," her lips formed a perfect circle as her eyes drifted down to the plate of scrambled eggs and mug. Something was wrong, I could tell in the way her jaw tightened and her expression changed.

"You don't eat eggs do you?" I assumed.

"No no..." she shook her head looking up at me. "I only drink coffee if it's basically dessert; cream, sugar, the works..."

I glanced at the black coffee and smiled. "Eat," I said, handing her the plate. "We have plans today and you aren't doing it on an empty stomach."

She took the plate, eyeing me as her fingers brushed mine for the fork. I backed away from the door and wandered back into the kitchen to check the fridge, which was empty of what she needed. I looked up at the list that she had left on the outside of it, stuck to the freezer door with a Hornets magnet that had seen better days. The list was all August's handwriting—nothing for Drew.

"Mmm," I grumbled, shutting the fridge before taking the stairs to the main floor and raiding Jensen's coffee creamer collection in the fridge. I swiped both the regular cream and the caramel that he hid in the back of the fridge. Bringing them both back downstairs for Drew.

She's sitting at the island in a hoodie and jeans when I return, her hair pulled back in a lazy bun and her eyes drifting to the two bottles.

"Why didn't you write it on the grocery list?" I asked her, setting them on the counter to retrieve her abandoned cup of coffee. She pointed to the caramel when I held them up to her.

"Because I can buy myself cream for my coffee, Silas," she said after a bite of food. "Do you know where August is?"

"Dean picked him up for the Cancer Walk in the city... I hope that's alright—"

"That girl, Daisy. Is she nice?" Drew asked, pushing around her breakfast with her fork.

"I don't have an educated opinion?" I said, raising my eyebrow at her. "Her mom is Cael's Aunt, she's a sweet kid. Quiet. Her parents aren't together anymore either," I explained and Drew nodded. "So maybe her and Auggie found some common ground."

"He's spending a lot of time at the baseball stadium for a boy that hates sports," she said.

"I grew up in that stadium," I defended gently, "it's a safe place for him to find his footing in Harbor. I promise"

"You're being awfully welcoming for a man working under contract," she noted, her smile brightening as she took another bite of food.

I held back what I wanted to say to her about the contract. That I was going to do everything in my power to make her want to destroy it.

"We've been out of sync and before we do any more dinners or events I would like to get us back on the right path," I said instead, skirting around the fact that my path looked very different from hers.

"Out of sync?" She stood from the stool, walking around me to clean her plate and I took it from her before she could.

"One thing I learned from growing up in the sport is that if a team isn't on the same page, they can't win the game. Right now," I paused, making sure she understood the next part wasn't her fault. "I'm distracted, I need a break. A reset."

"Fair enough," she said, clearly still a little confused by my remark.

"I wanted to take you somewhere today, to give us both a chance to do that?" I asked her, both my hands were fucking sweaty and I felt like an idiot. Asking her on a date like we were in high school made me feel juvenile and *nervous*. "Just the two of us."

"Oh," she said, pausing to look at me. "Maybe we shouldn't... the last time we did something just the two of us—"

"Just trust me?" I asked her and her brows furrowed. Trust was in short supply these days and that was alright because I had a plan to earn hers back.

It took her a moment but she nodded. "Alright."

Even her smallest yes felt like fireworks beneath my skin.

I changed quickly, throwing on a hat and grabbing the keys to my bike as Drew waited for me in the kitchen. Her eyes trailed over me from bottom to top, stopping on the head with a curious expression.

"What?" I looked down at my jeans and t-shirt.

"You look..." She paused and smiled, "normal."

"Normal?" I barked out a short laugh and strode toward her. "What's that supposed to mean?" I asked with the laughter still on my tongue.

She chuckled, inhaling slowly as I invaded her personal space. "You have two outfits, a suit and a Hornets polo. I've just never seen you so... relaxed."

"That's the point of today," I told her, "now move your butt, I need to get you on the back of my bike before you change your mind about today and break my heart."

Drew's green eyes sparkled with something other than sadness for a split second and I'd remember that sight, keeping it in my back pocket to remind myself that the woman she wanted to be was somewhere deep inside of her. Buried beneath all that survival.

There was no protesting about the bike that time, she just pulled the helmet over her head and curled around my body as I backed us from the garage. I took the back roads and let the speed climb on the empty concrete until the wind ripped away every ounce of tension in my muscles. The fresh air, the speed, Drew wrapped around me it was good. It felt fucking good. For a second I was able to forget about all the nagging responsibilities that waited for me at the Nest, at the stadium, the courthouse, the hospital and with my grandfather. The list felt endless but at that moment it was nothing but paper. Out here I didn't have to worry about a single one of those.

"What is this place?" Drew asked as she slid off her helmet and handed it to me. The building looked sketchy from the outside, a big concrete box that used to be a carwash had only two windows and was framed against the blue sky by a circle of junk and scraps.

"Keep trusting me?" I held my hand out to her, hoping that she'd go along with it.

She looked nervous but clapped her hand into mine and let me lead her into the conspicuous building. Inside there was a front desk. And a small brunette girl that looked maybe fifteen in a pair of coveralls and a big smile on her face.

"Silas!" She hooted.

"What's up tiny terror, where's your brother?" I asked her, leaning over the counter to see what she was working on in her journal. "What's that?"

"A poem about the sun killing frogs," she said confidently and I just shrugged. "He'll be back in a second, he went to go help a group of girls…" she said. "They were going to hurt themselves."

Drew cleared her throat nervously beside me, reminding me that she was there. I was so used to coming down here alone I had completely forgotten that I brought a guest.

"Drew this is Lyla," I introduced them.

"You're pretty... she's pretty Silas. Is this your girlfriend?" Lyla asked, her manners elsewhere making me laugh.

"Yeah," I answered confidently and felt Drew stiffen under my touch.

"It's been a while." A dark voice came from the hallway and I turned to watch Mercer pull off his gloves before handing me a dirty hand to shake. "Si," he nodded, shoving that same hand through a thick head of long, loose dark waves.

"How's the off season going?" I asked, knowing how much he hated small talk.

"Busy," he shrugged, chucking his phone on the counter by the register.

"Drew," Lyla cooed when Mercer's eyes scanned the room.

"Nice to meet you," he said politely, turning away from her and wandering around the counter. I looked over at Drew trying to figure out if she was making the connection only to realize that she wasn't a sports girl. She had no clue who she was standing in front of.

It was almost endearing to watch as Mercer grumbled, his famous face going completely unrecognized by Drew. Lyla on the other hand thought it was hilarious. When Mercer North wasn't keeping one of his family's four businesses running, he was on the ice as one of the NHL's roughest enforcers.

"That's cool," Lyla snorted, noticing the lack of recognition and how much it bugged her older brother before she went back to her writing.

"Is the usual room open?" I asked, trying my best not to take the jab at him over it. Mercer nodded, shifting behind the counter in a pair of brown overalls that had seen better days.

"There's some crates in the back room, if you need more you know where to get it," he said as I dropped a few hundred on the counter. Mercer chucked a pair of keys at me without looking up from what he was reading behind the desk.

"Go get yourself and Lyla lunch, she's the hardest working employee you have." I caught the keys effortlessly, backing away from the counter as Mercer's mean stare turned on me. I pulled gently on Drew and led her back through the building, the sounds of laughter and screaming echoing through the heavy walls loudly.

"What is this place?" Drew asked as I popped open the last door on the left.

Inside was shabby, the walls had seen better days and were covered in paint and chips. In the center of the room sat a couple pairs of overalls and glasses. Along with a large garbage can full of well loved tools.

"A rage room," I said to her, closing the door behind us before she could turn and run.

I knew the thought of it would scare her, hence the surprise. I had run through my speech to her about a hundred times before waking her up that morning preparing for this exact moment.

"Silas," her voice broke on my name.

"I haven't lied to you once since we met," I said to her, stepping forward to block her path to the door. Her eyes looked around the room and her heart was pounding so loud I could hear it echoing off the walls as she started to panic. "So I'm not going to start, I'm sorry that I yelled at you yesterday. I was overwhelmed, stressed out and distracted but it wasn't your fault and the glass breaking was bad timing. August told me…"

"Told you what?" I watched as she froze.

"He told me about your ex, breaking dishes…yelling."

"Bradley never hit me, I'm not some—" Drew started but I cut her off.

"I didn't ask," I said calmly, seeing the fear in her eyes. I wanted to. I wanted to know just how bad it was under some stupid pretense that maybe I could fix it for her. Fix everything. But for now, I'd try to just fix this. "I just wanted to apologize for making you feel so small. It wasn't my intention and I promise I'll be more careful going forward."

"I'm not some broken doll," Drew argued but there was no fight to her voice.

"Alright spitfire, listen," I said with a smirk on my face. "I brought you here because I wanted to show you it's possible to break the cycle."

She watched me carefully, surprisingly letting me continue as she processed everything she had heard so far. I could tell she was internally losing her mind but she was trying to hide herself behind walls she assumed I couldn't tear down.

"I grew up walking on eggshells," I said and she raised her brow. "Oh I know what's going on in there." I tapped my temple with one finger.

"*Boo hoo*, the handsome rich doctor had a mean dad. I was and will always be a business tool to my family, maybe not my mother. But I was never a child, and I've heard the sound of shattering glass more than you know."

Her eyes softened at my confession.

"I've watched my best friend attend baseball games covered in bruises, watched his mother shield her sons until the day she died. I've watched *my* own parade around like she was invincible even in the face of every man in her life trying to tear her down." I inhaled slowly, people had no idea. "Found out I had a brother whose life was…" I swallowed hard. "Watched a man lose his wife and a team of young boys lose a woman so special to them they're still mourning her death. They've gone through hell, we all have." I said quietly. "Before you throw that rock, know *my* house is made of glass too."

"So you're a hypocrite?" Drew asked when I went quiet, but it wasn't malicious.

"Sure, something like that. I judge people too quickly based on assumptions, and I'm sorry that I scared you yesterday. But this, this is how you get over that sound. It's how I did. It's the only place I could just come and let everything out that I had been holding on to. All that anger, all the grief, all the fear of not being good enough."

Drew wet her bottom lip as she thought about what I said. I don't know if I got through to her or if I was totally off base but I held my breath and waited.

"Give me the bat." Her voice was shaky, quiet—but her hand was steady and that was all I needed.

COURTNEY

I was shaking, absolutely terrified of what came next. Silas helped me into a pair of coveralls and I pushed the safety glasses down over my face and took a deep breath.

"So I just break stuff?" I asked him and he nodded, zipping up his own and grabbing the sledgehammer from the bin he rolled it in his hand.

"You just break stuff," he said with a bright smile.

Just not your heart.

No, that's special.

Silas watched closely as I stepped toward the table. The gloves were a little too big, every fibre scratching at my skin. He had laid everything out of the table and stepped back so I could pick what I wanted to break.

It felt silly, absolutely ridiculous that he wanted me to take out my anxiety on the poor chip plate in front of me. I stared at it, remembering every time Bradley hurled one across the house, the sharp shatter echoing off the walls.

Figure yourself out Drew.

Smash.

You've got to do better.

Smash.

You wanted this.

Smash.

Can't you just be happy?

"Drew?" Silas's voice was calmer than before as he came around to stand in front of me. He lowered his six-foot frame to come eye to eye with me. "Take control of the sound, remove the emotional trigger from it."

"How do you know all this?" I asked him.

"Years and years of therapy," Silas smiled. "You didn't think a man this regulated did it on his own, did you?"

I took in all the features of his face, the hardened ridges of his jaw and the soft swells of his cheeks when he smiled at me. The tiny flecks of dark blue danced along the light gray color that swallowed his pupil. Long lashes and tiny gray hairs poking out from his beard and around his ears.

"Shocking." I grinned at him, forcing the smile to my face in a pathetic attempt to hide how terrified I was.

"Just have fun."

"You go first," I suggested.

Silas shook his head at me, "you have to go first," he said, reaching out to push back a piece of my hair that fell loose. "If I go and it scares you, we're right back where we started."

"Okay," I huffed nervously.

"Hold the bat..." he mumbled quietly, shifting my hands around on the handle, "yeah that's better, and swing as hard as you can. Don't hold back."

Silas stepped out of my way, moving to the back wall as I counted myself down. I stared at the plate, more ready than I had been before. *I could do this, I could break a plate. Nothing will happen if I do. It's why we're here.*

I lifted the bat over my head and brought it down on the plate, shattering it into a bunch of pieces without remorse. I froze, waiting for the screaming, waiting for the panic, taking in all the fractured pieces. It had exploded across the table much like the laughter that exploded from me. "Holy shit," I turned to Silas, my heart racing out of my chest. "That was..."

"Fun?" He was standing with his arms crossed over his chest, the hammer hanging down at his side and a smug smile on his face.

"Can I do it again?" I asked, the adrenaline pumping through my veins.

"Have at it, killer." He shrugged and I turned back to the room, taking in all the things that were *meant* to be broken. Like someone had turned on a switch I just went at it all, swinging the bat around and releasing all the negative energy that I had been holding on to.

Silas watched on as I moved to the T.V. In the corner of the room, looking back at him to ask permission only for him to nod. I couldn't begin to imagine how Silas had stumbled upon something as ridiculous as this. It felt so out of how he typically carried himself in the public eye.

I swung through and smashed out the screen with a satisfying pop of glass and fibers. Silas strode across the room and, tapping me so gently on the hip with his sledgehammer to get me to move. I smiled, stepping to the side and leaning on the bat out of his way as he brought the hammer up and over his head. The muscles in his back rippled beneath his tight shirt as the hammer collided with the top and caved in on itself.

"Wow, you're strong," I said sarcastically with a smirk on my face.

"Don't patronize me," he huffed, no real heat in it, just light dancing in his eyes.

"It's not about the size of the dog."

"Sorry, sorry. Please continue," I stifled a giggle and put my hand over my mouth as he glared at me playfully.

Silas was anything but a small dog, his arms were wide with strength and his shoulders broad. The veins in his neck popped as he ripped through the side of the already dismantled television and sent it flying across the room.

It was clear that he hadn't just brought me down here to work through my own emotions, he was carrying heavy pains of his own. His face tightened with the next swing and I could see the stress building and releasing in his body with each hit. I was going to ask him earlier why he wasn't back at the hospital but the thing was, usually he would have just told me and it was like he was avoiding the conversation of what happened all together.

I could respect his space, even if I didn't want to.

"I can't smash all this stuff alone," Silas turned to me with an infectious smile, pushing back the doubts that maybe he wasn't enjoying himself. And even if he was masking the way he was really feeling, so was I, so I couldn't necessarily fault him for it. "We aren't leaving until you've destroyed everything so..."

I joined back in with him, letting every ounce of frustration out through laughter and destruction. He couldn't have been more right about letting it all out and taking back the subtle violence that was held in every broken dish of my past. Everything in the room turned to dust and it felt like all the tense muscles in my body were finally unknotting enough for me to breathe properly again.

Silas's hair was sweaty and sticking in every direction as he whipped off his glasses. I hadn't noticed the dimples in his cheeks before now, his smile pushing them forward.

"Better?" He asked, running a hand through his hair to smooth it down.

"Better."

And for once the word didn't feel like a lie. I honestly felt better, lighter even in the wake of everything happening outside of my control. It was absolutely insane that taking a bat to inanimate objects made me feel alive.

"How often do you come here?" I asked him as we stripped from the coveralls. He turned to me, taking mine and hanging it on the wall beside the door.

"I haven't been able to lately with everything going on. It's been hard," he explained. I watched as Silas retreated in on himself. "I probably shouldn't have even come today but, I just needed a second to breathe." His jaw tightened with every thought that popped back into his head and I hadn't meant to bring it all back up after he had left it behind with the broken dishes but...

"Have you checked on him?" I asked him as we wandered down the hallway back to the front door, the lobby was empty and I was grateful because it meant Silas couldn't use other people as an excuse to play a part and avoid the question.

"Riona called this morning." His words were tight and lacking any sort of emotion that might tell me how he really felt about the situation.

"Silas," I stopped on the curb as he walked around his bike to grab the helmets. "I thought we were supposed to be on the same page again."

"This is personal Drew, it has nothing to do with our arrangement," he said softly, not trying to hurt my feelings but I narrowed my eyes on him.

"Neither does this." I pointed to the building behind me and stepped up to the other side of the bike across from him. "Tell me the truth or stop giving me mixed signals."

Silas stared at me for a moment, clearly unimpressed by the demand but it worked, it shook loose something inside him that he had locked up.

"He's in rough shape, Cael is a recovering addict and while his addiction did not discriminate against any vice, now that he's sober he refuses any addictive medication," Silas explained and I listened, I knew the basics but what Cael was going through was exhausting and took so much strength I'd never understand. "He's going to have surgery and wake in more pain, and there's nothing I can do about it, but I could have *prevented* it."

His whole body tensed and I could see the water lining his gray eyes.

"It was an accident."

"Arlo hasn't called," Silas said, practically cutting me off. He had already rationalized his guilt. His teeth bothered his bottom lip and his eyes lifted to the sky. "That's how I *know* I fucked this up. Arlo should have called, but him and Ryan made Riona do it because I fucked up. It's my fault that Cael's injury went unnoticed, why he's..." His words trailed off tightly and I watched him turn away from me to hide his emotions.

"Have you tried to call them?" I asked, tip-toeing around the delicate relationship hierarchy they seem to have. The silence was deafening.

"Arlo warned me that I needed to remember what was important. I've been..." he cleared his throat, his hands running over his face with his back to me. "There's just a lot happening and I thought I could handle it all on my own."

"Isn't that why I'm here?" I said quietly, my fingers reaching across the divide, I gently tangled them into the back of his shirt and begged him to turn around. "Let me help." I said when he finally looked at me.

It was like it had never been offered to him before or maybe it had never been offered in a way that he listened or considered it.

"You helped me today, in the midst of all your own turmoil... you brought me here to rewire a part of me you didn't tangle Silas. Why?" I asked him, retreating back and resting my hand on the seat of his bike.

"I don't know," Silas said softly.

"You don't know or you don't have an answer that won't make this complicated?" I argued with a gentle smile forming on my lips. "Because it's okay if it's the second one."

Silas nodded.

"We should get back to the house," I said when he didn't have anything else to say. "But first, the hospital. Let's check on Cael."

"They don't want me there," he said with a weak shake of his head.

"We should bring them coffee." I ignored his protest and grabbed my helmet.

"Drew," Silas warned.

"I did something scary today," I told him. "Now it's your turn."

SHORE

Drew carried a tray of coffee in her hand and I followed behind with a bag of food, my feet practically dragging on the tile floor of the hospital. My feet dragged across the hospital tile, my heart hammering against my ribs. I was completely consumed by my guilt and I wasn't exactly sure how coming here would go but Drew was determined and her leverage was solid.

Cael was still in the same room, but when we arrived his bed was empty. I stepped into the room in front of Drew, Arlo was slumped against the wall with his eyes closed and Ryan was sleeping in the chair with his head resting over the back of it.

"Ar."

Arlo's eyes opened slowly at the sound of my voice and his jaw tightened but he pushed off the wall and walked toward me. I half expected him to hit me when his hand tangled into the collar of my shirt, I flexed, bracing for the impact but he just stared at me.

"Where the fuck have you been?" he asked, his voice low to not wake Ryan.

I swallowed tightly. "Taking care of everything else, it's not like you two wanted me here. Having Riona call was *cold*."

"You spent way too much money on all that education to be this stupid," Arlo snapped. "She called because Ryan is a mess and I don't have my fucking phone."

"Where's your phone?" I reached up and uncurled his hand from my shirt, taking a step back to breathe.

"I chucked it out the Fastback window—it wouldn't stop buzzing," Arlo muttered with a pissed-off look on his face. His tongue brushed over his bottom lip. "He's going to be okay Si," he assured me. "He was lucid enough to fight with Clementine when she wouldn't give him one last joyride before surgery."

"He said that?"

"Yeah, in front of his dad and about three nurses just trying to get him out of the room." Arlo shook his head.

I smiled, cursing myself for missing the look on Ryan's face when it happened.

"He made that one and about nineteen other jokes about his immortality. I swear by the end of this Coach is going to have a head of gray hair." Arlo looked over his shoulder at Ryan. "Why weren't you here?"

"When Riona called I just assumed it was because neither of you wanted to talk to me..." I shrugged.

Arlo stared at me with that hardened, confused expression and I, as much as I loved him, sometimes it took him a second to remember that it's not always black and white.

"You think this is your fault?" He scoffed, stepping forward and grabbing the back of my head to pull us closer together. "This isn't anyone's fault but that stupid kid in surgery right now. He's an adult, he had the opportunity to bring this to you, to Ella. And *he* didn't."

"I should have noticed the strain it was taking on his body," I argued and Arlo's fingertips tightened around my neck.

"It's fucking playoffs, there's strain on everyone and you aren't a human X-ray machine. The only thing preventing that tear was a permanent spot warming the bench." He scowled at me, and I knew he was right but it didn't make it any less hard to hear.

"Even if that was his last inning of ball, the kid went out swinging. The press will be talking about it for weeks and if it kills his career even longer," Arlo said. "You know what he said to Ryan before they took him out of here, tears in his eyes from the pain?" He asked and I swallowed tightly, expecting the worst. "He told his dad that playing again didn't matter as long as he had his family and his sobriety. He's here because of you, all that work you did to get him sober without destroying his life. You fixed every problem in that idiot's life for the last seven years, for once don't blame yourself for something he knowingly did to himself."

I clenched my jaw and tried to process what Arlo had said but the guilt was strong and it would be for a while. Even if it wasn't my fault. Until Cael was back on his feet, it would run rampant.

"I'll feel better once he's home," I breathed out. Just trying to give Arlo something to run on so he'd stop digging his fingers into open wounds. "I promise."

He eyed me for a moment but his grip loosened on my head and he stepped back from me with a suspicious look on his face. I know full well that I wasn't going to get away with that answer for long, so I was going to have to avoid him for a bit to figure myself out.

"Is that for me?" He asked, his head leaning around me to where Drew was standing with her coffee. His eyes flickered with judgement before he said good afternoon to her and thanked her for the coffee.

"Where's Riona?" I asked.

"Right here," her voice was like ice as she entered the room. "I had to drop off Daisy with her aunt," she explained, "in three years she's never once wanted to do that Cancer walk, I had to bribe her last year and now because of that silly little brown-haired shit head-"

Arlo burst into laughter, his eyes crinkling up as Riona ranted and Ryan was startled from his sleep.

"What the hell is going on?" He sat up in his chair, stretching out his back as Riona wandered to the corner to set her purse down.

"Riona is insulting Drew's son without knowing it and I'm enjoying the worst cup of coffee I've ever drank in my entire life." Arlo choked it down with a rough cough.

Riona's eyes went wide as she took in Drew, "I am so sorry."

"It's okay, if the roles were reversed I would have thrown in a few more choice adjectives," Drew said, allowing Riona an easy out. "Your daughter is also the only reason my son is up on a weekend and if he doesn't behave I'll lock him in his room for a week?" She gave her a weak smile.

"Well, it's nice to meet you, and I'm sorry I insulted him…" Riona crossed the room and held her hand out to her. Drew offered her a coffee but after seeing the face Arlo made, passed on the cup and took the bag of pastries out of my hand.

"How long has he been in surgery?" I asked, stepping back to rest against Drew, grounding myself to her and silently thanking her for the push.

"Half an hour maybe?" Ryan looked down at his watch with a grunt, "Clem should be back soon, I sent her home to sleep a while ago."

"El?" I asked Arlo.

"She drove Clementine home, and is going to bring her back," he explained. There were small moments of brightness in the dark, like Ella finding her confidence to drive again. It was only occasional and only when she had to, she still used her bike more often than not but she was working toward something and that mattered.

"She's just keeping herself busy so she doesn't go insane with worry."

"Clem will take care of her," I said to Arlo and he nodded.

Riona grumbled something in response to that as she started to chew down a danish. Ryan pushed from the chair and stretched out what could have only been exhausted muscles.

"Everyone go home, get some sleep." He looked around the room, old green eyes pausing briefly on Drew before they flickered to Arlo. "You too. He'll be groggy as all hell, coming out of this and I'm going to need your help in the morning."

Arlo opened his mouth to argue but got the glare of death and thought better of it. "One of us needs sleep and some patience or a bum shoulder will be the least of his worries," Ryan joked, earning a soft laugh from the room. The look of concern on his face was palpable. The first time he had injured himself, he had also quit drugs cold turkey and threw himself in a rehab facility. None of us had to truly survive the tidal wave that was enduring the pain he would no doubt be in when he woke up.

The next week or so would be the worst until the dull sting of metal instruments poking around inside of his muscles and scraping against his bones subsided. I couldn't imagine how horrible it was going to be without even ibuprofen, but we'll be lucky if we even get him to take that.

The worry was loud between the three of us, in a deadlock of fear for what was to come when he got out of surgery. Riona cleaned her hands off and cleared her throat after a moment and we all managed to get free of our thoughts.

"Come on, Cap. I'll give you a ride," Riona patted him on the shoulder, still referring to him as she always had and ushered him from the room after giving her brother a soft look.

"Silas," Ryan said as I turned to Drew, she smiled at Ryan and excused herself.

"Yeah?" I twisted back to him and braced for the scolding. It had been awhile since he had been coach and me a player but even I had my moments where Ryan was more father than friend. The look on his face told me that this was one of those times.

"The doctor said that Cael could have torn that muscle reaching for a can in the cupboard, it was as thin as paper when the injury happened. Barely hanging on under his skin. There was nothing any of us could have done to stop it. Do you understand?" He asked and I nodded. "I'm sorry I snapped at you yesterday, that..." he paused, struggling with his apology. "It shouldn't have happened but I was frustrated and *scared*. You were the first person I saw and it just came out."

"It's okay," I said. "I'm scared too."

Ryan inhaled, filling his chest with air before speaking again, "he's going to be fine."

"He's too stubborn to be anything else," I added as he wandered closer and gave me a pat on the shoulder. I stood with him for a quiet moment, the both of us taking the chance to settle our heart rates in the silence.

Ryan Cody never got enough credit for wrangling all of us. Lorraine was often the forefront of conversation when it came to her instincts and our upbringing within the Nest. But Ryan had watched us grow from the dugout, he'd watched boys come in and out of that locker room each one coming in a boy and leaving a man. He wasn't always eloquent with his words or loud about his love but he had always protected us from the monsters in the dark that none of us could see. Raised us to know how to fight them when he wasn't around to do it.

He'd stumbled with Cael—but raising your mirror is the hardest thing a man can do.

And unfortunately, Cael was running around in the world with the heart of Lorraine completely unprotected and unaware of how much it hurt Ryan every time he was in pain.

"I'll stop by the office, grab your duffle before I come back in the morning. Do you need anything else?" I asked him.

"A fucking vacation," Ryan joked.

"After playoffs," I smiled. Backing away to where Drew stood in the doorway. "I'll pay for the plane ticket."

Ryan shook his head, waving me off. "I'll see you in the morning."

By the time we get back to the apartment after running some errands and stopping at the stadium for a bag of Ryan's things, the Nest is full again and everyone is upstairs making noise. There's a massive banner on the kitchen table that Dean had started to paint for Cael's return and Drew giggled at the sight of it.

"He's got the artistic skill of a toddler," Arlo scowled, staring at it. Ella was tucked in his arms with her back against his chest, staring at it with her eyebrows scrunched together.

"But it's so cute, and telling him would break his heart," Ella said. "I still have my birthday one rolled up in the room. I'll treasure it forever," she laughed.

Drew's stomach grumbled from beside me and I looked over at her. "I guess we should get food..." I said, completely forgetting about it in all the commotion.

"You two go, Auggie is two hours into an intense Mario Kart tournament with the boys, I'll make sure he gets some pizza," Ella said with a smile, pointing to the couch.

There was a pile of boys spread out across the living room, August sitting in the middle with a hardened concentrated look on his face. Red, that stupid asshole cat, was sprawled out across the back of the couch with Josh's fingers pressed into its ratty fur. It stared at me like it could see into my soul and it gave me the heebie-jeebies. That cat was absolutely going to murder me in my sleep.

"Is that?" My eyes looked over the rest of the room, landing on a dark-haired girl with a massive smile on her face before turning back at Arlo.

"No idea how that fucking idiot pulled her," he shrugged. "Apparently getting half naked in the middle of playoff games is the new flirting."

"You should try it on your next girlfriend," Ella teased and Arlo dug his fingers into her sides making her laugh loudly.

"How about I try it on my current girlfriend," Arlo teased as we turned our attention back to the living room.

Adeline Sarah was sitting at Jensen's side laughing loudly and by the looks of things she was winning the race they were in the middle of and Van was screaming about her cheating while Josh watched on in amusement at Dean's misfortune with red shells.

"Good for him," I said with a smile. Drew looked hesitant to leave August for a split second but I pressed my hand to her back and she shifted her gaze to me. "We can order something?" I asked her and she nodded.

COURTNEY

Silas came back with two bags of food and it all smelled incredible as he pulled it out and set it on the island in front of me. "What is it?" I asked.

"Thai, I hope you like that... I probably should have asked." He stumbled around his choice for a second, losing that normal shield of confidence.

"I do," I said with a smile, plucking a sauce-covered carrot from the container in front of me as he reached for plates.

"Sorry it's not pickles," he teased.

"Don't bring them into this," I said, piling my plate with whatever looked good. The reality was, after telling him, three different types of pickles appeared in the fridge the next day. I was never telling him something was my favourite again.

We sit in silence for a little while, going back and forth with stupid little questions that have no actual point but it's nice to see him relax a little after the evening we had. Seeing him so wound up at the hospital had caught me off guard. The Silas I had come to know was a man of positivity, he always looked for the good in a situation but I guess that didn't apply to his own mistakes or faults.

I didn't know anything about baseball, or injuries but hearing that he truly believed that he caused the injury was devastating and it seemed his friends knew that he would feel that way and were quick to counter his thoughts.

"Thank you for today," I said quietly, "it's odd but I feel better."

"In all honesty, I didn't even think I was going to get you on the bike," Silas said.

"Why?" I asked, nibbling on a string of spicy noodles.

"I figured I had screwed up whatever friendship we did have. After dinner and then breaking the cup..." He shrugged.

"I'm not that fragile you know," I argued gently and it forced him to smile.

"Auggie sees it differently," Silas said and my heart stuttered.

"What does that mean?" I asked, trying to hide my panic.

"Do you know anything about Cael? About their family?" he asked me. It was almost infuriating that he just continued to serve himself food while my breathing had stopped. "Was it in any of the notes Ella gave you?"

"A little, it was mostly basic stuff," I said, and set down my fork.

Silas sighed. "Auggie reminds me of Cael," he said. "There's something so innocent and observant about him. Something so undeniably kind. I don't know a single kid that would choose a dumpster cat when he has more than one kitten to pick from."

"He's always loved the underdog," I said, trying to calm myself.

"That, right there," Silas pointed out. "Is why he sees you differently," he explained. "You're very good at hiding it, I'll give you that."

"Hiding what?" I scowled at him.

"Your sadness." Silas watched me, his chest rising and falling slowly. "Auggie sees it better than anyone and he spends a lot of time tip-toeing around it because it's afraid to hurt your feelings more."

"Wow, I'm glad this dinner turned into you judging how I raise my kid. What happened to throwing rocks in glass houses?" I went to slip off the stool and Silas grabbed my arm. "Let go," I warned.

"I'm not judging you," he said, not loosening the gentle grip he had on me. "I'm just saying he's protective of you, he's the first to stand up for you."

"He's my kid, he shouldn't be doing any of that," the words were tight and uneven coming out of me. I hated this, watching a good day turn sour.

"When he told me about what your ex used to do... It took everything in me not to say some horrible shit or pry into your life, Drew. I was ready to use a thirteen-year-old just for a little more information but I realized that he isn't the person I should be asking." Silas said. "It's not his responsibility to take care of you, even if he believes it is. Even if that's not how you raised him."

"This all sounds pretty condemning, Silas."

"From what I gather he's been raised to be kind, protective and helpful. To never make more work for anyone, to always be the first to offer a hand and to be polite even when someone isn't treating you with respect. And there's nothing wrong with any of that, but it's not Auggie. He's just a kid, he's doing what he's always done. It's what he knows. But it's not him, all of those things. They're *you*."

"Oh so this is more therapy, the rage room was just the first hurdle?" I sneered at him, hating how his thumb brushed over my arm and how easily I was distracted by the calming feeling it brought on. I was putting up walls faster than he could tear them down just praying that he didn't get to the route of the problem.

Figure yourself out Drew.

"You wear this mask, you never show anyone who you really are and at first I thought it might be because you were protecting yourself but it's not that," Silas said and my chest tightened. "It's because you don't know who you are."

I huffed out a frustrated laugh just to keep from crying. Why was it when I felt this way, crying was the only response my body came up with?

"I do know who I am and who are you to assume I don't?" I tried to fight back. "My fake fiance, who's using a woman to trick his dying grandfather into signing over his shares to his fortune?" I said harshly, instantly feeling like a piece of shit knowing that it was probably too far. "Who are *you*, Silas?" I countered. "Because from where I'm standing you don't even know."

His grip finally faltered and his eyes softened. "I deserved that," he nodded, "maybe not the dying grandfather part but the rest."

"I'm sorry," I sighed. I didn't want to be some frightened, depressed ball of anxiety. I had been formed into this over the years.

"You're right. I don't know who I am outside of the 'How can I help' version of myself. And maybe I'm terrified that if I don't get these shares it makes it hard to be that guy for everyone. Who would I be without that money? I can't fund the team, I can't keep harbor running, I can't donate to people who need it. All that fortune will go into my corrupt fathers pockets where he can ruin more lives and create more kids like Josh."

His frustration poured out, "and if he does I wouldn't even have the ability to help them down the road."

My brows knitted together tightly and I leaned over the counter, suddenly aware of how cracked his armor was. Silas thrived on being everyone's white knight but he genuinely believed that's all he was to them. A problem solver with an endless bank account.

I set aside my frustration because Silas had never once given a reason to be treated like that and I could recognize that lashing out wasn't going to solve anything. What hurt was knowing that's how others saw me: small, reserved, easy to be around because I never asked for much.

"You're more than that." The words came out so softly that I wasn't even sure he had heard them but he looked up at me again, brows crumbled together and jaw screwed shut. "You are."

"You're doing it again," his voice was smooth, almost cautious. "You make yourself small to avoid the conflict."

"I meant that," I argued back. He wasn't just his money and it was frustrating that he had been conditioned to believe that about himself.

"I know you did," he responded, "but you said it because you were scared of the argument, you were backing down because you didn't want to hurt my feelings but what about yours?"

"You didn't say anything that wasn't true, Silas." I admitted and the confession stung at the corners of my eyes.

"You can get mad, I won't..." he paused, "you can yell and scream at me and I will never lay a hand on you." The words came out with conviction and Bradley never had but I appreciated the tone in Silas's voice when he said it.

I rounded the island with shaky hands and a racing heart.

"I know," I said to him as he turned to face me. It was so simple, but honest and needed to be said. For him and for myself to hear it. "For the record, I've never been...hit."

"Auggie wouldn't tell me," he said, sounding upset. "I shouldn't have asked but I couldn't help myself. I needed to know."

I took a deep breath as his hand came up and his knuckle grazed my tight jaw, "I don't mean to, but I also don't know how to stop it," I confessed, "it's just easy to get small, familiar."

Silas studied my face, wanting to say something but clearly conflicted on how he should word himself to avoid restarting the argument that had sparked suddenly. It was odd because even though we had both contributed I didn't feel like I was being backed into a corner. Fights with Bradley had always felt me feeling like I didn't have an out. Like I needed to plan an exit strategy for every little mistake I made.

Meanwhile, Silas was sitting here staring at my lips like he wanted to kiss me but his face was twisted painfully with deeper intentions.

"Say what you're thinking Silas before you lose the nerve," I whispered and he swallowed tightly, his eyes finally drifting up to meet mine.

"I'm adding a condition to our contract," he said, reaching out and wrapping around me until I was slotted between his thighs and his palms were spread out flat against my back. The movement surprised me as much as his confession did. I was waiting for anger, more frustration or questions. Not that. I held my breath waiting for his newest condition.

"Anytime you feel the need to get small, come and find me?"

I opened my mouth to argue and he shook his head.

"Even if it's my fault, let me fix it." He was practically begging me to agree as his fingers dug into my back and pressed me closer against him.

"That feels a little personal for a contract," I whispered, tempted to run my hands through his unkempt hair.

"It's my contract, I can change it whenever I want," Silas argued.

"That's worrisome." I offered him a tiny smile and he finally took a breath of air, his chest brushing against mine. "And what about you?" I asked, trying to think of something that could help him wriggle free of his need to feel useful constantly.

"Me? Drew I've never made myself small for anyone," he huffed and I laughed gently.

"No, I mean, if I'm forced to work on myself, so are you. Once a day, you have to do something for yourself. And only you. It can't have motives. It has to be selfish."

"Feels stupid," he huffed.

"It's just one thing, Silas."

"It can be anything?" he asked me and I nodded.

He leaned forward, his hand coming up around the back of my neck as he brushed his lips against mine so gently it tickled. I hated how good it was, even sober, like the universe was laughing at me by dropping a man like Silas in my lap when it knew I wasn't good enough for him. When he pulled back he looked satisfied with himself.

"That was *selfish*, I'm sorry." Silas's voice was low and teasing, but he had a proud smile on his face.

COURTNEY

Eventually, I slipped from his arms, still dizzy from the unexpected contact but there was no tension or stress between us. Nothing left unsaid. It was a strange feeling to be able to argue with Silas and still come out feeling like I had won when the truth was no one did, we weren't even trying to compete. It was healthy despite being fake and it was infuriating that it was happening this way.

"Any fun scars?" He asked after some time, reaching for his second beer and offering me one. I shook my head, the last time I got drunk around Silas Shore I ended up naked.

"I grew up on a farm and we never wore shoes when I was little. We went from the house to the gravel to the grass without a second thought. I stepped on a nail when I was nine, it went right through my foot and now I have a perfect circle right below my big toe." I told him and his head tipped back in laughter.

"That's it that's your only scar?" He asked, absolutely bewildered by it.

No, but the others were from cleaning glass and accidentally cutting my hands and the soles of my feet. Scars that weren't fun.

"Yup, I look small but I have surprisingly strong bones. Never broken a single one," I beamed with pride.

"That's impressive, not even a finger?" He asked, bringing the bottle to his lips as I shook my head no. "I don't think there's a bone in my body I haven't broken..." Silas thought about it.

"Is that so?" I raised an eyebrow and insinuated.

"Alright, alright..." he blushed, the man actually turned an adorable shade of pink. "You and I both know that bone has never been broken."

"Hey," I scowled, "don't bring me into this, it was your story. I'm just double-checking the details," I feigned innocence.

"Mmhm," Silas hummed. Flirting, even for half a second, was a fatal mistake. I watched as Silas's expression shifted and turned hungry.

"Is that why you aren't drinking?" he asked me softly after a beat of silence. When I didn't answer he smiled, shaking his head and setting the bottle down. "The whiskey might have instigated that first time Drew but I have been having very sober thoughts about it for weeks." His eyes seemed to burn tingling circles into my skin that forced me to look away from him.

"Silas," I warned.

"Drew," he countered with a smirk.

"You can't tell me you didn't feel it," he said, his tongue brushing over his bottom lip like he was chasing the taste from our kiss. He pushed out of his stool to stand over the island and get closer to me.

"It's a show, and we shouldn't make more of it. Someone is going to get hurt," I argued gently despite the way he stirred up the butterflies in my chest.

"I have a high pain tolerance," he practically purred as his hands curled around the edge, his knuckles white, pushing all his frustration into the grip.

"That's not—" I scoffed, "what I meant. You can't be flirty and—"

"And what?" He smirked, his tongue darting out over his bottom lip, "use your words."

"Annoyingly handsome," I huffed, his hair was messy, his shirt was loose around his collar giving me the smallest hint of the tanned skin that ran beneath. I wanted to see his tattoo again, study his thighs and count the freckles on his back. I had been spending the majority of the day ignoring the urge to hold his hand and touch his face. The lovesick crush was making me nauseous. His smile grew, flashing his perfect teeth at me and he knew he won. I was fucking screwed.

"You want me to be selfish, and I want to make you feel good. Is that complicated to you?" He countered, those painfully beautiful eyes watching my every move, each shift in expression was caught by them and I couldn't stand it.

"You make it sound like it's black and white," I sighed.

"It isn't, I know it's not. But I want all the gray in between too, Drew. Sober, drunk. I want them all." He waited, and I knew if I didn't give him a solid answer he would either climb across the island and take it himself, or he'd spend the next week convincing me otherwise.

"I have a son." I whispered, "a very grown son who sees through every single one of my lies."

"One who is very much passed out on the couch upstairs with Van," he turned his phone to show me a picture from the group chat. A tiny giggle leaving my lips at his nickname. "Hey, very serious, time-sensitive conversation happening here, don't you laugh at Cat Daddy."

"We can't," I shook my head, but the smile on my face gave away my cracking resolve.

"Why?" He asked. Silas smelled too good, he looked too fucking good. I needed him to stop before I crumbled under the pressure.

"Because," I weakly countered.

"Not good enough," He took the pathetic rebuttal as an opening and took a couple steps around the island toward me. "Give me one good reason why I shouldn't kiss you again."

"My pain tolerance isn't as high as yours," I said quickly, stepping back from him despite the want to curl into his touch. Terrified of getting attached, needy for the feeling he brought down on me.

"I'll be gentle," he said, pausing in his movement to truly mean what he said. So many implications behind those three words.

How could I trust myself not to fuck this up? What happened the day he decided we weren't worth the hassle? Was I just another problem for him to fix?

"What happens when you get the control you need, the shares?" I asked him, I couldn't help myself. I needed to hear him say it before I ultimately gave into those rough hands and bright eyes.

"This isn't about that." He dropped his tone.

My head was spinning with what-ifs that I couldn't control.

"That's what this is all about, it's what started it!" I said loudly with a shaky voice.

"This." He stepped forward, linking his finger into the front of my jeans and tugging me into his gravity, "isn't." His head lowered to mine and he used his other hand to hold my jaw in place as he approached. "About that." The kiss that followed was deep, slow and intoxicating as his fingers tangled into my hair and pulled it from the ponytail it was in.

His tongue swiped over my lip and into my mouth as his fingers worked at the button of my jeans and popped it free without breaking his concentration.

"It's infuriating how easily you make me change my mind," I hummed against the kiss, losing myself in him with each small ticklish movement.

Silas chuckled softly, the vibration sending a shiver down my spine. He unzipped my jeans slowly, pushing them down my hips in a swift movement. His hands moved so softly I gasped when they slid around my ass and lifted me effortlessly to the counter, spreading my legs wide. His lips found my neck sucking softly as one finger pushed the damp fabric aside and he slipped inside of me, testing the wetness.

"You make it too easy," he grumbled, his words hot on my neck as I arched back and braced myself on the countertop.

"We can't do this—" I choked on the words as he added another finger and they curled against my walls. "Here."

We were going to get caught.

"They're asleep, it's fine," he whispered against my collarbone. His fingers continued their slow pace, driving me wild. At this rate it wouldn't matter because I'd be completely undone in seconds. My entire body betrayed me with each tortuous plunge his fingers took, I was a mess from the way he carefully stroked every nerve.

"Silas." His name was nothing but a deep moan off my tongue.

"Quiet," he warned with a mischievous smirk. His thumb pressed down onto my clit sending me over the edge. He watched with satisfaction as my mouth dropped open completely speechless from the pleasure coursing down to my toes. He pulled his fingers out and pushed them into his mouth, sucking them clean.

Fuck.

"You're being reckless to prove a point," I huffed breathlessly as he pulled me from the counter into his arms and walked me to his bedroom.

"And you're too stubborn to admit this is exactly what you want." He kicked the door shut behind us and tossed me onto the bed. "No more thinking," he said, pushing the hair away from my face and then wrapped gently around my throat as he kissed me again.

I shut everything off as he kissed down my neck, his other hand curled around my hip tightly. He hummed against my skin like he could feel my surrender and it only fueled every wet peppered kiss he left behind. His hand on my throat tightened slightly, not enough to hurt but enough to remind me it was still here.

Bradley had never touched me like that. He was so quick about sex, like he never wanted to be there. But with Silas it was slow, each touch meant to rattle me to the core. He broke the kiss, his eyes searching mine as I tried to hide the memories away and focus on how he touched me, how he looked at me.

"Turn over," he demanded, his voice husky and commanding.

I slipped from my shirt, tossing it away from me and rolled onto my belly, sinking into the mattress. Completely unsure about what he was going to do but trusting him completely.

I felt the bed move and heard the sound of his clothes falling away before it dipped again. His hands skimmed down my back, fingers trailing over every curve and dip. His fingers hooked into the underwear in his way and rolled it over the swell of my ass and down my thighs. Once gone he settled between my legs, his hardness pressing against my ass as his lips brushed my ear.

"Such a good girl," he whispered and my body tensed as it rolled through me, it was freeing being completely at his will. He groaned, his hands spreading my legs apart slightly. The wetness pooled between my thighs and my stomach clenched as he leaned down and pressed an open mouthed kiss to the small of my back, his tongue snaking out to taste my skin.

My hips sank into the mattress and I burned my face into the pillows as he took his time exploring my body with his lips, teeth and tongue. His finger undid the clasps of my bra with a simple flick, leaving it limp against my skin as he continued to move. Sucking, kissing and nipping at every inch of exposed skin as he slowly worked his way down my back. He moved lower, his tongue dipping into the crease of my ass before moving further down to my soaking core.

Silas moaned against my skin, his tongue swirling and lapping at my clit, teasing and sucking gently. He wanted to draw out every ounce of pleasure from my body before taking what he wanted. His hands gripped my ass firmly, spreading me wider to give him more room as my toes curled tightly. I tried to hold onto my dignity but it felt so good that I didn't care how pathetic it was to come again, that time on his face instead of his fingers.

He growled in satisfaction, the sound rumbling from his throat. My body trembled with pleasure, every skillful stroke of his tongue pushed me closer to the edge. My fingers clawed at the sheets as my hips rolled back to meet his mouth, needing even more from him as the orgasm exploded through my body harsher than the first one. He slowed his tongue, lapping gently to prolong the shocks with a tortuous pace that heightened the already insane pleasure racing through my veins. His hands would leave bruises on my hips from the grip he was using to hold me against his face as I came.

Only after I was completely spent, my body shaking gently from the release did he pull back and admire his work. I looked over my shoulder at him with heavy eyes and pushed to my knees, presenting myself to him as his hand reached out to brush the swell of my ass.

The submissive pose turned his admiration into hunger, desire. His face hardened as he kneeled behind me, his large hands gripping my waist possessively. He rubbed his hardness between my quivering thighs, coating himself in my release before he positioned himself at my entrance.

I stretched out my arms above my head, sinking into the bed to lift my ass even more as he reached across for condoms in his nightstand. My fingers brushed against the headboard as I buried my face into the pillow and waited with nothing but euphoria calming my thoughts. His hand brushed against my raw skin, a groan leaving his lips before he thrust forward, impaling me on his thick length. My moans were muffled by the pillow, low and needy as he filled me completely.

His breath caught at sounds and I completely surrendered to his mercy. With one hand on my waist, he guided himself in and out slowly stretching me inch by inch. His other hand tangled in my hair, pulling my head back slightly to look at him.

"Is this what you need?" He asked, his voice soft and husky, a harsh contrast to his sharp, unrelenting movements. I nodded in his grip, the hold on my hair tingling my scalp as his cock touched every single raw nerve inside of me.

He started moving more, his hips snapping forward with a delicious force. The sound of skin slapping against skin filled the room as he thrust into me relentlessly. His hand in my hair kept my head pulled back, forcing me to arch my back and take him impossibly deep.

I gasped loudly as his movements became sharper, unable to form words or even think I sank completely onto him. The feeling of him buried that deeply inside of me completely erasing every thought I'd ever had for a brief moment of absolute silence. I tightened around him, unable to help myself and it drew the deepest moan from his lips, causing his hips to buck forward erratically. His cock throbbed, ready to lose himself completely buried in me. His hand left my hair and I whined at the release only for him to find my throat, cupping it with a perfect grip he lifted my chin with his fingers and leaned over my body so his lips met my ear.

"You're mine, do you understand Drew?" His voice was low, demanding and unwavering in his command. "I'm ripping that fucking contract to shreds because you are all mine." Every word was met with a sloppy thrust that made my mouth fall open in silent ecstasy.

His grip on my throat was making me dizzy in the most perfect of ways as his hips snapped forward and hit the spot inside of me that made my eyes flutter shut. His thumb pressed against my skin, as his tongue flickered across my shoulder, pushing the bra strap out of his way. His teeth dug into my shoulder with just enough force to make me cry out in pleasure as he claimed every fucking inch of me as his own.

"Say it," he demanded, his words breathless and choppy.

I clenched around him, unable to stop it, unable to find the words as the third and final orgasm ripped through me like a strike of lightning. My knees barely held me in place as my body writhed beneath his thrusts.

"Drew," he growled, his fingers digging into my waist. Silas wanted an answer I couldn't give to him, not like this. He crashed into me again and again, chasing his own release. His body dripped with sweat, his muscles shining in the dim lighting casting through the curtains. It was all too much, I was too sensitive, he was too perfect and he looked like an angel as he lost all control.

With a final deep thrust he came with a guttural moan that tore from him as his hips stuttered. His forehead rested against my back as he slowly caught his breath, one hand still possessively around my throat. He carefully nuzzled my neck, placing soft kisses as he softened and retreated from between my thighs.

I was sore but in the best kind of way. I had absolutely never felt that good, Silas touched every part of me and left nothing to complain about. I rolled to my back, my fingers brushing over the small imprint of his teeth on my shoulder. I could feel the bruises forming on my hip from his fingertips.

He watched me with hooded eyes as I touched the mark, a satisfied smirk tugging at his lips. He leaned down, pressing a kiss to the indention before shifting to lie beside me. One arm draped possessively over my thigh and rolled me into him, resting my leg over his hip as I curled into his side. There was no chance of me sneaking away from him in this position and he knew exactly what he was doing as his fingers dug into the underside of my ass to hold me close.

"You like doing that, don't you?" I looked at him, his throat damp with sweat and his mouth red from kissing. I didn't have to say anything more because his eyes flickered to my shoulder with pride.

He chuckled low in his chest, the vibration rumbling against my side. His hand slid up to my neck, thumb brushing over my pulse point. Even the thought of the primitive act had him purring with excitement and I thought I would hate it but seeing him so insanely possessive made me both nervous and excited.

Silas's smirk deepened, and he pressed a soft kiss to my forehead, "do I like leaving marks on you? *Yes.*" He admitted without hesitation, his voice low and rough. "I didn't hurt you did I?"

I shook my head no, not quite ready to admit that I enjoyed the possessive display of affection. He searched my face for an answer, probably seeing right through me but if he did, he said nothing about it.

"You're quiet," he said, resting against his pillow.

"Were you serious?" I asked, "about the contract?" I was so quiet, nervous to even broach the subject with him now that we had gotten it all out of our system.

His eyes locked onto mine, the intensity in his gaze making my heart skip a beat. He was silent for so long, his thumb idly tracing patterns on my skin. When he finally spoke, his voice was firm, leaving no room for doubt. "I don't say things I don't mean."

Panic surged but it was different than before.

Were we actually going to do this? Take a run at something that should clearly stay professional? I studied his face, so serious and hanging by a thread for what was next. I brushed my thumb over his bottom lip and he chased it, kissing the pad gently. So patient even if the answer would break his heart.

I was either a massive idiot or the smartest woman in the world. But leaping off the cliff without the confirmation of a parachute was terrifying.

"I'm yours." I said quietly, finally answering his question from before. He eyed me carefully, like any movement from him might startle me. "But don't you dare fuck this up Silas Shore." I scowled with as much fire as I could muster. I knew the likelihood of him screwing up was low. It was me that brought on my concern, scared to do or say the wrong thing but when he looked at me like that... with all the confidence in the world and even more trust. I wanted to try.

His eyes flashed with a mix of amusement and respect at the warnings. He leaned in, his top lip catching my bottom one in a small, languid kiss. "I wouldn't dream of it," he paused, his breath hot on my lips as his finger brushed gently against my jaw.

"I should probably go to my room," I said, only this time I didn't want to leave.

"Please don't," he said so quickly that it shot a searing wave of heat through me that wrapped around my heart and squeezed. His arms were around me and our chests were tight together before I could even try to escape his bed.

"Okay, but you should probably go get my pants before anyone sees them on the kitchen floor..." I pushed my free hand through his hair and kissed the worry line between his eyebrows.

Silas chuckled, a lopsided smile forming as he came down on top of me for another kiss before climbing from bed and leaving me to the silent dread of accidentally breaking his heart.

SHORE

I was on cloud nine walking into the hospital the next day. Arlo had called, from El's phone, to let me know that Cael was out of surgery. I collected some breakfast for them and headed over with my head in the clouds and my thoughts on Drew.

She hadn't left.

I woke with my nose pressed into the side of her hair and my hands wrapped around her body as she slept soundlessly. It almost pained me to unwind from her but I managed to get out without waking her.

She rolled onto her belly, her hair spread out over my pillows and the sheets slack around her hips. I brushed a knuckle down her spine, taking in the way her breath lulled from my touch before taking a cold shower and getting out the door. But I just wanted to get back to her as soon as I could.

I brought what I could from the office for Ryan, as well as some paperwork to go over for other players that still needed eyes on them. Ella was running appointments when I got there and she let me know she could handle everything, all she asked was that I took care of Cael for her while she did.

An easy enough promise to uphold considering the guilt was still eating at me despite everyone continuously telling me it wasn't my fault.

There were two voices coming from the room and much to my surprise my mother's laughter floated down the hallway toward me. I shifted Ryan's bag on my shoulder, cradling breakfast and work in the other as I wandered through the door.

Cael was asleep in his bed, his arm completely wrapped up and tight to his side. Mom was leaning against the window with a smile, her face looking more dressed down then I'd ever seen her in jeans and a Harbor hoodie I didn't even know she owned. Her face was flushed from laughing and Ryan was talking in a quiet tone with a soft expression on his tired face.

"Morning..." I announced myself and watched her take a step back from Ryan, her posture straightening out as he cleared his throat. "I brought breakfast but I didn't realize you'd be here or I would have brought more."

"She can have mine," Arlo's voice directed my attention to a chair out of my sight, forcing me to step further into the room. "Ella made muffins," he held up his half eaten one.

"I just came to check on you three," she smiled at me. "I wanted to drop off some heating blankets and things to help with Cael's recovery."

Mom was talking but my focus was on Ryan, his hands curled into the seat under him like he was trying to keep still. In seven years of knowing that man, I had never once seen him fidget. A rumble formed in my chest out of nowhere when she touched Ryan's shoulder gently with her fingers.

"I should get going, give Cael my best." She grabbed her purse from where it was resting beside a large glass vase of lavender before kissing me on the cheek and excusing herself.

Ryan rose from his chair and grabbed his bag from me as I set down the breakfast on the small table across from Cael's bed.

"I'm going to go take a shower and then we can run through the subs for the week?" He asked me but I was still stuck on my mother flirting with one of my friends...

"Yeah," I said, eyebrows pinched together tightly as he threw a couple pieces of bacon between his teeth and left the room. "What the fuck was that and why were you just sitting here letting it happen?"

"She was in here when I got here." He shrugged, "she brought me jello she stole off one of the carts in the hallway to ignore their very private conversation. So I did."

"You disloyal rat," I swore at him.

"I'm not a snitch and it was blue... that's the best flavor." Arlo wasn't going to budge and I hated that cocky grin on his face. The fact that he knew something I didn't, was making his whole morning.

"Fuck you! If he's fucking my mom I swear—" I threw my hat at Arlo who just laughed at me.

"You fucked his sister, asshole," Arlo countered, his laughter only growing.

"Quit fucking laughing, prick!"

"Lower your voice, Grandpa, some of us are trying to sleep," Cael's sleepy, scratchy voice interrupted my panic attack. "Did Arlo just say you stuck your east coast foot long in my Aunt?" He asked next and Arlo practically fell out of his chair.

"No," I said at the exact moment Arlo said yes.

"Bold move considering her ex is the size of a fucking grizzly bear," Cael weakly laughed and shifted in the bed with his eyes still closed.

"Yeah Silas, bold move." Arlo snorted, enjoying the situation a little too much.

"I will make sure you end up in one of these beds if you don't shut the hell up." I flipped him off and wandered over to Cael to take a look at his arm.

"As much as I love seeing you two fistfight, I have a raging headache and if I don't get my hands on my Clementine in the next twenty minutes. I'm performing a half-cocked jailbreak and going to find her," Cael's words were strung together in a slurred string. The pain no doubt making it very hard to stay awake.

"Van is on his way with her and Zoey," Arlo answered his question, "and stay in bed you aren't wearing pants, no one needs to see your ass."

Cael scoffed, "*everyone* needs to see my ass"

"Respectfully disagree, Loverboy." Cael practically popped up from death at the sound of Clementine's voice. "Keep that perfect ass in your bed, I'm not fighting any handsy nurses today."

"That's my cue to take my leave," Arlo scowled, pushing from his chair and disappearing into the hallway.

Clementine was successful in calming Cael down and it made me feel a little better about everything that was going on. I opened my mouth to say something when my phone vibrated in my pocket, I pulled it out hoping to see her name flicker across the screen but instead it's a reminder that despite how I felt today, nothing was going right in the rest of my life.

"Tobias," I answered, leaving the room to chat with my lawyer.

"I hate doing this so early on a Monday, Silas but your father is withholding sensitive information that we need if we want a shot at winning this trial." Tobias explained. Winning for us meant keeping my father in prison, something that not a single member of my family understood. If Grandpa knew I was working with the prosecutors on Dad's case I'd be shunned; but they needed an inside man. Someone who could get information legally out of my dad.

"What do you want me to do about it, Tobias?" I sighed, stepping into the hallway. Arlo pushed off the wall at the sound of my annoyance and stepped closer to listen as I put Tobias on speakerphone.

"I need you to go to the prison, I need more information on his relationship with DeeDee Logan." The line went quiet at the sound of her name and I swore under my breath. "It would have been a lot easier to convict him with her alive but now all I have is conversations through illegible high texts and word of mouth from your brother. We need more, I need your father to admit to funneling money to more than just DeeDee. It'll prove that he held no regard emotionally for any of the people he was 'supporting.' I need you to talk to him."

Arlo grimaced. This was bad.

"There's no way I can get him to talk about that, he's been buttoned up since she died. He's terrified to get slapped with charges related to her death." I said, and it was a reasonable fear because it was exactly what they were trying to do. He was all but a drug runner for her, supplying her with enough cash monthly to keep her high enough that she didn't go to the press or the cops.

"I think it's time you consider taking Joshua down there for a conversation, it might be the cracking—"

"Find a new route." I cut him off. "I'm not subjecting Josh to that and you know it, *stop asking*."

"If you can think of a better way to get that information Silas, I trust you but from where I'm standing our time is running out and if you want to keep him in jail as much as I think you do, Josh might be the only answer." Tobias's explanation was diplomatic and well worded but it didn't matter.

Even Arlo shook his head no at the mention of putting Josh through something like that, worse, Josh would do it if I asked. But I couldn't do that to him, he was finally starting to have a healthy life with the Hornets, at the Nest. With Dean. I couldn't undo all the hard work he had been doing to feel normal for the first time in his entire life.

I wouldn't.

"I'll go talk to him, push him harder this time but leave Josh out of this," I ordered and Tobais fell silent. "I mean it, if I find out anyone in your office called him about this, my helpful visits end and you guys can do the dirty work on your own."

"Understood," Tobias confirmed, but I could tell from the way he paused that his confidence was wavering. "It's time sensitive, Silas."

"Yeah, I'll go today." I hung up the phone and sighed. "I slept with Drew again," I blurted to Arlo and turned my head toward him.

"Sloppy." Was the only thing out of his mouth, "did you at least buy her dinner this time?"

"Thai," I responded, shoving my phone in my pocket as Arlo nodded in approval. "I swear someone is playing a joke on me, every time I think I have my life sorted or I find just a shred of happiness. The universe turns out the lights and I'm back to square one."

"We cancelled practice today, so it looks like you and I are going to the prison," Arlo said. I opened my mouth to argue that he didn't need to come along for the ride but he shut me up with a glare, "and the universe doesn't control your life, you do. Stop whining and handle your shit." He slapped a hand to my face. "And if you like Drew, own it. Stop acting like sleeping with her is shameful. Idiot."

"Hey, too far." I sighed.

"You're right, I'm sorry." Arlo feigned sincerity, putting his hand on my shoulder. "You're still an idiot."

"You don't have to come today," I shook my head.

"Oh, I wasn't giving you the option for company, let's go. I'd like to be back before lunch." Arlo didn't budge on his intentions for the day and before long we were driving out of the hospital parking lot up to the county detention center.

"I didn't know you were helping them with the case," Arlo said, emptying his pockets into the buckets provided for our personal goods as I signed us in for a half an hour meeting.

"I'm the only person he'll willingly see besides his lawyer," I said, my phone vibrating as I took it out. It was a text from Drew detailing her plans for the day and it made me smile at my phone like an idiot.

"What a dotting son," Arlo cleared his throat.

"Yeah, that's the point." I dropped my phone into the buckets without responding and allowed the guard to pat me down before stepping out of the scanner. "He has no idea I'm funneling information back to the lawyers, and by the time they call me for testimony it'll be too late for him to realize that he nailed his own coffin shut."

"You're serious about this?" Arlo stopped me just before we entered the common visiting room.

"I don't have anything left for him, Ar. After hearing Josh's story, after helping him bury his Mom, consoling my own. Charles is dead to me." I assured him and he nodded.

"Alright," He tapped two fingers to his chest and I mirrored the motion. *I'm here if you need me* was left unsaid as the door buzzed loudly and we were let inside.

SHORE

"Si!" My father wrapped me up in a tight hug that made my skin crawl. His hair was getting longer and there was so much more gray now that he couldn't dye it brown once a month. He turned to Arlo who's jaw tightened in discomfort as he too was offered a suffocating hug. "It's good to see you King," He looked him over, hands on his shoulders. "Looking good, it's a shame about that pitching hand. You had a promising career in Pittsburgh," he noted. "Guess not all of us are cut out for the show."

"Dad," I sighed, "sit."

"You don't bring anyone to see me, I'm just making conversation," Charles sneered and gave Arlo another pat. "I miss you King boys, what are Luc and Sawyer up to?"

"Working," Arlo clipped with a forced smile. "Luc has a baby on the way, due in the fall."

"That's incredible! Fingers crossed for a boy, we need more talent flowing out of that family and into the Hornets legacy."

The ignorance of this motherfucker.

He turned his dark eyes on me and I knew what was coming before he opened his mouth because every single time I saw him he asked and every time it filled my throat with vomit.

"How's Joshua?"

I had been expecting the question, but it had come as a surprise to Arlo who tensed beside me as his brows gave away how pissed off he was that it even rolled off my father's tongue.

"He's fine, he graduates soon." I tried to keep my answers short, mostly because he didn't deserve much more, but even worse, any accomplishments that Josh made constantly turned into my father patting himself on the back.

"That's my boy, he's resilient. Smart as a whip," he said to Arlo, "luckily he got his brains from the Shore side and not from the Logan side."

"Ms. Logan was a nurse dad, she was plenty smart," I reminded him, trying to shift the conversation so he was forced to talk about her.

"Was," he corrected, "before she ruined her life with drugs."

"Before *you* ruined her life with drugs," I said, staring him down. His joyful mood dissipated and his jaw tightened.

"I didn't buy her drugs, Silas."

"You put the money in her hand, once a month to keep her quiet and the only way she managed to do that was by filling the void with drugs that made her feel less broken," Arlo interjected. Playing the bad cop without skipping a beat. He leaned over the table and demanded my father's attention. "You don't feel guilty at all do you?"

"All I did was send her money to support my child, Arlo." He rebutted.

"You sent her money to shut her mouth," he sighed.

"Who are you to judge? You would be *nothing* without our money." Charles snapped, slamming his hand down on the table. One of the guards stepped forward, warning him to behave.

"What was the point in sending her money, did you know she was killing herself with it?" Arlo asked him, allowing me to stay innocent in his eyes while he took the blunt of the aggressive behavior from my father. Arlo didn't care what insults Charles flung at him, he had worked hard to get where he was and while his journey might have been fostered by my family. His skill was not. Baseball had been coursing through his veins the second he was born, if we hadn't poached his father in high school, Arlo could have played anywhere.

The legacy he carried around wasn't a blessing, it was a curse.

"I didn't give a shit if she was killing herself, that was her choice. She knew why the money was coming and she never once said no to it." Charles defended his actions venomously.

"So you had no idea that in between cheques she was using Josh to make money to support the drug habit. The habit that you created when you drilled into her head that she was disposable?" Arlo kept pushing and I could see my father starting to crack.

"You'll end up just like your daddy, drunk and dead to the world in a dusty recliner," Charles snapped.

Arlo smiled, knowing that the argument had worked and we had won. He had admitted out loud to the two of us what he had been doing. Arlo scratched his chest over his heart with two fingers and I knew that if push came to shove, he'd get up on the stand.

"At least I won't be dead in jail, forgotten by the world," he added just to drive it home.

"Get out, this visit is over." Charles shot from the table and a few guards yelled at him causing him to raise his hands in the air only to get restricted by the shackles around his wrists.

"Orange isn't your color, Mr. Shore," Arlo chittered, pushing from the table with a grin. Never happier than when he was insulting horrible people or starting fights.

We were ushered from the visiting room as they took him back to his cell.

"You didn't tell me he was that fucking delusional," Arlo said on the way back to the car.

"He genuinely doesn't believe he's in the wrong on this and that's why I'm working so hard to keep him in that orange jumpsuit. He's all sunshine and butterflies in there for show. If he gets out..." I wet my bottom lip.

"He'll go straight for Josh." Arlo finished, understanding the dangers.

"I have to protect him," I said.

"We will." Arlo tapped the top of the fastback. "Together."

By the time we got back to the hospital, I had about six meetings I needed to be across town at the stadium for. I was so exhausted I barely noticed the sun going down or my stomach screaming for food. It was nearly seven when I parked my bike in the garage and found the Nest virtually empty.

I had been back and forth on whether or not I was going to tell Josh about what was happening with our father. There was a good chance they asked him to take the stand in a few months and if that happened, I would have to prepare him for the fake bullshit that Charles was peddling to everyone that would listen.

But I found him and Dean at the island smiling, picking over a container of french fries and I couldn't bring myself to ruin their mood. Dean was eating, he was healthy. Josh was smiling and his hand was knotted into the back of Dean's sweater like he never knew anything but stable, loving relationships.

I couldn't let my father ruin something Josh had been working so hard for.

"Stop hovering," Josh said before I could announce myself, he was the only person on the team or perhaps in Harbor that could always feel my presence. It was like he had a radar for it and it went off whenever I got within twenty feet.

"How was your appointment with Ella?" I asked Josh, hand out to look at his elbow like it was a natural routine between us now.

"Fine, muscle is good, no signs of stress. I'll be good to go for the next series," he confirmed and I believed him. There was no bruising or swelling in the normal areas and he had full range of motion. "Doesn't hurt, I promise."

"Mm," I hummed. "Last idiot that made that promise broke it."

"It was Cael." Josh shrugged.

"Cael doesn't make promises he can't keep," both Dean and I sang the tune we had heard from him a million times simultaneously and Josh rolled his eyes at us.

"Sorry if I don't take anyone's word for it right now," I said afterward.

"How is he?" Josh asked.

"Pretending like he's okay but he's definitely sore. He's going to need all the help he can get in the coming weeks. He's going to be in a lot of pain but the hospital is going to get him through the worst of it before we bring him home."

I explained and the two of them nodded at me. "You should go see him again tomorrow, he needs family."

"Sure, Doc," Dean tapped his chest.

"Are they home?" I pointed to the basement door.

"Auggie for sure." Dean shoved a few more fries in his mouth. "Haven't seen Red."

"Don't call her that," I scowled. "She has a name."

"Sorry, I haven't seen Drew." He corrected himself. "Auggie is out on the back deck, has been for awhile. We bought him food but it's getting cold."

"I'll take it to him." I grabbed the takeout container off the island and made my way out to the deck to win over the other side of the Courtney duo. If I was going to convince Drew that I was serious about her, about all of this in the way I thought I was, I needed August's help.

He was laying on his back staring at the stars with his arms underneath his head to get comfy and didn't flinch when I set the container beside him.

"What are you doing?" I asked, tilting my head back.

"Watching the stars," he answered without acknowledging me but his face curled up in an annoyed expression. "If you're out here to ask me if you can keep making out with my mom, don't bother."

"I—" I opened my mouth and closed it again, rubbing the bridge of my nose between my fingers.

"You aren't sneaky and my mom was singing in the shower this morning," August sneered.

"She was?" I smiled, quickly wiping it off my face when he shot me a dirty look.

"You don't get it do you?" August sat up and stared at me. I could feel his upset in his glare. "Sure it's all fun for you, but she hasn't been happy in a long time and if you're the only reason she's happy again and you do something to make her sad then she's going to move us across the country again." The words came out furious off his lips and he huffed in anger when he finished.

"Whoa, okay." I squatted down to meet him eye to eye. "What if I told you I was taking this seriously?"

He watched me nervously but didn't say anything in response to the question.

"I really like your mom, Auggie," I added to the silence. "I like making her happy enough to sing in the shower," I said.

"Adults lie," he countered. "How do I know you aren't just saying that to take advantage of her?"

"How do you even know how to use that word in context?" I scoffed.

"I'm thirteen! I have basic vocabulary skills." He grumbled and cursed me under his breath for having to continuously repeat himself.

"Well, I'm not lying," I said to him, making sure that I sounded as sincere as possible because it was the truth. I liked seeing Drew smile and I wanted to continue that win streak if I could.

"I like it here." He confessed after a second, his shoulder slumping. "Everyone is nice to me, no one bugs me for not liking sports, I like my teachers, I like Daisy and I like this house." He turned his head up to the stars again. "I don't want to leave because you kissed my mom and didn't mean it."

I chuckled. "I like this house too. I won't give your mom a reason to leave and even if I do, I promise to do everything to make her want to stay."

"We've never lived anywhere I can see the stars from the backyard, but they're so bright here." He ignored my promise but I could see him thinking about it and that was enough of a win for the evening in my eyes.

"Do you want to see something cool?" I asked him and he turned to look at me again with a small nod. "Come on," I pushed to my full height and extended a hand to him, when he took it he held onto it for a moment.

"Don't make my mom cry," he warned. "I mean it."

"I hear you, Auggie." I guided him inside toward the back of the Nest to the storage room off the sitting room. I told him to wait outside and entered the room with a deep breath. I hated this room, long after the machines and bed had been removed I could still hear the beeping that echoed against the walls now covered in shelves and boxes. I would never see it as anything more than the room Lorraine Cody died in. I spun around, looking for something important when my eyes caught the carton with her neat handwriting sprawled across the piece of masking tape.

"Found you." I hauled the box up from the floor and carried it back to where August was waiting in the sitting room. Dropping it gently on the coffee table he moved closer to inspect what was inside.

"This box belonged to Cael's mom," I said softly so my voice didn't crack, "she liked the stars too." I wiggled out the itch that formed in my nose from my eyes watering as I popped the box off. I reached in and gently pulled out the glass angel used to live on the windowsill in the kitchen. It had only been retired to the box because we didn't want to break it but staring at it now I felt like we needed it back.

I rolled it in my hand as August started to lift other stuff out.

"Whoa," he flipped through the pages of one of Lorraine's journals dated from 1996. Inside there were hundreds of soft, sketch drawings all more intricate than the next and every single one a constellation she had wanted records of. "This is like thirty years old," August gasped, running his fingers over the yellowed pages. "It's so detailed."

"There's another box in the storage room too, it's got her old telescope in it. I'll set it up for you tomorrow?" I asked him and he looked at me with wonder in his eyes, looking more like Drew than ever as a bright smile plastered to his face. I was just happy to give him a space in the Nest that felt like his, and Cael would be over the moon that someone had found joy in his mom's old journals. Suddenly it felt like the Nest was a home again, and not four walls housing a bunch of self proclaimed orphans, and misfits. August unknowingly filled a gaping hole in my chest I never knew existed and now more than ever the stakes were high.

I couldn't screw this up.

"Please?" He asked.

I nodded. "You'll have to show Cael how to use it when he gets home."

"Deal."

COURTNEY

"How's this?" I spun in a small circle, and the bottom of the light blue sundress kicked up around my thighs. "I know it's a barbecue, but it's a barbecue at your family's estate…I don't want to be too casual…"

Silas looked up from buttoning his shirt, "it's perfect, stop fussing."

I stepped forward and shooed his hands away, correcting the button he missed by unbuttoning everything and starting again. "Maybe you should take your own advice?" I smiled up at him sweetly. It had been a nice few weeks of quiet, probably too nice and out of that serenity anxiety bred. But I was doing my best to push it away and stay present with Silas, with August.

Silas huffed, "Sorry, I'm a little distracted."

"Cael comes home tomorrow, the new series starts Tuesday and you have to call Tobias back about your father. You've been avoiding his calls," I said, straightening out his shirt and stepping back to inspect it.

Silas stared at me.

"I pay attention, here." I held out his keys and phone, he'd forgotten them the last four times he left the apartment and had to come back for them. He smiled at me and I felt a warmth spread across my chest. "It doesn't help that your grandfather sprung today on you."

"It doesn't," he agreed. "This week is going to be hard."

"So let's make the most of today?" I asked him.

"I think I can handle that," he agreed, reaching out to wrap a hand around my waist. "With a little help," he whispered and lifted my chin to meet his lips in a soft kiss. He pulled away, licking the taste of me off his lips and smiled. "If we're late Mom will have my head. You ready?"

"Just need to make sure August is settled, I'll meet you outside?" I turned, grabbing my bag. I found August sitting at the counter listening intently to Dean as he tried to run him through his homework.

"Hey boys," I said on approach. "How you doing?"

"I'm finally understanding what the hell all this means," August swore.

"Language," I scowled.

"They swear all the time, hell isn't even that bad," he argued and Dean threw his hands up in surrender, backing away from the island before he could get a scolding too.

"Thank you for teaching my son math *and* swear words," I said with a soft smile, messing up August's hair in my fingers.

"In my defense he already knew that one," Dean said, a cheeky grin forming on his face. "Did I mention you look very pretty today?" He added, for brownie points.

"Thank you," I said, kissing August on the head, "I have that work thing this afternoon, you'll be okay with Dean?"

"He's going to teach me how to make quesadillas and salsa," August said without looking up from his homework.

"Ella is going to teach *us*," Dean said quickly, like I was going to accuse him of not being able to use the stove. I eyed him for a second before nodding.

"Have fun boys," I said. I couldn't exactly tell if August was in one of his *I hate Mom* moods or if he was just finally settling into a pace where he felt comfortable enough to relax. And both had me worried. If it was just a mood, what had I done? Did he know about Silas and I... and if it wasn't, what happened when we had to leave? Disrupting him again felt like torture.

"What happened?" Silas asked, knocking me from my thoughts. I hadn't even realized I'd walked to the garage and was standing in the doorway with my lip between my teeth until his voice echoed through the darkness.

"Nothing," I straightened out and made my way down. He handed me my helmet, not taking no for an answer when I opened my mouth to protest about the bike.

"Just sit tight against me," he said, helping me over the seat. He settled down and reached around to grab my thigh, pulling me flush against his back. "Tuck your dress between your thighs," he instructed and I did it, "good, now forward more," he said and I scooted impossibly close holding everything in place as I tangled my arms around him. "See," he hummed, proud of himself for being right.

The bike rumbled to life and I pressed my face against his back as he pulled from the garage. He was getting cockier about his speed with me on the back, and at first I wasn't sure I liked it but now, as he took a corner and our bodies moved together. I kind of enjoyed the rush. For the twenty minutes we were on the bike we were untouchable by all the nonsense going on in our lives.

For that short time, it was just Silas and me.

He pulled up to his family's house and I sighed quietly, sad that it was over and he absolutely noticed. "Do you want me to circle the block?" he chuckled, lifting the helmet off his head and smoothing out his hair.

"No," I whispered, doing the same. "Well kind of."

"We can take the long way home." He smiled at me and all the locks clicked back into place, keeping the anxiety at bay for a little while longer. "Most of the board members will be here today, don't let them get to you. Remember that they're assholes."

"I'm sure that's not true, you're just sick of seeing their faces," I said softly, "let me handle them today, just don't leave me alone with your mother for too long. She terrifies me."

Silas laughed, looking up at the house and then back to me with a more serious expression. "When Ryan started with the team he used to do this thing after conversations and speeches. And I never quite figured out what he was doing so one day I asked Rae, his wife." Silas smiled, his fingers nervously playing at the straps of his helmet. "It was their code," he explained. "The Lorraine I knew wasn't quiet but I guess at some point she was and it was a way for them to communicate without so many words."

"It's that thing you all do?" I asked him.

"Yeah," Silas confirmed, "so today if you need me."

I tapped my chest twice. "And you'll do it if you need me?"

His head tilted to the side but a soft smile formed on his face as he returned the gesture. "Exactly," he said with a nod before taking my hand and leading me into the house.

I wasn't sure what to expect but there were staff moving like bees inside the walls as he brought me back through the kitchen and out into the massive back yard. It was decorated in small tables scattered around and tons of florals that added to the already impressive nature backdrop.

"Wow," I breathed out and Silas looked over at me with a nervous expression. "Drinks?"

"For you, I have a feeling staying sober is in my best interest today," Silas laughed, already annoyed with the crowd. I could see it on his face as he took in some of the people that his grandfather had invited, there wasn't a single one his eyes landed on that made his face soften. And I knew it because the second he found his mother, his eyes changed color and his jaw went slack.

He navigated the crowd, avoiding speaking to anyone until we were face to face with Sylwia. "Mom," he gave her a kiss.

"It's lovely to see you, Drew." She offered me but her eyes were constantly moving.

"Is there anything I can do to help?" I asked, knowing the face of a woman with a hundred things on her mind.

"Oh," Sylwia's lips parted and her focus shifted back to me. "I'm waiting on a delivery of wine, do you think you could go find out where it might be?" She asked me, giving me the name and number of the person she was in contact with.

Silas watched me carefully as I wandered back into the house where it was quieter. I called the number, was given an answer and not five minutes later the driver was standing at the front door with a few cases of wine.

I was helping one of the staff line them up on the island when Seymour sauntered in, a drink in hand and a cautious look on his old face. He looked like he wanted to scold me for helping and not enjoying the party but when he opened his mouth he started to cough violently. His hand gripped the wall next to him and I crossed the kitchen, tucking my body against his and leading him through the kitchen to the lounge and into a chair.

"Do you need water?" I asked him and he held up his scotch glass but I ignored that and found him some water anyways. "This," I said, taking the scotch away and setting it out of reach until he drank. "You shouldn't be drinking that." I said softly, offering him a napkin as he coughed some more.

"The scotch isn't going to kill me any faster, girl," he groaned when he was finished.

"It might, the way you drink it," I said. Only smiling at him when he started to chuckle at my jab.

"Don't tell Silas but I like you," he said, waving his finger in the air. "You've got bite."

"Not always," I said.

"Oh if you're talking about that disastrous dinner party, don't you let those relics get to you. They have no idea how the world works anymore," Seymour said before coughing some more. It was pretty clear he was declining in his health faster than any of them were prepared for.

"I could have handled it better," I offered politely and handed him some more water.

"Handled, what better?" Seymour scoffed, "I've never seen Darby so silent after you shut him down."

I laughed gently, "I think Mr. William needed to remember where he came from."

"See there's that bite!" Seymour pointed, leaning forward in his chair. "You're good for him, he's too soft."

"Oh I don't think so," I argued gently. "I think he's just juggling a lot right now. Taking care of too many people."

"It's nearly impossible to get him to stop," Seymour cleared his throat. "It's like he's trying to erase all the sins of his father."

"He is." I nodded.

"There you two are," Silas's voice travelled over the lounge as he appeared from the opposite end. "Mom thought you died somewhere in the house and we were going to find a body," he said crossing the space.

"If I'm dying in this house I'm doing it butt naked and face down in a pile of scotch Silas." Seymour joked, and I laughed but Silas just sighed. "Maybe you can teach Silas about the power of dark humor." He coughed again.

"I'm glad you both think this is funny." Silas kneeled in front of his grandfather. "Have you been going to every doctor's appointment?"

"Your mother never lets me miss one," he groaned.

"Entertain her caution." Silas urged.

"There's no stopping what's coming," he said to him and I watched Silas's expression flicker with sadness before it hardened again. "She can't fix this and neither can you."

"No we can't but it doesn't make it any less hard on her." Silas warned, *on him*, was said silently.

"Heard," Seymour coughed. "Now, help a dying man up so he can spend the evening entertaining party guests with a pretty girl on his arm."

The last thing I wanted to do was be paraded around again but I could see the worry that laced Silas's features and knew that it was something I needed to do, not for Seymour. But for Silas. He needed something to be taken off his plate and if I could bear the load of his sick Grandfather for just the night, I would. For him. After some coercion from the armchair, Seymour managed to get to his feet and I offered my hand to him, tucking it into his elbow. He held his hand out for the scotch but I handed him the water instead.

"Tell them you've switched to vodka." I smiled at him.

Seymour laughed wildly but took the glass from me. As we started toward the backyard I could feel Silas's eyes on my back. I looked over my shoulder at him as we turned the corner and watched as he quietly pressed two fingers to his heart.

Thank you.

SHORE

Two weeks after Cael's surgery, he's slamming into the house with Clementine and August on his heels and a massive, goofy smile on his lips. "It's raining outside," he declared.

"It's been raining for a week, Cody." Josh slammed the fridge closed. "If it keeps up, they're going to cancel our games."

"We can have them moved to Harbor," I interjected, "I'm sure they won't mind and it will prevent a week of rain delays in the schedule. Everyone wants this season over, not just us."

"You're the only person that wants the season over," Jensen said, sliding onto the counter and shoving a sandwich in his mouth.

"Can you blame a guy, every time I blink one of you has a new injury. Cael is barely lucid at this point," I said and he gave me a dirty look, "these games are going to be the hardest you've played in a while and you're down the best shortstop in the league."

"Awe, Gramps," Cael's tune changed.

My eyes focused on the glass angel, back where it belonged and the rain hitting the window outside in a rhythmic pattern that filled the momentary silence. Cael had only been home for a few days, Clementine followed him around like a guard dog making sure he wasn't doing something stupid completely drunk on pain. They had picked August up from school because Cael begged to be let out of the house.

The thought of August in a car with either of them driving gave me heartburn but Drew had to work and I couldn't let the kid walk home in the rain. It had been two solid weeks of bliss with her, most nights I snuck into her bed because I couldn't find sleep without knowing she wasn't going to run. And maybe that was stupid but I hadn't figured out a way to stop myself from wandering in the dark to find her.

We had suffered through three more very important outings. Each time she was more beautiful than the last and she was impressing everyone constantly. It was like she floated, moving around a room, working a crowd with a smile and soft voice. Somehow giving me everything I needed without a second thought and all while still working at the stadium and finding time to spend with me without prying eyes.

"Earth to Doc," Jensen said, "you alright?"

"Yeah, Jenny... Fine." I assured but everything was either really incredible, or a fucking shit show. There was no in-between. In a few weeks the trial would start for my father's charges, and each day we got closer to them asking Josh to get up on that stand and testify against his father. It'll be the first time he's seen him since the beginning of the season, and it made me sick to my stomach to even ask him to do it.

But we needed his word.

His voice, his story, is what would lock him up for good. We had no choice.

"Yeah," Cael looked at me suspiciously. "There is nothing fine about you," he narrowed his eyes on me. "You know what you need?"

"We aren't doing that again, it made a mess last time," Dean said as he dug through the fridge.

"Shut up, not that," Cael grumbled, his face twisted in pain for a second. He did his best to breathe through the wave before speaking again. "It's a puddle jumping day."

"We aren't kids anymore," I said instantly, "and you can't get that cast wet."

"Okay, buzzkill." He smiled wickedly and turned to the cupboard, hauling out a massive box of garbage bags with a hiss of pain and a loud thump. "Don't be silly, wrap your—"

"Do not finish that sentence," I said looking between him and an innocent August.

"Problem solved, Grandpa." He whipped out a bag, ripping the bottom with his teeth to make a hole and pulled it down over his head like a poncho. "No wet cast, we can still have fun and you can't say no because if Momma had asked, you wouldn't have even thought about it!"

"We aren't—"

Arlo cleared his throat from the archway, "we were never kids." Ella stepped up behind him. "The best part about puddle jumping was that it gave us permission to be kids *again* Si, and you know it. If Rainy was here she'd be pissed we were wasting time arguing over it."

"It's stupid," I said looking around the full kitchen at my family.

"That's the fucking point," Van said, leaning against the counter in a sleeveless t-shirt with a approving smile on his face. "I'm in."

"What is going on?" Ella asked.

"Lorraine believed that the rain could wash away all our stress, she believed in the power of rainy days because they only showed up when one of us really needed them." I explained because the rest of them had gone silent. "She said the weather man was a glorified overpaid psychic and Mother Nature was healing."

"It's raining for a reason, Doc." Dean said. "We'd be stupid not to go play in it."

"No slip in slide, if any of you get hurt it's on me and—"

"We know!" The kitchen erupted and they all started to toss their phones on the island one by one before piling out of the kitchen. "I'm going to wake up everyone else," Cael yelled, jogging through the house noisy and crashing to the upper floor.

"How is he?" I asked Clementine as the house emptied out.

"He's a menace." She smiled at me, "he's in ton of pain but he's the same talk first, think later, fuck hard and play harder Cael. Just a little unbalanced at the moment."

"Do you need anything?" I asked her after a good laugh.

"We're fine, Silas," she said and for once I genuinely believed her.

"Alright, well if you need anything," I started and she gave me a dirty look.

"I'll call his dad, you have enough on your plate. Now get your ass outside before he finds out you aren't out there and throws a fit," she warned, her brown hair swaying as she turned to leave the kitchen.

"I'm glad you're here, Clem." I said to her as she walked down the hallway, only for her to raise her hand and wave me off. I pulled my phone out and slid it on the counter, stripping from my dress shirt to join the boys in the pouring rain.

I stood on the step watching them utilize the holes in the gravel driveway as they started to fill with water. Cael found the stereo and set it up on the porch with Van's help, blasting some of the worst ninety's music they could find over the lawn. I smiled to myself as they danced around, letting everything loose and just enjoying themselves the way they should at that age. Ella was singing at the top of her lungs dancing around a stiff August who took a second to get into the groove.

My heart slowed in my chest as the rain hit my outstretched hand and I closed my eyes, stepping down off the step to let it wash away all of my stress exactly the way it was meant to. My muscles relaxed and my breathing became even as if I'd never experienced a moment of worry in my entire life. I felt bulletproof in the moment. The sound of the music, the rain and the laughter flooded my soul in a way I didn't know I realized.

But Cael had.

Pain riddled and fighting for his life he had seen the need.

He shook his hair out like a dog in Clementine's face who squealed and backed up about ten steps from him before jogging forward and jumping into the puddle at his feet. Water flung up around them and coated them in tan mud. I sighed, I was going to have to take him to the hospital tomorrow and get his cast changed. There was no way it wasn't soaked beneath that garbage bag, but the smile on his face told me it could wait.

Arlo looked over at me, rain dripping down his face and nodded, *this is what it was about it.* This was who I was fighting for. I nodded back and joined in on their playing until a set of headlights came up the drive and Drew got out with a bewildered look on her face.

"What are you guys doing?" She asked.

"Jumping in puddles." August announced over the sound of rain and the music that roared from the porch. "You should try it," he smiled, he was covered head to toe in mud and water, staring at his mother like she was the insane one for not immediately agreeing.

"You're going to get sick," she said to him, but she was overruled by a loud chorus of boos and jeers from everyone. I thought for a second it might harden her, or embarrass her but she looked over at me for help and I just shrugged.

"It's therapeutic," I said to her with a smile.

She closed her door and chucked her purse on the porch, pulling off her hoodie and returning to the downpour to stand next to me with a small sigh.

"What now?" She whispered to me as everyone went back to jumping around and playing. I didn't give her verbal instructions, instead I jumped forward into the puddle just ahead of her and splashed dirty water up over her clean jeans. She inhaled a sharp breath as the cold water hit her skin, a scowl forming on her lips but her eyes were lit up like a fire as she took her turn to jump in a nearby puddle.

Her laughter was loud and infectious, bubbling up from her chest with each splash, step and hop. Eventually she was muddy like the rest of us, spinning August around in circles and singing alongside Ella to songs she recognized from Cael's party CD.

At one point August made eye contact with me and I could see the warning flash across his expression as Drew rang out the bottom of her hair between her hands. I wanted to say to him, *don't worry kid, I'll make sure she keeps singing.* But instead I tapped my fingers to my chest, a gesture that meant nothing to him but everything to me.

"Silas Andrew Shore," my mother's voice stirred me from sleep. I sat straight up, the blankets falling around my waist as I checked the bed for Drew. I was so exhausted that I had fallen asleep and not moved the entire night which meant I hadn't gone in search of comfort from her. "Where is your fiancée?" she asked, her head turning to the side.

Shit.

"She wasn't feeling well last night, so she slept in the guest room so she wouldn't get me sick before the next series." I lied as quickly as I could. "Why are you here?" I mimicked her movements as she stomped across my bedroom completely ignoring the outrageous crossing of boundaries she was committing. "Mom," I barked and she stopped digging through things.

"Why are none of her things in here?" She asked me, "isn't this the guest room? Why is she in *your* room alone?"

"I don't know! I'm half awake! Why are you at the Nest so early?" I rolled my eyes, "visiting someone special?" I huffed pushing out of bed.

"It's noon, Silas." She glared at me. "And you're being cagey."

"Her things didn't fit in this closet with all my things, so she took the master closet and the ensuite to get ready in the mornings, she sleeps in here normally. Thank god she wasn't in here when you decided to make a surprise visit to your grown son's bedroom." I groaned, grabbing my keys and a shirt from the dresser.

"Are you done with your hissy fit?" She asked me.

"Are you done snooping?" I countered, opening the bedroom door. "Out," I said to her and she huffed, turning in her heels and leaving.

"I came over to take Drew for lunch, there's wedding plans we need to discuss. If she's going to be part of this family, I'm having a party." She declared.

"Is a party really the smartest idea right now?" I arched a brow at her. "Dad's trial starts soon and I barely have any free time to do anything, let alone plan a wedding and be involved in it."

"It's the perfect time, it shows urgency and commitment to the board members. A man not planning his wedding is suspicious, Silas," she said, narrowing her eyes on me.

The fact that she was right woke me up. Not planning or picking a date left room for them to ask questions, to dismantle the credibility of the relationship.

"Fine." I agreed, "stay here." I warned, knocking on Drew's door before I cracked the door open and locked it behind me. The shower was running, and I could hear the soft sounds of Drew humming a song I didn't recognize. It made me smile, sinking into the acoustics of her happiness. It took me a second to invade her privacy but I stepped inside and closed that door behind me too.

"Drew," I said softly, causing her to yelp from the surprise. "Sorry," I said, as she stepped around the fogged up glass. My jaw clenched at the sight of her damp skin and soft morning smile. "Hi." I whispered to her and the smile grew.

"Are you okay?" She asked, "you don't usually come in here..." I cut her off with a kiss, wrapping my hand around the base of her throat and gently willing her closer as I stole the air from her lungs.

When I let her go, I stepped back to get control of my emotions before explaining to her why exactly I bombarded her. "My mother is in the kitchen, she wants to take you to lunch," I said.

"What?" Drew stuttered. I pulled my keys from the pocket of my shorts, taking her engagement ring off them and setting it on the counter where she could see it. Her eyes flickered from the diamond to my face with dread. "She's going to eat me alive, Silas."

"No she won't," I assured her, "she just wants to plan a wedding. So we're going to let her and it will be fine."

"How is that fine?" Drew hissed. "We're barely dating, we're definitely only fake engaged and your mother wants to plan a *real* wedding." She turned off the water, reaching for a towel and I grabbed it for her holding it out as she stepped from the shower. "Not to mention I work tonight at Hillys."

"I told you to quit that job," I scowled, a little offended that she hadn't.

"And I didn't," she said quietly.

"Call in sick. Just for today. It will be fine." I put on my best, charming smile. Kissing the corner of her mouth and then her damp jaw just to feel the way she relaxed against the contact. "You're so beautiful and smart, and I owe you my life." I praised, just hoping to wear her down a little more as I wrapped the towel around her.

When she opened her mouth to protest I grabbed her face, kissing her lips one more time before backing out of the bathroom before she could yell at me some more.

"She has a son?" My mothers voice was laced with vicious confusion, I knew the tone well. The last time I had heard it was when I broke my leg sneaking out of the house with Arlo at the age of sixteen to go to a Green Day concert on a school night. Mom had a school agenda in her hand with August's ID and name on it from the highschool.

"Yeah," I said, trying to act like I wasn't scared of my mother at that moment. "No, you can't meet him, he's at school and you are suffocating."

"Excuse me?" Her glare was hot and burned my skin the longer she stared at me.

I was being too short with her, too angry. It wasn't my intention to offend her, and it didn't happen often but I had made her feel like she wasn't good enough. I could see it all over her face and I felt like a massive piece of shit for doing so.

I am not my father.

I opened my mouth to apologize but Drew came out of her room with her hair pulled back in a neat bun and wearing some of the clothes we got her for situations like this. She smiled at my mother and played nervously with the ring on her finger.

"It's nice to see you," she said, "it's very nice of you to invite me for lunch. Silas says you want to discuss wedding plans?"

"Among other things," my mother's scowl was threatening and it only made me more nervous for what the afternoon held.

COURTNEY

"For two please," Sylwia said to the young girl at the hostess desk. She led us back through the busier part of the restaurant to a small table against the window. She ordered us both a coffee and water, setting her bag down and settling into the chair.

I had never met a woman so intimidating, and it didn't even make sense why I was so nervous. Everything that Silas and I were doing was a lie. Other than sleeping together. But that could only sell the story…right?

"Are you nervous?" She asked me as if she could read my mind. I kept forgetting that she had been a mother for nearly twice as long and all her instincts were sharp. She was going to be harder to get around with lies.

"A little," I went with honesty.

"Silas makes me seem like a monster, but I'm not. I raised him after all," she said in a voice that was a little softer than before. "Do you like coffee?" She asked as the waitress returned and I nodded.

"You raised him to be very kind," I said once we were alone again. I filled the rest of my coffee cup with cream and brought it to my lips.

"I did my best," Sylwia smiled at me and I felt that worry in the base of my chest like an explosion gone off. It was all we could ever do when it came to raising children. Our best.

"It's hard raising a son who refuses to take care of himself," she added after a moment of contemplation. "He's always been like that, finding little projects to keep his hands and mind busy, I have no idea where he got the notion that if he stops he'll die. It's exhausting to watch him pull apart at the seams for everyone else."

"That is very much the Silas I have come to love," I smiled, spitting out the word to cover our lie but unlike before it felt like sandpaper against my skin.

She studied me for a moment with a soft expression on her face, "Arlo was a project you know," she said, stirring her coffee and I only noticed then she was drinking it black.

I didn't know Arlo extremely well, he was quiet and always watching everyone. He gave off the aura that he didn't want to be approached most of the time. But I did know that he and Silas had been best friends since the beginning. Inseparable, was the word Silas had once used to describe them.

"Seymour was somewhat of a mentor to his father, Arthur, when he was playing at Harbor. From what I hear that man had more talent than any player of his time. I married Charles after Sawyer was born, we had Silas a few weeks before Nicholas came. I had unknowingly married into the baseball version of the Brady bunch. Their mother and I never really got along, but she was a very strong woman for all it was worth. And in the end I got four extra sons out of the deal, she noted with care, pausing briefly to order us a few appetizers.

"Sounds like taking on projects is a family affair," I said, and she smiled at me with a tiny shrug of defeat. Her and Silas were more alike than either of them cared to admit.

"Arlo..." Sylvia sighed. "Silas was barely walking but the day that baby was born he had one sole purpose in life. Keep Arlo at his side."

"Even that young?" I couldn't stop the gentle bubble of laughter that spurred from my chest.

"Arlo didn't have a choice, Silas never gave him one." Her face softened as she recalled the two. "On paper Silas was an only child but that became untrue the day Arlo was born. They're brothers in every sense of the world. Given his necessity to stay close to Arlo, his decision to work with the Hornets didn't surprise me. He was a player when the Codys came to us. He came home that night and talked about Cael for the entire dinner and I knew right there he had found another brother."

"And then Josh," I said softly and she nodded.

"Both in blood and heart, he has been searching for Josh unknowingly his entire life. It was like he knew before anyone else. He was always restless during

Lorette games, looking around the stadium like he was searching for a feeling he couldn't figure out." She sounded sad but I let her continue, the insight on Silas was refreshing with how little he talked about himself. And if she was talking about her son then she wasn't digging into my life.

"Intuitive," she noted, "when he gets that instinct he follows it and I gave up trying to shield him from it a long time ago. Despite the trouble it can bring, he usually has a method to his madness."

And just like that she had gone from Silas back to me. It was obvious what she was getting at. She thought I was a project, and she wasn't wrong. I just wasn't unaware of Silas's little after-school hobby to save his family's fortune.

"I thought maybe one day he'd grow out of it," she chuckled, "but I don't think there's much truth to that."

"I wouldn't want him to," I heard myself say but I had no idea where it came from. "I hope he always has a heart big enough to help, the world is bursting at the seams with selfish people, it needs more like Silas."

Sylwia stared at me for a moment, no doubt surprised by the boldness of my voice but a smile crept to her stern face and the softness returned. "He'll need someone to protect the heart he leaves unguarded." She said, our eyes never left one another's. After a moment she inhaled slowly, and I felt the conversation shifting.

"That's enough about Silas, I want to talk about you," she said gently, "I feel like he hasn't told me anything, which is unlike him. I want to know everything you've ever dreamed of for your big day. I've been hosting parties for so long I tend to start micromanaging everyday life and I want to make sure it's perfect."

"Silas said that you want to help plan the wedding, that's very generous." I just needed to get through lunch with her.

"If you're okay with that, I don't want to overstep if you have plans with your family," Sylwia cooed. "I remember planning my wedding with Charles' mother. It was a horrible experience and nothing about the wedding felt like mine."

"No family to step over," I assured her.

"What about your son?" She asked and the question was like an unexpected shot to the chest. I hadn't even found the courage to tell August I was spending more time with Silas, let alone break the news to him that everything was a deal just to get us an apartment. I chewed on my tongue for a second, trying to come up with a reasonable answer that would satisfy her.

"August is thirteen he's at the age where everything I do is embarrassing," I offered.

"Thirteen?" She sipped on her coffee. "That is a hard age. Silas brought home his first girlfriend at that age and I remember being a mess about it."

My heart calmed for a second, knowing we did in fact have things in common.

"August has his first crush and I'm beside myself trying to figure out what I should do," I confessed. "Do I over parent and ask him a hundred questions or let him figure it out and wait for him to come to me?"

Sylwia chuckled, "I'm a fan of the hundred questions," she winked at me. "Is it a girl from school?"

"They go to the same school but they met at the stadium," I told her and she nodded.

"It's Riona's daughter isn't it? Daisy?" She asked.

"It is." I made room for the waitress to set some plates on the table and thanked her. Everything looked so delicious.

"She's a sweet girl, you have nothing to worry about," Sylwia said with a smile.

"I'm not worried about her, I know how boys can be," I sighed. Raising a son was hard enough, raising a son when he had a toxic father was another. I had no idea what August learned from Bradley in those times when we were apart. My only fear was that he turned out like his father and from what I could tell I had done enough to prevent that…

"I know that look," Sylwia said, sliding her knife across a piece of toast. "I worry about the same thing, you raise them to be kind and observant but sometimes no matter how much you try it can go wrong. Keeping them from turning into their fathers is exhausting."

I nodded, mostly staying quiet to keep from crying and I only needed to cry because of how easily she had pegged my emotions. It caught me off guard.

"So you were married previously?"

"Yes, for six years," I said.

"What happened?" She asked, her eyes casting on me. She knew she was overstepping but she didn't care. She needed the story from my mouth and she needed it to calm the raging doubts that swirled around. She was protecting her son the same way I was trying to protect mine.

"I had August and got sick," I said slowly to keep from choking on the words. "Postpartum depression ruined my marriage."

Sylwia's face hardened but it wasn't concern or annoyance, it was understanding and sadness.

"I take medication for it," I lied, I used to take it when I could afford it. Now I was just barely hanging on until the next episode hit and riding it out from the safety of my bed. That's typically how a move started, the depression rolled in and once it did there was no stopping it. I spent weeks, willing myself out of bed until one day I just couldn't, missed shifts would end up with me being fired shortly after and in desperation mode to find work. "I took," I corrected myself when she arched her eyebrow. The facial expression was similar to Silas and I could see where he got his attitude from at that moment. His spectacular need to always be right and informed no matter how uncomfortable the information.

"You stopped, why?" She asked. I knew she would.

"Because I couldn't afford the medication but Mrs. Shore, I want you to know that I am by no means with your son because I think it's a payday." I said, not giving her the chance to object with that idea because I knew it would be swimming around in her head the second I told her. Lying felt wrong, especially when she was sitting here just trying to make sure her son had the best. I would have done the same thing.

"So why are you with Silas then?" Sylwia questioned gently, her expression never shifting. "Because if not for his money I would love to know how a woman, with a grown child ended up with a ring on her finger and living with my son when two months ago he was spending every night of the week with a different Hilly's waitress."

I swallowed roughly, I had heard the rumors about Silas. Kayla had run her mouth more often than not about all of the time they had spent together tangled up. Back when she told me, I barely listened but now where indifference once bred, jealousy blossomed.

"I was one," I answered honestly. "The newest."

Sylwia stopped drinking.

"Silas is very charming, very sweet. I refused his offers, most of them at least," I smiled, that part was true enough.

"Until you didn't," she asked.

"He made an offer I couldn't refuse," I said, "he can be persuasive."

She finally laughed and I felt myself relax a little. "That's the Silas I know," she shook her head. "Drew I have been through my fair share of hardship this past year and I hope you understand that all of my questions come from a place of wanting to protect my son from the kind of heartbreak it is to never really know the person you're marrying."

I nodded, listening carefully.

"I had the wool pulled over my eyes for years, and I love my son for all he is, even when he's being blinded by the need to do what he believes is right. His heart is too big and too soft," Sylwia cautioned. "Promise me that you'll do your best to take care of him."

The question struck me as strange considering she could have asked me for anything. Not to marry him, to be honest, to be loving. But she had considered what her son needed and asked for that. *Take care of him.* All she wanted to do was make sure that Silas was looked after in a way that he'd never look after himself.

My heart was pounding in my chest again, terrified to make the promise when I knew there was a chance I couldn't keep it. The question that kept rising up, *what if I screwed up?* But she had added, do your best on purpose, I could see it in her eyes. She was giving me grace when I probably didn't deserve it.

I swallowed roughly and wet my bottom lip.

"I promise."

I held my breath, terrified that she could see right through me. Panicking deep down about fights, and situations that hadn't even happened yet. My anxiety clawed at my insides screaming to get control but I inhaled slowly, pushing them down. She waited a moment, her lips pressing into a tight line as she watched me, "good, let's plan a wedding then."

SHORE

"Take it slow," I said to Cael, trying to get him to ease into the stretch but much like my own, his mind was everywhere today. He groaned into the motion, his shoulder shaking. "Stop, stop," I said, pressing my hand to his forearm to keep him from moving. We had been at this for thirty minutes and we weren't getting anywhere because he was trying to do movements that his shoulder wasn't ready for.

"I can do it," he fought, not looking up at me but he put pressure on my arm and tried again to get through the stretch. There was sweat beading around his temples, his eyes exhausted as he worked through the pain he was going through.

"Cael," I warned him.

"It's just a stretch, I can do it." His words were strained, and he barely got them choked out between a ragged breath.

"Your will power and your ability are two very different things," I snapped, my frustration slipping through the cracks where it shouldn't. "I'm sorry," I said, taking a step back from him. I should have learned my lesson by now but my mind was swirling with a thousand problems and my focus wasn't on Cael. "Let's try something else with less impact."

"Or you could tell me why you're mad at me?" Cael mindlessly rubbed a couple fingers into the skin around his healed incisions. His blue eyes were so bright with pain it took everything in me not to convince him just to take something. *You can't*, I bit down on my tongue and turned away from him to a bottle of water.

"I'm not mad at you," I said, swallowing tightly. It was the truth. I couldn't have been further from mad at him. I handed it to him on the wrong side and cursed myself as he raised his good arm.

"I'm sorry I hid it from you," he said next, scratching like a needy cat on a door I shut in his face. I had worked through my guilt and didn't want to rehash it because Cael thought I was mad at him.

"Cael," I said, the annoyance in my voice was thick.

"It started getting sore after the game against Boston," he continued, "I was using hot showers and ice baths to soothe it and keep the swelling down like you taught me. I thought I could get to the end of the season, go out on a high note."

"Boston?" I looked up from the ground with a scowl on my face. "That was before playoffs," he had been hiding the pain for so long and I never once noticed.

"You had all that family stuff on your plate, with your dad and Josh. I didn't want to add to it, I should have let Ella handle it but she would have brought it to you anyways..." Cael sighed.

All the family stuff. I wasn't sure if it made me feel better or worse that he was trying to protect me from burnout in the middle of hiding his injury. But I knew that nobody came out on top when we stopped communicating with each other. It's a common argument with Arlo and yet there I was not following my own advice.

I inhaled slowly and turned back to face him with a tight expression just trying to hide how much his explanation tore me to shreds.

"Listen to me," I said to him. "There will never be a reason why I don't have time for you, you call, I'm there. No matter what's on my plate, who's causing trouble, how distracted I am. If you need me, I'm there. And I'm sorry I wasn't, I'm sorry that this happened because you were protecting me when I should have been looking out for you."

"I am a grown man you know." Cael's lips curled into that stupid goofy grin. "I'm not your responsibility, you don't owe it to anyone to keep me alive."

"I do," I stopped him. "I owe your Mom." I stepped forward and pretended to inspect his shoulder but really I just needed to ground myself to something, distract my thoughts to keep from crying in grief and frustration.

"Mom wouldn't blame you for this." Cael's face twisted in confusion.

"No she wouldn't," I said, my voice losing its fight. "She wouldn't have let it happen in the first place."

The silence was thick as Cael's chest rose and fell slowly.

"I get it now," he said, "you're trying to fill her shoes." He said it like it was the most obvious thing in the world but he was wrong. I could never fill Lorraine's shoes, that was an impossible feat. "What did she say to you that day?"

The day she died.

"Come on, Si. Tell me, I want to know. You've never talked about it," Cael's voice was tight. She had left every single Hornet with something but she hadn't left me with anything but the responsibility of keeping her family together.

"Nothing," I said, "we read the end of the outsiders book for the hundredth time and even though she could barely hold the book she insisted on reading Johnny's letter to me just like she always did." It was the truth, I hadn't really gotten a good bye.

I expected Cael to push for more information but there was a smile on his face, soft and knowing. Almost irritating. "What are the last lines in that letter again? I forgot."

"No you don't." I shook my head.

"No, I haven't read it in so long I have no clue." Cael shrugged, his face scrunching in pain from the motion.

"Uh," I stopped to think about it, "something about having lots of time to make yourself what you want to be and there's lots of good in the world, and to tell Dally. Which was irrelevant at that point because Dallas was dead. What was the point in this?" I asked as he rubbed a towel over his head to wick away the sweat in his hair.

"She was telling you something, she was reading the letter to you." Cael said.

"That's ridiculous and you know it. She just didn't have anything to say to me, I don't blame her. She had to see my ugly face every day until she died, I was nothing more than her doctor in the end," I said, leaning against the wall.

"Bullshit, she refused to be anywhere but the Nest, *because* you were taking care of her," Cael swore. "She trusted you with her life," he said. "You've always been a bit of a pessimist when it comes to your own worth, she saw through you. All that studious, responsibility crap. It's always been us and you making sure we were all in one piece but you've never slowed down enough to enjoy the sunsets. That's what she wanted to tell you."

"You're reading into it, it's just a letter out of an old book." I said tightly. I hated how easily the topic of Lorraine got under my skin. It wasn't like I didn't have a good mom, I was lucky to have one. But a woman like Lorraine left lasting impressions.

"I'm not," Cael pushed, "she wouldn't have left without telling you something, she gave us all something to hang onto. You just forgot what you were supposed to do somewhere along the way and it's time you stop moving so fast and just enjoy what you've built."

"The pain is messing with your head kid," I scoffed, but a small smile formed on my lips.

"This wasn't your fault," Cael said, pointing to his shoulder. "She never wanted you to fill her shoes, you wouldn't fit them anyways." He laughed. He wasn't wrong, no one could fill those shoes, ever. "Mom wanted you to fucking slip into your own for once."

I stared at him for a second, appreciating how ridiculous he was about everything. He could win any fight, even the ones he didn't start and never even throw a fist. No wonder my soul was covered in blisters, I'd been walking around in shoes that didn't fit.

"I might have lost them along the way," I admitted and he smiled at me.

"Buy some new ones, you're stupid rich, remember?" He joked.

TRUE HONEY

I dropped the last box for donation into the bed of Van's truck and closed the tailgate. I was sweating through my t-shirt in the sun while I moved old crap out of the apartment that I didn't need anymore, leaving room in my closet for Drew's belongings.

I tugged the sweaty shirt over my head and shoved it into the back pocket of my jeans while I walked back through the house and downstairs. It was going to be a fight, I knew that. Standing there staring at my half-empty closet I knew she would argue about the move I was going to propose.

But for the sake of the lie, she needed to be in my room. We needed to be together. *For the show....*

The apartment door opened and Drew sauntered in with some bags in her hand headed towards her room. Her eyes stopped on me, dragging over my chest and back to my face. I pushed my hat off my head with a hand and curled it into my palm to keep from reaching out and grabbing her.

"Like what you see?" I smiled at her.

"Shouldn't you be at the stadium," She said, shaking off the tension in the air. Her red hair curled around her face gently. She had been wearing it down more often and it made the green in her eyes brighter. I was working very hard not to cross the room and tangle my fingers in it.

"Did physio with Cael, had a meeting with Ella and then cleared my books," I said to her, leaving out the part that the reason I cleared my books was because I couldn't focus on anything but her being out with my Mother. Alone. It had me so worried that I wrote my first name on email ten times before I realized I was typing the same thing over and over.

"How is he?" She asked, waiting by her door.

"Alright," I answered, tossing the hat on the kitchen table. "He's sore, more sore than he's ever been but he's also Cael, so he's determined to do all of this with a smile on his face."

"That's good." her voice was soft, understanding, but her knuckles were white gripped around the handles of the bags. "Are you going to stand around half-naked all day?"

I looked down at my bare chest and chuckled, "Why? Am I distracting you?"

"Silas," she warned as I stepped closer, tempted to reach out and pull her forward to me. "I have to go pick up Auggie soon," she said, knowing exactly my intentions.

"I know," I said, closing the gap between us. My fingers grazed her jaw, tickling down her throat and around the back of her head to lift her lips to mine. It was soft, and lasted longer than I expected as her fingers pressed to my chest, allowing her to lean into the contact.

"What was that for?" She asked breathlessly when I retreated.

"You're going to yell at me and I wanted a kiss to remind me how much you like me," I smirked at her, watching her brows furrowed in confusion. "You have to move into my room."

"What?" She stuttered.

"It looks suspicious that we aren't sharing a room," I explained. "We're so close to the finish line with all of this and I hate to have it messed up because someone questions the legitimacy."

"What exactly do you expect me to tell Auggie?" Drew scowled.

"He doesn't need to know," I assured her, "one of us can get up early everyday or sneak around some more just so it doesn't raise any flags. Drew," I was ready to get on my knees to beg her.

I could see the reservations whipping around behind her eyes and I hated how easily she became unbalanced. I just wanted to help her keep both feet on the ground and the confidence in her decisions.

"We're almost out of the woods," I said, running my fingers down the side of her throat. Her heart was racing beneath her skin and the apprehension on her expression was loud. "You've been sleeping in my room for a week, just move your clothes in. *Please.*"

"You're serious?" She asked, the begging breaking her down just a little and hopefully in the right way. "This is a bad idea," she added.

"Everything has been a bad idea since the day I ran into you, we might as well be consistent," I reminded her, inhaling slowly. I wanted to kiss her again, badly but with Drew it wasn't ever as easy as convincing her with make-outs and flirting. Instead of asking again, I reached down, taking the bags out of her hands and walking toward my room.

I heard her sigh, and could picture the annoyed look on her beautiful face without even turning around but when her footsteps grew louder I knew I had won. I set the bags down in the closet, looking at the half-empty side with a triumphant smirk.

"Will you grab the hangers from my— the guest room?" She stumbled over the transition standing in the doorway to the closet with her hands on her hips.

"It's the least I can do," I kissed her on the way past and jogged down the hall to her room. I stepped inside her room and unlike that morning I took a moment to look around. It was like she hadn't even moved in. There were two unopened boxes in the closet on the floor, a quarter of the closet filled with dress clothes. I ran my hand over the folded jeans and shirts she had brought with her.

I grabbed the hangers, breathing in the perfume that lingered on the fabric and carried them back to my room...*our room*... I scrunched my eyebrows together at the thought. "I think this is everything hanging, I'll grab a basket for the rest." I said laying them on the bed and turning to her. She was running her fingers through my clothes and it made me feel like less of a weirdo for smelling hers when I pulled them down.

"You have too many clothes," she looked over at me and it pulled on all the strings of my heart how soft and mundane she was. Beautiful as always but there was a familiar comfort to Drew that I think my heart recognized long before my brain did. The way she was standing there, waiting for me to respond to her lighthearted jab, I could see it. A future.

"I packed up three boxes before you got back," I grimaced and walked toward her leaning on the door frame. "I have a bad habit of buying clothes and then wearing my Harbor polo eighty percent of the time."

"I like this color," she said, running her fingers over a dark red dress shirt that I'd selfishly bought but never wore because it would give Seymour a heart attack to see me in Lorette colors. Drew glanced at me over her shoulder with a knowing smile and I just shook my head at her.

"Thank you for doing this," I said after a long pause. "I know it's asking a lot more than was originally discussed."

When she looked at me that time I expected a smug look or a snide remark about the contract but nothing like that came. "I admire how much you're willing to do to keep your family together Silas," she said, "besides I thought you ripped that contract up."

I dropped my head, smiling like an idiot at the floor and gave her a soft, gladly-defeated nod. "It was the first thing I did this morning," I admitted.

"Good," Drew sighed, continuing her exploration of the closet. "What is this?" A bubble of disbelief exploded from her chest in the form of the sweetest laughter. She pulled down a hanger holding it up to her small frame, eyes wide in shock. "Honk and I'll cum?"

The black sweater had never been worn and had been sitting in the closet for two years but I couldn't bring myself to throw it out. I started to laugh, stepping forward and taking it from her to hang back up. "Cael gave it to me for Christmas a few years ago."

"I like that kid, he's funny," she hummed.

"Yeah me too." I said, rubbing the fabric and remembering what he said to me today.

"Does it work?" She asked next with a cheeky grin.

"I've never worn it," I admitted, "it would work for you though, wanna test it out?" I leaned forward to grab her but she moved out of my reach.

"I don't need to honk to make you cum," she laughed, her eyes sparkling with amusement, "I've got that covered on my own."

COURTNEY

> **Ms. Cody is taking us to dinner. Can I go?**

I stared down at my phone, terrified at how fast my little boy was growing up and chewed on my lip. A warm chest pressed to my back and like he knew something had bothered me Silas's arm wrapped around my stomach and pulled me back.

"He's safe here," Silas whispered, his eyes flickering to my phone sensing my hesitation.

I hovered over the keyboard, unsure if I believed him because it had been a long time since I felt safe anywhere and the doubt doubled when I thought about August's safety.

I took a necessary breath in and texted back that he could but to keep his phone on.

With August occupied and given a rare night off I wasn't even sure what to do with myself but I closed my eyes, setting the phone on the island. I leaned against Silas who didn't protest the affection but instead placed a soft kiss to the side of my neck.

If you had asked me months ago where I saw my life going I would have laughed at you and plotted out our next road trip. I would have had August in the car, running away from whatever the hell was going on in Rhode Island. Silas had a way of masking the worry, dampening how loud the mean little voices were in my mind even if it was just temporary. My only fear was that I was using him as a band-aid, covering up damaged goods and pretending to be something I wasn't just to keep him happy.

I was so terrified that I was single-handedly turning him into another Bradley.

We were safe now, but down the road when I inevitably fucked this all up beyond repair would he be willing to work this hard to prove me wrong. Or would the fight become too exhausting? The battle against my mind seemingly always won out over all the good. Did the safety stand a chance against the war I was waging against myself? The spiral was like hitting black ice and suddenly I was slipping out of control again.

"Riona is the most responsible person he could be with, I promise." He said, fingers splayed out over my stomach as he matched his breathing to mine and slowed us both down. He was too good at that, whether it was accidental or he knew what he was doing. He could throw on the brakes and take the wheel when I started to spin out of control. "Do you want to go for a ride?"

I snorted, it bubbled up so fast there was no stopping it and Silas laughed at the noise, his fingers digging into my side. It was honest and raw because he had caught me so off guard with the question, and dirty thoughts flooded in washing away everything else.

"What's so funny?" He tickled my ribcage and I squirmed free of his grip, backing up a few steps that he slowly closed with a predatory look in his gray eyes.

"What kind of ride?" I chewed on my lip, looking him over. He was unusually naked, his bare chest damp from his shower and a pair of loose sweats low on his hips that did nothing to hide every inch of him. My mouth went dry. I watched as his neck and ears turned a funny shade of pink and his tongue darted out over his bottom lip.

"The bike," he said, wet strands of hair falling against his forehead begging to be touched. "Unless…" he stepped forward again but I put my hand out to stop him.

"Later," I laughed.

"Oh so you're a pervert *and* a tease!" He barked out a laugh and surged toward me wrapping me up in his arms and lifting me to the counter. He slotted between my legs like he had always belonged there and I was starting to think maybe he did.

"You make it a little hard to be anything else," I wrapped my legs around his waist, pulling him closer trying to ignore the little monster in my head telling me to worry, to panic. Silas studied my expression and I did my best not to show him what was beneath the flirty and fun Drew he was chasing around after. I wanted to be better, for him.

"The bike will clear your head," he said, and it soothed over the worry. He could have as easily asked me what was wrong but he didn't because it wasn't what I needed. Read like a book left open for anyone to see. "Ice cream from Hilly's will cure your blues, and if you're still wound up when we get home…"

"Mhmm," I purred and unlinked from him. "But listen, you can't go out like that." I looked at him as he went to reach for his keys.

"It's like 96 degrees out, Drew, not even the wind can mask that heat…" He practically whined. "I ride the bike shirtless all the time, it's fine."

"Nope. I don't care about your chest, Silas. You're giving everyone a free show," I said with a smile, pointing to his dick pressing against the soft gray material. He locked down and back up at me. The last thing I needed was the urge to deck Kayla if she even so much as made a passing comment about him in those sweatpants. I hadn't officially quit because I was still nervous about not having a plan B and screwing myself out of a decent job out of pure, childish jealousy would be stupid. Very, *very* stupid.

Silas tilted his head at me, a smirk forming on his face causing me to roll my eyes knowing the comment that was coming next.

"Oh she's jealous…" he stalked back to me, spinning his keys around on his fingers and letting them fall against the back of his hand only to cup my face in both palms. His nose brushed against mine and I surged forward to take a kiss without asking but he moved back with a serious look on his face. "I'll change," he whispered, "but I want to commit this expression to memory because jealous Drew…" his eyes flickered from mine to my mouth, "is my new favorite." His smile was so bright it showed all his perfect teeth and blossomed lines around his eyes as he kissed me once, slowly and carefully.

"Not jealous," I called out to him as he jogged to the bedroom. "Protecting your modesty!" I said and heard him laugh wildly from the hall.

When he returned I was still sitting on the counter, staring at the wall trying to keep my mind out of the dark corners. He was wearing a pair of shorts and a sleeveless t-shirt that hung off his frame and gave easy access to his torso, his graying hair pushed off his head with a hat.

"Better?" He asked with a smile.

"Better."

I had no clue where we were going and I didn't really care. With my arms wrapped around Silas and my face pressed to his back I let the wind from the highway drown out everything. He was right, a ride would clear my head. There was no nagging voice when I was on the bike, just the hum of the outside world whipping past us as we sped around the outskirts of town. My fingers curled against his stomach, beneath the fabric of his shirt and I felt him tense as he took the corner that leads back down toward Hilly's.

I noticed Kayla's car in the parking lot when we pulled in and before I could follow him, he slipped off the bike. "I'll get the ice cream, stay here." He pointed at me in warning.

"Silas." I grabbed the back of his shirt and held on until he turned to look at me. "If Kayla flirts with you all bets are off." I glared at him and he laughed, reveling in the jealousy that poured from me.

"I'll be good, baby." He winked, pointing at the bike to get me to sit back down and I let go. I felt like a child. I wasn't going to do anything even if Kayla decided to cross a line. But I was also a little disappointed that I'd miss the look on her face when she realized that Silas and I had shown up together.

Silas took longer than expected but he returned with a cone for himself and a paper bowl for me filled with strawberry ice cream and chocolate flakes. I was leaned up against his bike picking at it, the creamy consistency melting against my tongue with each quiet bite.

"We know why *I* needed a ride on the bike, why did you?" I asked him finally and he paused the assault on the waffle cone to shrug at me. "Don't shrug, answer." I pushed gently, knowing that I had very little right to do such a thing given how hard headed I could be about discussing my feelings.

"Cael said something to me the other day that's chewing away at me," he admitted. "In not so many words, he suggested that I need to find myself. But I don't know what that looks like anymore."

"What did it look like before?" I asked him, trying to help him the way he's helped me.

Silas scratched his eyebrow, his hat ending up lopsided on his head as he thought about the question. The ice cream I hadn't finished was starting to melt in the paper bowl and was turning into a soupy, sugary mess as I waited for him to answer.

"You said that you didn't want baseball to be your answer, that you chose differently than your father and grandfather for a reason." I said when he went quiet. "What's stopping you?"

Silas chuckled, fixing his hat and squinting at me in the sun. "How do I trust anyone anymore?" He asked me and it hit like a ton of bricks against my chest. "My entire life was curated so I could carry on some legacy, a family name that meant something and now…"

I set the bowl on the seat of the bike to listen to him while he worked it out for himself. It was rattling to know the man of stone was made up of nothing more than thousands of tiny cracks, waiting to be picked at, seconds from crumbling into dust.

I knew the feeling.

"It means nothing, he made sure of that when he destroyed our lives and here I am still trying to recover from his mistakes to right the wrongs of my father. He doesn't deserve salvation," Silas frowned. "But it's the only path that saves the Nest, that keeps the team together."

"That's not true," I argued, shaking my head gently and stepping into his space with a napkin, the remainder of his stupid bright orange ice cream melting down his hand as he vented. I ran the napkin up his wrist slowly, cleaning his skin from the sticky mess he had made. "If it was, I wouldn't be here. You saw a solution to your problem, a way to cut your father out of the equation and save your home. You did it your way. Even if it meant doing it in the most dramatic fashion." I said to him, not looking him in the eye but focusing on his hand. "And for the record," I cleared my throat as it started to get tight. "You saved more than just the Nest."

Silas tensed as I pulled away my arm to put the napkin in the garbage and to give him some space but his hand caught my wrist and pulled me back against his chest. Without a word his mouth was on mine and his fingers were in my hair tugging tightly to keep me as close as possible. He was funneling every ounce of himself through our connection, it tingled like being too close to a bonfire and left me breathless in his arms.

"What was that for?" I swallowed hard, trying to inhale as he pulled away.

"I like when you're honest with me," he whispered, his eyes focused on mine and his hand still wrapped around my neck, "lets me know where I stand."

The look in his eyes terrified me but it also left a last electric feeling that coursed down my spine and made me feel alive in a way I'd never felt. I was falling in love with Silas Shore and I didn't know how to stop it. His attention was like quick sand and suddenly the idea of being suffocated by him was intoxicating.

"You taste like orange soda and black licorice." I whispered, choking down all the other words I wanted to say as I licked my bottom lip. Silas's grip loosened and that soft, smug smile returned without effort to his handsome face.

A loud crash came from the dumpster beside the building and I turned my head in his hand to see Kayla standing there looking pissed off. If glares could kill, I'd be dead.

"I think I just got fired," I giggled, as he pressed a kiss to my jaw either completely oblivious to our audience or purposely adding fuel to the fire.

"Good," Silas hummed, his fingers dug into my skin, turning my face back to his so he could continue to kiss me without a care in the world.

COURTNEY

The office was a mess again. It felt like every time we managed to get it organized, a new rush of papers came across the desk and the phone rang non-stop with sponsors, scouts and press wanting to be transferred internally.

Susanna had left to get us lunch and thankfully the phone had stopped ringing for the time being, giving me the chance to separate the papers into urgent and easy. We could get to the important stuff within the day and the rest could wait until tomorrow.

I turned around, searching for the silver bin that Susanna liked to use for the easy papers without luck. "Where did you go?" I mumbled to myself and wandered back to the storage office, flicking the light on and staring around at the chaos of towered boxes and old merchandise left to collect dust.

In the corner on the bottom shelf there was a box, old and water damaged but opened that caught my attention. I knelt down, pulling it out so I could get a better look at what was inside.

"Oh my god," I laughed, scooping up the box and carrying it out into the main office.

Susanna was setting paper bags on the desk when I appeared from the hallway, "now where the heck did you find that?" she asked me as I stopped in front of her.

"It was in the storage room," I said. "What is this?"

"A few years ago, the baseball team did a fundraiser to raise money for cancer awareness. It was just after Lorraine died." Susanna pulled a copy out and flipped through the pages. "I didn't think there were any more boxes of those things around."

"There must be like a hundred calendars in here," I said in disbelief.

"They sold about a hundred thousand," she said looking up at me, "it raised so much money they had to print a second run to keep up with the demand."

"Is—" before I had the chance to finish she was flipping to the image of Silas in a doctor's coat practically naked and bringing a blush to my cheeks. "Do you think I could take a fifteen-minute break?" I asked her, my mind turning with ideas.

"Of course." She shrugged, "I'll put your lunch in the kitchen." She called after me as I started through the stadium. I had to follow the signage back to the medical wing because I'd never been this far down but eventually I popped out down a hallway leading to two giant doors. Beside it was a smaller, empty office with Silas's name on it and of course it was left unused in favor of the very public medical room.

I turned my back, pushing open the doors with the box still in my arms and spun to see him working with an athlete, "sorry," I mouthed, not realizing I was interrupting until it was too late. He didn't look upset, more surprised that I was there as he excused the player, walking them out and locking the doors behind him to give me his full attention.

"Well hello to you too." Silas circled me and the box, swiping his clipboard off the bed and tossing it on his bed after marking a couple things in pen.

"You need to do another one," I said, digging into the box and holding the calendar up and letting it fall open to Mr. August.

"No." Silas jumped toward me but I held it out of his reach with a smile on my face.

"Why not?" I asked, sincerely confused by his immediate refusal.

"Let me rephrase, *hell no*." He reached for the calendar again but I stepped back and narrowed my eyes on him.

"*Why not?*" I repeated, my tone dropping.

"It was humiliating the first time and we will never outlive it!" He sighed, "where did you even find that box?"

"The storage room." I shrugged, "and are you going to listen to *why* you should do another?" I set the box down and crossed my arms over my chest. Silas stared at me, locking us in a silent standoff.

"There's no good reason for it," he argued.

"Susanna said last time you sold over a hundred thousand copies," I said. "At what price?"

"Twenty-seven dollars and ninety-nine cents," Silas said.

"And what was the printing cost?" I asked.

"Local place in Harbor did it, I think it was like six bucks per..." He said, his brows knitting together as I did the math in my head.

"So close to two point five million dollars in revenue, give or take?"

"Give or take," he chuckled at the fast math.

"Two million dollars that didn't come from your father's name. Two million dollars that only existed because of *you*." I tapped my finger on the calendar. "You want to show people that there is still good in the world? You don't need him, you don't even need their money if you don't want it. You just have to get creative," I said with a smile.

"How?" He asked, and I knew that he was interested because his shoulders relaxed.

"Reshoot the calendar."

"Drew, no," he laughed and if I wasn't so determined to get my way I'd swoon at the way his eyes scrunched up and created little lines around his face.

"Silas," I grumbled and he quieted. "We donate all the proceeds of the new calendar to Women's funds, shelters and programs in Harbor. To the people that don't have the support your mother had, or your brother. To the ones that need it the most."

He watched me for a moment, his fingers tapping the desk he was leaning on as he thought about it. "You're good." He hummed, staring at the calendar. "Do you think you can give that speech twice?" He asked, looking up at me and I chewed my lip. "I'm not the only one you have to convince."

The players. His friends. *His family.*

An inkling of confidence blossomed in the base of my chest and like he always did Silas caught it first, grabbing the crumbling box off the table and shifting it into his arms.

"Come on," he said, motioning with his head toward the door. I hesitated for a second but he was patient and eventually I picked up my feet and slipped through the door behind him. I went left, in the direction of the office but Silas went right and my brows knit in confusion as I switched directions and followed him.

The sound of rowdy men got louder as we went and I realized he was walking toward the locker room. "I didn't think you meant like right now!" I said loudly as he turned his back to the door and smiled, pushing it open.

"It's now or never," Silas said, like that was actually the only option. I inhaled slowly, listening to the chaos abruptly go silent the second he dropped the box on the floor loudly.

"Good afternoon to you too, Doc," Dean said, his hands on his hips and a towel wrapped around his waist. In fact most of them were damp and without clothes making me turn my eyes to the ceiling.

"Get decent," Silas said loudly and a few of them covered up with towels or shorts in a mumbled shuffle. "Most of you know Drew, she lives in the basement with me, and works with Suse in the front office." He explained, looking over to me still standing awkwardly by the door. "She has something she wants to talk to you about."

When the entire room turned their eyes to me the temperature in my body rose significantly and my throat closed over tightly but Silas's expression was encouraging and if I only focused on him I could find the courage to do it.

"Um—" I cleared my throat. "I was thinking that maybe it was time you reshot the Harbor Hornets Calendar..."

The room erupted and it was overwhelming with noise for what felt like minutes.

"Shut up!" Arlo barked from the corner. I hadn't even noticed him standing in the locker room but he was leaning against the wall near Josh with his arms crossed over his chest.

"Go on," Silas said softly, his eyes drifting to his best friend in thanks.

"It's not a secret that the calendar is important to a lot of people, and the last time you did one you raised a crazy amount of money for a good cause." I tried to sound confident in myself but my voice shook a little.

"And never lived it down," Van said with a soft laugh, causing a few of them to chime in.

"So I'm learning," I chuckled nervously and looked to Silas for help but he just gave me another soft smile and mouthed *keep going*. "Harbor needs your help again," I said, trying to find my voice. "All the donations from the new calendar would go to the women's shelters, and programs that help rehabilitate women affected by domestic violence. I promise it's for a good reason," I added to the end. "It's something I know is close to my heart, but also Silas's and I think now is the perfect time to remind Harbor why they love you all so much."

The room was silent, I expected more arguments but not that. The silence settled against my chest, the anxiety building the longer they remained quiet in the face of my proposal. I counted myself backwards, my fingers folding into my palm as I made it around to ten and started again.

"I'll do it."

I turned my head to see Josh standing up with a serious expression on his face. Arlo was staring at him and I couldn't pinpoint the emotion on his face but his jaw was set tightly and there was a sense of admiration in his eyes.

"Fuck it, I'm in," he stepped forward, unfolding his arms. "Blondie is going to flip."

One by one, the Hornets fell in line with their participation, and eventually the entire room was in agreement to help with the new calendar. Silas beamed at me with pride, his smile stretched from cheek to cheek and it did something to my heart that I wasn't familiar with. It wasn't anxiety, the heavy feeling of dread wasn't present but my heart was racing all the same.

"I have the perfect person to help you set it up," he said to me.

COURTNEY

Over the course of nearly two weeks, I went back and forth with Cael. We had figured out everything for the photoshoot. He had known what to do for every step we took, and even though I could tell he'd rather be on the field with his friends during the games that week. He was teaching me more about baseball than I'd ever cared to learn.

He sat with me in the stands for five of the seven games they played and explained anything I asked about while we came up with ideas for new calendar shots and tried to figure out exactly what months everyone could be.

I hadn't realized before, but he really was a sweet guy. He just loved attention. He was standing off the field with August as the photographer set up his gear and the rest of the volunteer Hornets stood around nervously.

"You guys are wearing way too many clothes!" Ella yelled coming onto the field with a big smile on her face.

"Who let her in here?" Arlo said, pointing to her with a scowl.

"You didn't think you were going to get away with shooting this without me? Did you!?" Ella laughed wildly, "that's cute."

"Get her out of here." Arlo pointed, shaking his head at Silas as I ran the cloth over his shoulders, making his skin shiny under the hot sun. Arlo continued to whine as Silas turned to face me with his arms out at his sides and an amused smile on his face.

"I didn't think they actually rubbed you down with oil?" I said, running the cloth over his chest.

"I thought you were going to tackle the makeup girl when she told me to strip," Silas said, his smile wide as he watched me spray more of the sweet smelling spray on his skin. I couldn't tell if it was baby oil, or watered-down sunscreen but it tickled my nose and made his tanned skin glow.

"I was not going to tackle her..." I mumbled. My jealousy had gotten the better of me when she decided she was going to touch him. Seeing the excitement on her face, I took over the job with a few choice words that had Silas laughing at me.

"She doesn't get to wash it off me later." His voice was low as he leaned down and caught my eye, tapping the underside of my chin with his finger. I froze at the tiny show of affection, knowing August was probably watching but Silas had thought about that already. "He's busy."

"I don't like hiding it from him," I whispered, my voice growing sad despite the promise of private affection later.

"Then tell him," Silas pushed.

"That's asking for disappointment," I responded softly and I could see the hurt in his eyes but it was the truth. It was one thing to have my heart broken, but to break August's was a whole other ballgame. I couldn't do that to him, no matter how much I loved the way Silas looked at me, or how safe I felt around him...around them all.

"I'll win you over eventually," he said, masking the sadness quickly as the wolfish smile returned to his face. "You can't get rid of me that easily."

"It's your turn." I tapped his chest, ignoring his statement with a knowing look on my face, "go before we lose Arlo and he doesn't want to do it anymore."

He stared at me for a second longer and it was obvious that he wanted to say something more but didn't want to start an argument or ruin the day. I tossed the cloth and spray bottle to the table beside me and went to stand with Ella who was watching intently as the photo shoot unfolded.

"I can't believe you got them to do this," she said, crossing her arms as Silas grabbed a bat and mimicked Arlo's pose. Both of them stood with their feet wide in low-hanging baseball pants with the bats over the back of their shoulders. The angle made Silas's arms grow in size as his muscles tensed from the stretch, his stomach flexing as he laughed at something Arlo grumbled.

"They're good men," I said, "that's how."

"Mmm," Ella agreed quietly. "All of Harbor thanks you for your service."

"I have one more person to convince," I looked over my shoulder at Cael whose face was a little grumpier than usual but still doing his best through the pain to entertain August.

"He loves getting naked, it won't be too hard," Ella encouraged as I turned away from the delicious show that was Silas and Arlo. I walked across to the dugout, leaning over on the banister. "Can I talk to you for a second?" I asked, both of them looked over at me, "Cael."

He handed August the book he was holding and pushed off the bench to join me.

"What's up? Do you need me to grab something?" He asked, his eagerness to be useful even now was impressive. It wasn't hard to see that even though he was healing and starting therapy with Silas, he was still fighting waves of pain. Intense soreness that a normal person would take medication for but he was handling without help.

"I need you to get on the field," I said and his expression turned from eager to apprehensive.

"No it's a team thing, they don't need me out there." Cael said, stepping back from the banister. Not a single dirty joke or playful remark was made. Even I knew that wasn't like him.

"Cael," I said, pulling his gaze up from the dirt. "Get on the field."

"Listen I know you mean well and I appreciate it, but... It's a baseball thing," Cael sighed, running a hand over his shaved head roughly. "I'm never going to play again, which means I'm not on the active roster and I don't have a place in the Hornets calendar. Not anymore."

His eyes drifted to Silas and Arlo having their photos taken and I could feel how heartbroken he was. I stared at him for a second before nodding, backing away but only to move to my bag with my notebook to show him something.

"I figured out what the front will look like, did I show you?" I asked him and he turned back to me with a soft shake of his head, reaching out for the notebook. His eyebrows scrunched together and his jaw tightened with a visible tick as he studied the messy sketch.

"The Nest," he said, a tiny smile creeping on his face. "That's clever."

"You live there don't you?" I asked.

"Yeah," he sighed.

"What's your excuse now?" I challenged and he looked up at me with that fire returning to his blue eyes. "You're up with Dean next, and if you keep wasting time I'll send Azo over here."

"You're a fast learner," Cael laughed, throwing his hand up in retreat before handing the notebook back.

Instead of the Harbor Hornets, the calendar would be called The Nest. Meaning Cael's reasoning was thrown out the window because he may not play again, but he'd always be a part of the Nest.

"Don't make me use the mom voice on you," I warned and that got his feet moving. August stood up and joined me at the banister. "How you doing?" I asked him, brushing my fingers through his hair until he swatted my hand away.

"How are *you* doing?" He countered and I gave him a funny look. "What? It's not like you've ever gotten involved in anything like this before...I'm just asking."

"This is the job," I said, "I work for Silas, this was just work."

August eyed me, "okay," he said after a minute. "You're happy though, it's..."

"Nice?" I said, instead of saying, unusual, weird, out of character. Deep down my skin was still crawling with anxiety, worried profusely over how today would go and we still had eight hours left of photos to take. It should have been an easy job, it was my idea after all but once the players had signed on to help the stakes raised and suddenly it was elevated to a very important job.

"Yeah," August admitted. "Mom," he said quietly, "are we going to stay?"

I want to.

"It's pretty perfect here, isn't it?" I said.

He's pretty perfect.

I watched as Silas scanned the crowd of players and professionals until his eyes landed on me. He always knew when he was on my mind. He winked, the sun catching in his eyes as they were shuffled out to bring in the next group for photos.

"It is." August said, his voice tight and confident.

He was thriving here and I would do anything to keep his life this full, I just wasn't exactly sure how when it felt like it was on a winding clock and at any moment the time could be up and we could be evicted from the perfection.

Work harder.

"I should get back to helping," I tapped the banister and leaned over to kiss him on the head, "dinner later?" I asked and August nodded as I backed away. Cael had been helped out of his shirt and was being prepped to do a few shots with Dean, as Josh looked on with a grumbly expression.

"Don't worry, you'll have your turn," I said gently. "You're going to have to get wet though..."

Josh's head snapped in my direction.

"You don't want to get shirtless, I can respect that, but you've got to get wet."

"Wow, this is the thanks I get for volunteering first," he jabbed but it wasn't meant to hurt because there was a small smirk on his face. "No ring today?" He asked, his dark eyes trailing down to my hand tucked across my chest.

"Uh, didn't want to lose it..." I said, trying to keep my tone flat.

His eyes flickered back up to mine and I could see the question behind them.

"My brother is pretty smart but there's a whole lot of stupid going on lately, don't break his heart. He won't survive anymore betrayal." Josh's words were heavy and meant with purpose, looking away from me. Lately it felt like everyone wanted something from me that I couldn't promise. And all the requests involved Silas's heart or well being. It was a lot of pressure to put on a woman who could barely keep it together for herself.

"Dean and Van are going to dump a tub of water over you for the photo, are you okay with that?" I tried to deflect the conversation.

"Yeah," he said with a nod. "I'm sure they jumped at the chance when you asked them." His eyebrows flickered upward.

"They have a bet on whether or not you're going to punch one of them," I said.

"Pretty sure you aren't supposed to tell me that," Josh responded dryly.

"What are sister in-laws for," I said softly, knowing what it meant. Whether or not Josh had figured out what was happening between his brother and I, didn't matter. Because he wasn't the type to blow something up unless he thought it was going to hurt his newly found family. And that wasn't my intention, it never had been. In fact I had been brought into the circle for the exact opposite reason. With the intention to keep the Nest together, to save harbor. *So far, so good.*

"Hey Top-gun!" The assistant to the photographer called to Josh and I watched as a few of the players turned to look who she was talking to. It was like the entire field had been fed laughing gas the way they all lost it laughing.

"You know you kinda of look like the other one," I said to him as everyone continued to laugh. Josh's jaw tightened, "From the new one, Auggie loves that one. What's his name…"

"Don't say it." Dean tried to stop me but it was too late.

"Miles Teller!" Ella's head whipped around, finishing my sentence with a wicked grin formed on her face when she pointed at him. "Oh you are never getting away from that one, *Rooster*."

"Seriously?" Josh growled. "Don't call me that!"

"Oh that's your new nickname, *Rooster*!" Ella drove it home, giggling.

Josh flipped her off without so much as warning or a word.

"This is a perfect day, naked baseball players, insulting Josh…" Ella leaned against Arlo and sighed.

"Way to go," Josh said, rolling his eyes at me. He went off as Dean and Cael finished their simple pose. Dean's arm propped on Cael's good shoulder while Cael squatted in the sand shirtless. His incision was still raw but the tips of the wiry scars were turning pinkish and white. They had been sprayed with water and droplets were running down their handsome faces.

"What did I do?" I laughed.

"Nothing, don't listen to them," Arlo said. He tossed Cael a towel as he approached the side of the field and ran his hand over his head with a proud look on his face.

"Thank you," Silas murmured from beside me, so quiet I hadn't even noticed he'd circled around to my side. "For talking him into it."

"It was more of a threat." I smiled. "Besides, he's just as much a part of all of this. On or off the field, I know that much," I said, looking over my shoulder at him. His gray eyes were soft and appreciative, I could tell he wanted to kiss me but he behaved himself and settled with his fingers sneakily brushing against my side.

"You don't give yourself enough credit. This, *today*... It wasn't just Cael that needed it. We all did." Silas's touch disappeared as a few of the players wandered by laughing and pushing. The two of us watched as Dean and Van, both shirtless and smiley, dumped water down over Josh who was positioned with his legs hanging over the dugout top. His dark curls stuck to his forehead and neck but he had that smug smile on his face that would make for a perfect calendar shot.

The rest of the afternoon was spent rotating pairs and trios, Cael and Arlo took a few shots and Cael snuck in a kiss that would definitely make it into the calendar if Ella had a say because her laughter was infectious when it happened. Dean and Jensen showed off their party trick of backflips that would make a perfect July page, and then I had to send August away because Cael got even more naked and had Van hoist him up on top of the dugout.

They all were getting into it and by the end, Jensen, the catcher was on his knees at home plate with Van Mitchell pouring water down his throat but making more of a mess than anything else. When the boys cleaned up, Silas bought dinner, filling the Nest with the smell of Italian food and the sound of pure euphoria.

They all piled around the table, leaving an empty chair that after some explaining I learned was a spot in honor of Lorraine Cody that no one used. But as I looked around I realized just how important they all were to each other. It wasn't just a college baseball team. They were a family. My heart squeezed uncomfortably in my chest.

I couldn't screw this up.

COURTNEY

I grabbed a clean pair of pajama shorts from the drawer and wandered back into the bedroom where Silas was pulling off his shoes on the edge of the bed. His hair was damp from trying to wash out the beach spray they used to give it texture. He complained all dinner about it and was still grumbling as he pulled off his socks and sighed.

I collected my shower bag and went to leave the room. I needed a minute to think that I wasn't consumed by the thought of him. His hands, his smell... his heart. But his hand wrapped around my wrist and stopped me before I could get away.

"Where are you going?" His voice was soft, his body stretched out and his chin tilted up looking at me with confusion. I opened my mouth to explain but he tugged on my arm and pulled me into his lap, locking me in place with his arm.

"I was going to go shower," I whispered, letting him hold me against him and dropping my bag to the bed with a soft thud.

"I have a shower in here," he argued.

I needed space to think, to panic in private.

"That's your shower," I said.

"It's a shower, they're all the same," Silas chuckled, tilting his face up more to brush his lips against my jaw. He had a way of distracting my thoughts, shutting them off and making everything quiet but it also meant I wasn't thinking about the consequences. The fallout if anything went wrong and eventually something would go wrong. Something always went wrong.

"What's really wrong?" He asked a second later, pulling his face back to study mine.

"Nothing." I shook my head gently.

"Alright..." he sighed, but there was no frustration in his expression. "This may have started as a lie Drew." Silas's eyes watch mine like he's searching for answers, "but I've been able to read you since the day we met. Something is bothering you." Loosening his grip around my waist one of his hands took my chin to keep my eyes locked with his. "You can talk to me," he said.

Could I? I wasn't sure I could without my emotions exploding and I certainly couldn't tell him the truth about how I felt. It could have the potential to destroy his trust in me, a trust so steady and strong it scared the shit out of me.

"Today was just... a lot." I confessed, trying to be as truthful as possible with him. "I'm used to it being just me and Auggie."

"Right," Silas said, "and I have twenty something brothers..." he chuckled.

"I was just searching out a familiar comfort," I said.

Silas watched me for a moment longer, his jaw ticking and his fingers flexing around my back. "I can be that," he whispered. "You just have to let me."

"Silas..." I wet my bottom lip.

"No," he stopped me. "Don't do that, you always do that," he said and I wanted to argue but I couldn't even figure out what he meant. "You get cagey on me and I can handle that, Josh has been that way since the day I met him. His trust is like a wet piece of paper, but," he said, brows furrowed as he explained his train of thought. "Yours is flammable..." he whispered. "It's like every time we get closer you find a reason to pull back and I don't get it because you lie about what's going on up there," he tapped my temple.

"I'm trying," I whispered back.

"I know," he said quickly, "I know." A kiss followed, quick and reassuring in a way I wasn't expecting. It started at my lips and then he gently took my wrist in his hand, placing a kiss to my palm with his eyes still on mine. "I see it. Anytime we get into these... positions you go somewhere else. It's like you aren't here anymore, aren't with *me*."

"It's sex, Silas." I chewed on my lip trying to ignore the blossoming warmth that flooded my chest.

"No it's not just that," he replied quietly. Another kiss, warm and welcoming to my wrist. He lingered there watching me. "I just want to know where you go."

He wasn't even asking too much. He was asking for the bare minimum.

"I want to know what to do to keep you here, with me." He said, rephrasing his needs.

I swallowed tightly, slightly unsure about what information I could give him that wouldn't absolutely terrify him away from me. He was being so patient though, his gray eyes studying my face to catch every single expression change. How could I fault him for wanting to learn, to help? *I like to fix things.*

"You aren't asking because you think you can fix me right? Because you think I'm some kind of charity case." The words came out quiet, nervous and tight. I watched Silas cock his head to the side, his eyes flickering back and forth.

"I'm asking because I want it to feel good for you, as good as it feels for me. I don't want you retreating, I want you." He didn't even give me time to spiral about it, two more kisses both trailing down my inner arm were placed gently, with purpose. "What's there to fix, Drew? What are you so worried about?"

"My head isn't right Silas," I whispered. "Sex makes everything less noisy, sex with you..." I sighed. "It sounds horrible—"

"Go back," he huffed gently, the noise almost a laugh. "What do you mean your head isn't right?" He placed a kiss to the ditch of my arm, soft and needy he didn't stop the barrage of affection.

"It's screwed up, it's loud with fears and thoughts that I have no control over," I explained. "It always has been and while the sex wasn't ever anything special before it helps, it's a few minutes of quiet."

"Oh," Silas's brows kissed and he looked up from his path stopping on the soft curve of my bicep to lock eyes with me. "What if I can chase the fear away?" He asked.

"Only you would try." I cupped his face, digging my fingers into the scruffy edges of his jaw. "It's not that simple, even when I'm happy," I whispered, "even when I'm with you..."

"It's always there." Silas's eyes flickered around my face. "Does the fear have anything to do with us...with me?" He paused, wanting to make sure.

How do I tell you the truth?

"Sometimes," I swallowed tightly and watched his face fall. "But it's nothing you've done wrong." I'm quick to remind him. "It's all of my own insecurities. It's very clear to me that I do deserve your kindness and your attention, Silas. Whether it's the contract or whatever this is... I'm aware—"

"There is no contract, not anymore," he grumbled, his jaw tight. When he looked at me again there was a new light burning in his eyes. A worrisome one. Without a single confirmation of my feelings Silas rose from the bed with his arm around me and flipped me back onto the mattress. "Stay with me," he said, "for you to understand you need to be here, just... stay with me."

I stared at him for a moment, drinking in the serious tone in his voice.

"Can you do that?" He asked when I didn't have a response.

I nodded gently, unsure if I could actually follow through.

"No, answer me. Can you stay here? With *me*." He asked again.

"I'll stay," I whispered.

"Good," Silas huffed. "Now don't move."

"What are you going to do?" I asked, pressing back into the mattress as he pushed my knees apart to slot between my legs.

Silas ignored my question, instead leaning down to press his lips against my neck. He kissed and sucked at the soft skin, taking his time like he's mapping out every inch with his mouth and tongue. It's torture to lay still, to remain calm while not understanding the point he was trying to make.

I wanted to stay present but it was so much easier to fall into the lush and let the sex consume my messy thoughts. I know he could tell, it was in the way his hands roamed over my body, the way his fingers gripped my thighs possessively. He bit down on my neck, hard enough to cause my hips to lift off the mattress toward him. *Hard enough to leave a mark.* His tongue smoothed out the sting and he rocked his hips against mine hard enough that I could feel his growing hardness over my shorts.

"Silas," my voice was low, pleading. I couldn't do this, I couldn't be so serious about us. Not like this. I was panicking at the thought. He wanted something so much bigger than my capabilities. He wanted commitment and a relationship but I didn't know how to give him those things. I couldn't provide the stability he wanted, the partnership he deserved. I would fail him, just like I failed everyone else.

He paused, lifting his head to look at me. His eyes were intense, searching my face. He must have sensed the panic rising in my eyes because he sighed. "Overthinking, you're always overthinking." He released a frustrated breath but his grip on my hips eased. His thumbs traced soothing patterns on my skin. "I want to worship you and I want you to remember every single second of it."

"Keep reminding me?" I asked him in a whisper.

"I will. Every single second. You're going to feel my mouth, my hands, every single inch of me so deep inside of you that you'll remember it every time you close your eyes." Silas pushed my shirt up to expose my stomach, bending down to kiss my belly, sucking gently on the skin.

I arched into his touch as he marked a new path across my skin, his fingers trailing behind hooked into the top of my shorts. I could do this, I could stay present with him. Feel it all. I focused on the way his skin felt on mine, the delicate strands of gray that tangled into his dark brown hair, the scratch of his scruffy jaw as he passed over my stomach with his lips.

He looked up at me, his eyes dark with desire as he slowly pulled my shorts down, taking my underwear with them. He tossed them aside without breaking eye contact. Silas kissed the inside of my thigh, then the other, moving closer to my center but not touching where I needed him the most.

I wanted to complain, to huff and make him hurry but he had a point to prove, a memory to make. So I let him continue with his relentless slow pace, inhaling slowly to keep myself still with every touch.

His fingers spread me open, exposing me as he blew cool air over my warm skin before leaning in and licking a low, long stripe up my center. He hummed against my body, the vibrations sending sparks of pleasure through me.

"So sweet," he said, placing a gentle kiss.

My fingertips tingled, begging for more contact but trying to follow his instructions to remain still. It was torture. Silas continued his slow exploration, using his fingers to spread me wide and giving my clit a gentle flick of his tongue. He looked up at me again, checking to make sure I was still there, that I hadn't let myself slip away. His eyes locked on mine as he sucked my clit into his mouth, applying just enough pressure to make my hips twitch.

"Still," he whispered, his breath warm between my legs.

"You're being cruel," I complained quietly, it wasn't serious but I needed more from him. None of it was enough to numb the anxiety coursing through my veins. It was going to ruin everything if I let it get the best of me.

Silas chuckled against me, the vibrations sending another wave of pleasure through me. When he finally added a finger, curling it up to hit that spot inside of me and sucked hard on my clit, I shuddered. My breath shook and my fingers pressed into the mattress if only to try and keep still.

"Cruel?" He asked, "or making sure every touch is memorized. I want you to feel me in your dreams, Drew."

"I'm always dreaming when I'm with you, Silas." The words came out before I could stop them. Soft and low but with conviction I didn't know I possessed.

Silas stilled, his finger paused and his mouth retreated. Watching me like he didn't fully hear what I said for a long moment. He pulled his finger out, leaving me empty and needy as he sat up and brought his face inches from mine.

"Say that again."

"You're a dream, Silas." I dared to lift my hands and wrap them around his face. Battling every dark thought that pushed around in my mind to make sure he knew just how incredible he was. "A dream I never want to wake up from."

Silas's pupils dilated, swallowing the gray of his irises. He leaned into my touch, his forehead pressing against mine. For a moment he just breathed me in, his hands gripping the bed sheet tightly. When he kissed me it was slow, gentle and unlike anything he'd ever given me before.

He had no idea what he was doing to me. The kiss left me completely breathless but the sex that followed ruined me in every single aspect. It was slow, each thrust deliberate and deep, his eyes never leaving mine. He worshipped my body like it was made of porcelain, whispering sweet words with each delicious movement.

I allowed myself to feel it all, my fingers tangled into his hair roughly as he thrusted forward and our bodies melted together into one. He eventually broke the gentle pace, snapping his hips forward harder, chasing his high. One hand slid under my back lifting me into him while the other gripped my thigh pulling my leg higher around his waist, opening me completely.

"Like you were made for me," he huffed, his body growing tense.

Silas pulled me up against him, kissing a line across my throat and pulling out briefly to roll me onto my stomach. Wrapping himself around me he sat back on the bed, tugging me with him until my back rested against his chest. Once we were flush, he pressed himself back inside slowly and continued the rocking motion as his hand slid under my shirt and pushed it over my head.

He palmed my breast gently, his thumbs rubbing over my hardened nipples. His teeth found purchase on my shoulder painfully before he soothed the sting with his tongue He spread me wide with his knees, going deeper and slower. He was making love to me like it was the last time and he wanted to imprint himself on my body forever.

He had more than accomplished his mission.

I'd never forget tonight.

I wasn't going to last much longer in that position, his head rubbed against my tightening walls over and over causing the heat to build rapidly. Silas could feel it because he rolled his hips forward and stilled, grinding himself against my ass. He squeezed my breast a little tighter, thrusting his hips in a circle. He was hitting that sweet spot over and over as his teeth sunk into an untouched part of my skin on my back.

The orgasm hit like a tidal wave and without much warning, my body tensed in his grip as I came completely undone in his arms. It was euphoric to feel it like that, everything all at once. No holding back, no hiding in my own head.

I felt fucking alive.

"I understand now," my words came out a gasp, mumbled in repetition like a chant and Silas tensed but smiled so brightly I could feel his lips curl against my skin.

He followed quickly, all his resolve snapping. Groaning loudly against my shoulder as his own release hit him hard. His hips jerked forward, pushing his length as far inside me as possible. He wrapped his arms around me tightly, holding me in place as he pumped out his orgasm in heavy pulses.

He peppered hot, wet kisses to the back of my throat. His fingers spread possessively over my stomach, marking me with his fingerprints. He pulled back slightly to watch himself slide in and out of me slowly, already semi hard again. He growled quietly, nipping at my shoulder as his hips moved in slow thrusts like he couldn't get enough.

"Better?" He asked after a moment of us catching our breath.

"Much better." I smiled, feeling lighter than I had in nearly thirteen years.

SHORE

I thought that the cutest expression Drew made was when she was jealous but I was wrong. The sun poured in through the row of rectangle windows that ran along the wall of my room and bathed her in ethereal light that made her look like an angel.

She was pressed against the pillow, her red hair messy around her peaceful face. I could trace the few freckles and sun spots that painted her skin, across her cheek and around her jaw. Last night was different, it felt like I had finally gotten through to her. Something had broken down inside of her and she finally let me in. I understood her fear, the hesitation surrounding actually feeling her emotions toward me. There were zero assurances but the word of a man that had started a fake relationship with her signing a piece of paper. Asking her to lie to everyone, all so she'd have a place to live.

Playing it back in my thoughts it sounded even worse.

But Drew had knocked the wind out of me and I didn't care. I let her.

I almost wanted her too.

For years I walked around taking care of everyone else but she had shown up and within weeks had become the first person to really stop and see me. I was well taken care of in every aspect of life, wealthy financially and in my relationships, but crumbling mentally under the pressure of solving every problem. Especially the ones I didn't create.

I was falling apart under the mountain of issues from my father and worse, my grandfather's prideful neglect to see his son was a piece of shit. I wasn't aware of how bad it'd become until Drew came into the picture. She lit up every dark corner with light and even though she had monsters of her own, she took the time to help me get rid of mine. I was determined to help her do the same. It was going to take more work than previously thought, but I was willing to put in the hours.

Last night she stayed present, her eyes on me, her mind focused on us. She didn't slip away from me and I had hoped that she felt safer to try again without so much convincing but I wouldn't know until we crossed that bridge. She stirred a little in her sleep like she could hear me thinking about her.

"Your phone is ringing, Silas," she said in a mumbly, adorable voice and I clued back into reality to the sound of birds chirping from my side table.

"Sorry," I said, kissing her forehead and reaching over her to grab it.

Harbor Correctional flashed across the screen and I sighed, muting it.

That asshole would ruin a perfect morning.

"Why didn't you answer?" She asked, prying her eyes open. I inhaled her sleepy beauty to calm the anger that simmered over the interruption. I thought about lying to her, telling her that it was nothing...

"It was my father."

Drew was more awake at the confession, "at nine am? What if something's wrong?"

How do I look a woman so soft and empathic in the eye and tell her I just don't give a shit if there is?

"He's calling because I'm not on the visitor list for the weekend, I have to go to New York for a meeting and don't have the time to listen to him whine about how hard his life has been," I said, reaching out to tuck a strand of hair behind her ear. In reality I didn't want to do anything but lay in bed with her. I especially don't want to waist what time I do have thinking about him. "Hey," I paused, having a great idea. "Why don't you come with me?"

Instantly she retreated into her shell.

"There will be a dinner or two, it would be nice to have you join me for," I said, "and not because it's good for the board to see us together, but because I *need* you there." Attempting to convince her before she argued was a new strategy that seemed to be working. She narrowed her green eyes on me and I could feel her thinking of excuses.

I picked up my phone, scrolling to the group chat and choosing *Shithead*, letting it ring twice before a grumpy Cael picked up on the other end. I turned on the speakerphone so Drew could hear.

"What are you doing this weekend?" I asked before he could even say hello.

"Snorting coke, maybe go on a binger, hire some hooke—"

He was cut off by a loud slap. I heard him mumble on the other end before the phone switched hands.

"Morning Si." Ella's voice was a much more welcome sound.

"I forgot you guys had an appointment," I said, "sorry for interrupting."

"It's fine, Cael was whining more than working out," she grumbled. "What's going on this weekend?"

"I have to go to New York and I want to take Drew with me." I explained. Drew watched me carefully, still not remotely convinced and Cael's stupid outburst hadn't helped.

"I'm actually horribly offended that you called Cael to look after Auggie before me." She barked something unintelligible at Cael who had started to laugh.

"Lapse in judgement," I said softly, "Friday evening to Sunday evening?"

"Arlo's going to be so grouchy about this." Cael finally piped up.

"Luckily Arlo's not the boss," Ella said sweetly, "of course that's okay. If it makes Drew feel better we can call every night."

"I'll also be around," the voice was a surprise to my ears.

"Ryan?" I questioned, "why the hell are you there?"

"I took Cael for breakfast," he said, sensing my hesitation when I didn't respond right away he continued, "I'll check in on them this weekend. Make sure everyone still has their heads and all ten fingers."

It spoke volumes that he was willing to go up to the Nest to keep an eye on them. I could tell that it also soothed Drew's rampant worry, her anxiety taking control as she picked at her nails and kept her eyes on the pillow. She was doing a terrible job at hiding her concern.

"Oh actually I have this funny looking mole just under my nut—"

"Cael keep your pants on," Ella snapped and I heard Cael laughing in the background as she scolded him.

"Thank you, Ryan." I cleared my throat, "that would be wonderful."

I flicked my finger under her chin to force her to look at me. I knew leaving would be hard for her, she'd clearly never been away from August for long but we both needed a second to just be together without hiding it. I needed a chance to prove to her that I wasn't faking, no joking, that I wanted this, I wanted her.

That I needed her.

"Okay," she whispered, barely audible but it was the best sound she could have made.

All I had to do was keep reminding her that it was good.

We were good.

"I still feel like I'm forgetting something." Drew looked over her shoulder into the backseat of the SUV and scowled. She had been more distant than usual all week and I had just been counting down the days until I got her alone. I knew she was fussing over her own thoughts again because her nails were bitten to the bed of her fingers and she was unable to sit still for more than thirty seconds. She had pulled her hair up, let it down, and pulled it back up again all before I pulled out of the city.

"You aren't, you triple checked before we even left the Nest." I took her wrist gently and pulled her hand into my lap. I pressed my palm flat against hers and inhaled slowly, begging her to follow suit. *Calm down. Breathe.*

About half an hour later, it comes out. "It's August, I'm forgetting, Auggie."

My heart squeezed painfully in my chest as she figured it out.

"I shouldn't have left him there alone," she said, staring out the window.

"He's not alone," I reminded her. "He's at home. He's with the people I trust the most."

"And here I am running away from him to have a relaxing weekend away with my secret boyfriend..." She huffed under her breath. "I think this qualifies me for the worst mom of the year award."

I chuckled, "you've never been a bad mom, Drew. I don't think you'd be capable of that."

"It's not funny Silas! He knows I left him," her voice strained. "And he knows I left him for you."

"There was no leaving," I said, trying to reassure her. "We're returning. And I'm going to quote your son here, but... He's thirteen." That got a small smile from her, a lazy one that I'd never seen before but definitely wanted to see more often. "If anything he's babysitting Cael, and they're both completely distracted. I set up the telescope for them before we left."

"You did?" Drew looked up from her lap at me.

"I promised him I would," I said and felt the air shift as another suffocating knot loosened in the rope wrapped around the box that she kept her trust in. She didn't say anything else but her shoulders relaxed a little. "I told him we'd bring him back some books so before we leave we have to stop at a store."

"He likes you," she said quietly.

"He *tolerates* me." I glance at her again, taking in how nervous she looks, "for you."

"Same thing with Auggie," she let a quiet laugh go. "Thank you for trying though. I see you trying and it's been awhile since anyone did that for him other than me."

"I think that's true for both of you," I said. Drew didn't respond, whether or not she believed me wasn't for me to question. She was quiet the rest of the drive and I didn't push for conversation. If she wanted to talk to me she would. I could tell she was still mulling over what I said, tangled with her own insecurities. It was going to take a lot more than just words.

I led her to the top floor of the hotel, shamelessly I had upgraded my room to impress her once I knew she'd be joining me. I scanned the card and let her into the massive space. There was a king size bed centered on the west wall and a nice couch, and sitting area to our right as well as a huge, pristine spa-like en-suite that was the size of my entire apartment at the Nest.

"This is..." Drew inhaled slowly, her eyes taking in everything as I set down our bags. She wandered through, pulling back the curtains on the room to expose the expensive view of New York city. I listened as her breath caught and she crossed her arms over her chest nervously.

"Just a room," I finished her sentence, coming up behind her. I wrapped my arms around her waist and pulled her back against my chest, burying my nose in her hair. "I have meetings tomorrow," I whispered, "but I booked you a day at the spa downstairs."

"Silas you didn't." She tried to spin in my arms, trying to argue face to face but I held her tightly, not letting her turn even an inch.

"I did, and you can have whatever you want. All day. We're switching places, you're going to do something selfish and I'm going to do something brave," I said to her.

"What's brave about you going to meetings?" I could hear the pout in her voice.

"The meetings are with the prosecution, the lawyers working to keep my father in jail. We're going over my testimony and the defense's possible questions for the trial," I said to her and felt her body tense. I wasn't scared of it, but she didn't need to know that.

"Okay," she conceded like I knew she would. Her conscience not allowing her to let me do something scary or selfish on my own.

"That's my girl," I whispered in her ear and placed a kiss on her neck, digging my fingers into her skin. I would show her one day at a time that she deserved the world, even if it meant fighting against her intrusive thoughts every step of the way.

Drew was worth it.

SHORE

"Mr. Shore, I need you to focus." Eileen, tall, blonde and bossy, stared at me from across the room, tapping the manila folder on her knees. She was more than impatient with me. "If there's even a crack in your statement they will find a way to free your father with it."

"I don't know anything about his time with Deedee Logan," I reminded her, trying to control my frustration. Tobais stood in the doorway of the massive glass conference room on the thirty-third floor staring at me like I was causing problems on purpose.

"This question isn't about her, it's about your half brother."

"Brother," I cut her off and sighed, "*just* brother. I didn't know about his trips to Lorette, it's a void zone in his history that wasn't written down or recorded. There are no pictures, no memories, there's only one paper trail that connects my father to Deedee and it's the money."

"There has to be something you remember, Mr. Shore, I need you to connect some dots." She pushed harder, throwing the folder on the table between us.

"Did he ever bring Josh to the games you attended? Did he ever bring you to Lorette when he visited Deedee?" Tobias interrupted.

"No." I said quickly but a heat spread across my chest.

"Stay in the car, Silas." Dad looked at me in the backseat and I thought nothing of it as he parked the car in front of the shabby apartments. It wasn't like him to bring me to this side of town and we were supposed to be going to the movies. The new Hulk movie was out today.

I waited until he was walking into the door to follow him. There were so many stairs in this building, I'd never seen that many in my life. When I got to the top

Dad was talking to a lady and I pushed myself against the wall out of his sight. Part of me knowing that it was better to stay hidden. I knew the tone of his voice, he was upset about something. Sometimes he talked to mom like that and it always made me angry in a way I couldn't understand.

"Dee I warned you I didn't want to see him today," Dad said.

"Are you ashamed of him?" She hissed, she was pretty but not pretty like Mom. She was pretty in a sad sort of way.

"Yes." He barked, "I came to see you and if you don't—"

"No no!" She cried out quickly, cutting off whatever he was going to say to her. "He'll be okay out here for a few minutes..." she sounded funny like her tongue was too big for her mouth and after a couple moments she returned to the door.

I pressed tightly to the corner as my father turned around to look at the stairwell and counted my breathing to keep quiet as the door clicked shut. When I peaked around the corner again my dad was gone, and so was the sad lady but in the hallway, sitting on the floor with a few toys was a baby.

I stared at him for a second, confused by his head of dark hair and sad brown eyes. I didn't know much about babies but even I knew that you weren't supposed to leave them alone. One time I got yelled at for taking Arlo into the backyard without telling Mom and she got so mad at me for going alone. And Arlo was bigger than the baby in front of me smashing his hand into the rubber duck.

Creeping from my corner I approached the baby and got down on my knees, careful not to scare him or hurt him. His shirt was dirty with rings of drool and his face was covered in a sticky mess that might have been jam.

"Hi baby," I said, sticking my hand out to him and letting him take my finger. It took him a long moment but a bright smile formed on his chubby cheeks and it made me smile in return. "What's your name huh?" I poked his belly making him laugh and looked around at the toys on the ground. He was on a blanket covered in pickup trucks that looked old and dirty but in the corner a few letters were sewn into the fabric.

JOSHUA

"Joshua?" I said to him and he smiled again, "I'm Silas." I don't know why I told the baby my name, it's not like he was going to be my friend but he laughed again, his tiny body giggling.

I sat outside with him in the hallway, playing with the toys and checking the numbers on my watch tick by until he started to get fussy. It started as just little grumpy whines but soon he started to cry. When Arlo used to do that, his mom would feed him or change his diaper but we were alone in the hallway and I didn't know what to do.

Standing up I thought about knocking on the door, more than once, only to sit back down and try to calm him down myself. I was working up the courage to knock again only for the door to swing open.

"What the hell?" Dad's words were harsh as he appeared from the door. His hair messing and his hand working his belt. "I told you to stay in the car!" His hand wrapped around my arm and yanked me from the floor, shoving me toward the stairs. I looked back to see the sad lady scooping the baby into her arms and gave him a small wave, knowing deep down that something was very wrong.

"I was out here for almost an hour!" I said, showing him my watch. "What were you doing?" I asked as he shoved me into the car.

"Business," he slammed the door shut.

"We're going to miss the movie," I said sadly as he climbed into the driver's seat.

"What movie?" He scowled, pulling away from the curb too fast as I fumbled with my seatbelt and tried to sit upright.

"You told me we were going to see the movie!" I said, upset with everything that was happening but unsure how to ask the right questions.

"Grow up, Silas. You can't always get what you want. Consider it a punishment for not listening to me."

"Mr. Shore?" Eileen's voice was like a loudspeaker, snapping me from the memory.

"I remember something," I said, "I don't know how credible it'll be. I was only ten at the time."

"Everything helps," she gave me a patient, empathic smile.

I unbuttoned my shirt with one hand as the hotel room door clicked shut behind me and I tossed my bag on the long table in the entryway. The bed was still messy from our lack of sleep last night and for a second I thought maybe she hadn't returned from the spa but she appeared from the bathroom door.

"Hey beautiful," I whispered as she appeared in a white robe, her hair falling around her face in soft red waves.

"What's wrong?" She looked me over, sensing the stress radiating from me.

Ignoring her question, too tangled with trauma I wasn't ready to process. The hurt of my father's indiscretions were crashing down around me and Drew was the shelter I needed from the debris. I tossed the sweat drenched shirt onto the bed and crossed the room, unable to control the urge to get my fingers beneath that robe and against her skin. "You're so soft," the words came out as nothing more than a vibration as I buried my face against the base of her throat and inhaled.

It was the only thing that could regulate my frayed nervous system.

"They gave me just about every treatment downstairs, I've been touched by about seven strangers and smell like coconut," she giggled.

"Mm," I hummed, "I like it." My fingers travelled over her hips and into the soft skin of her ass cupping tightly and bringing her as close as I could without melting together completely.

Her hand went into my hair and I thought that would be the end of me, my whole body shuddered from the contact and my eyes fluttered closed as she tugged gently pulling my head back.

"Better?" She asked in a tender tone.

"Better," I hummed, trying to retreat back into her.

"You have to get ready for dinner," she whispered, coaxing me back a touch but I wasn't ready to break away completely. "You have to feed me Silas," she said with a laugh. "If you don't I'll wither away and who will you hold hostage then?"

I looked up at her, green eyes playful and observant, the lights from the windows reflecting back at me like stars. "You ate," I teased, nodding to the room service tray from this morning.

She narrowed her eyes on me and I knew I wasn't going to win the fight, she was right I needed to get ready for dinner. We were meeting with a few of my classmates from school that I hadn't seen in a few years. It was another opportunity to cement the relationship that no longer felt fake but for the sake of everyone involved should have remained that way.

"Shower with me?" I asked her.

"I already showered," she hummed.

"Shower again." I smirked, digging my fingers deeper into her skin.

"I'm not going to play your little game.," She smiled back, the corners of her lips begging to be kissed. If I had it my way, I'd keep her locked up in this room for the next twenty four hours.

"You know it's not little," I teased and she tugged on my hair harder. "Okay, okay. I'm going." I finally relented, letting go of her ass only to wrap my hands around her jaw and pulling her toward my lips for a needy, hungry kiss. Her fingers tightened in my hair and her hand pressed against my chest as I stole the air from her lungs.

"Shower," she gasped, pulling free. "Now."

I sighed, closing my eyes as she slipped away from my grasp and went back to getting herself ready. I ran the shower cold, letting it deal with the sexual frustration that was pumping through me. But nothing killed the vibe like remembering that day.

It was as if I had blocked it out completely. I thought that the first time I'd met Josh was the day I found out about him from my father's paper trail. But that hadn't been true. I'd come in contact with him so much earlier than that, I'd just forgotten that day. Whether it was trauma or ignorance that kept it tucked away, the memory was free now and it was going to eat away at me.

I got out of the shower, bending down to grab my phone from my back pocket and dialed his number.

"What?" Josh answered after one ring.

"We need to work on your phone manners," I said, rubbing the water from my eyes and leaned against the counter as I wrapped myself in a towel.

"If I know it's you, why would I need manners?" Josh challenged.

"Okay well," I sighed, pushing my wet hair back with my other hand. "Nevermind."

"What do you want, Silas?" He asked, reminding me why I dialed his number in the first place.

"I need to apologize to you," I said, trying to control my tone.

Josh huffed. "For what now? If it's something Charles did that you're taking responsibility for... don't bother, I don't want to hear it."

"You're going to hear it eventually and I want you to hear it from me," I explained. Josh went quiet and I could feel the tension that flooded him from across the phone. "I remembered something today during my meeting with the lawyers."

"The prosecution?" Josh questioned.

"Yeah."

"They called me twice this week, they want me to go to the prison."

"No," I said quickly, "under no circumstances are you going to go there."

"I'm not a child," Josh argued, "if it needs to be done to keep him locked up, I'll do it."

"I said no," I snapped harder that time.

Josh swore on the other end. "Fine, what did you remember?" He asked after a long stretch of tense silence.

"Dad took me there when I was younger, probably about nine, maybe ten. I met you before you were even out of diapers and I didn't fucking remember until now." I felt like a fucking disappointment. I knew he was there, knew he existed and I had forgotten about him. "I'm sorry Josh."

He laughed, tight and cold. "I warned you not to apologize for things that Charles did."

"I should have said something to my mother, to anyone. But I was scared." I said to him, just trying to be honest.

"You were a kid," he reminded me. "Call me when you have something to apologize for that isn't *his* bullshit," he said, I could hear the smile on his face.

"Yeah," I sighed.

"Silas," he said before hanging up. "There was nothing you could do back then and the second you were able, you changed the entire trajectory of my life."

I swallowed down the guilt, using his words to create a barrier between me and the overwhelming feeling that I was letting him down again.

"You looked like me," I said to him suddenly, "when I get home I'll bring over some pictures, we looked alike…"

"Alright." Josh agreed. We were still working on what it meant to be brothers, but we were getting better at it each day.

"Alright," I repeated back to him.

COURTNEY

Silas went down to the bar ahead of me, too antsy to stand still while I finished getting ready, and he was making it nearly impossible to do so with every kiss, touch and bite. He was relentless, he had come out of his shower worse than he'd gone in. It was obvious that he was bottling up information about what happened today and it wasn't really my place to ask him what was wrong but I had tried anyways only to be met with his lips or his tongue.

I was aware of the timeline of our relationship, cautious with knowing that it had started because we both needed something from each other but I was scared that it was changing into a different type of need. One I wasn't sure I was able to handle. The little voices in the back of my head persisted. Repeatedly telling me that I wasn't good enough, wasn't strong enough, wasn't smart enough to be adored by someone like Silas Shore.

The noise only silenced when he was around with his constant reminders. It was when he wasn't around they flooded in knowing Silas' strength wasn't protecting me. What kind of life was that? Subjecting him to a job he never signed up for, at least willingly. How long would it be before he got frustrated with my little progress, or bored of the struggle that came with shut downs. How could he see through the storm when it felt endless?

I stared at myself in the mirror, the dark green dress hanging off my shoulder by two tiny straps that did nothing to hide the fresh mark that he had left that morning. I changed three times before circling back around to it, it hung off my body in silky waves that felt so nice against my skin after being treated to such a good day. I'd never been taken care of like that and it was an addicting feeling.

Downstairs the lounge was full and it took me a moment but eventually my eyes fell on him standing at the main bar with a half-full glass in his hand. He was wearing the burgundy dress shirt from his closet with a dark pair of pants and his hair was pushed back off his face in the soft messy waves courtesy of my fingers after giving in to his protests for affection.

His eyes caught mine from across the room and softened as he angled his body toward me, leaning on the bar with his elbow and pushing that smug, handsome smirk to his face. Silas Shore was a god, bathed in bar lights and drenched in the sound of old money laughing at the jokes of women too young for them. He stood out among the wealth, his gaze never leaving mine as I navigated the tables and glances of other men.

"God damnit, Drew." His hand reached out to me and yanked me close with a gentleness I wasn't expecting, his eyes falling to my shoulder. "You're going to kill me." His eyes flickered up to mine.

"I thought I was meant to show it off?" I whispered, leaning in closer as his hand wrapped around my hip to my lower back. He inhaled slowly, whatever answer was on the tip of his tongue stayed there because we were interrupted by someone clearing their throat. Silas brushed his hand up my back, finding the low cut hem and pressed his fingers into the bare skin between my shoulder blades. I turned to give my attention to who he was looking at and smiled politely.

"Drew this is Donny," Silas said.

"Don, no one calls me Donny anymore." The blonde haired man held out his hand showing off the expensive watch on his wrist. "It's nice to meet you," he said.

"Preston and Troy," he said to the others. Both dark hair and dark features smiled and shook my hand. All three men screamed old money and reeked of whiskey. "We all went to school together."

"Oh, did you all play baseball too?"

Preston barked a loud laugh that made me flinch. "She's cute," he said, bringing the glass to his lips. "No sweetie, we didn't. That was always Silas's thing. Waste of time really."

Silas tensed but I just laughed like I was being paid to do it.

"The guys who play baseball at Harbor, *need* baseball. It's a scholarship not a hobby. And guys like us don't have time for hobbies unless it includes running trains."

"Running trains?" I said and all three of them stifled laughter as Silas told them to shut the hell up. The conversation that followed included a vicious dick measuring contest about who had done more in the last few years since they graduated university.

I learned quickly that they were all doctors, varying in their fields but all just as egotistical and rude. I did my best to keep a smile on my face but it was pretty obvious that none of them wanted anything to do with me. For the most part all I got was funny looks and the rare snide remark. They never asked me what I did for a living, they barely spoke to me at all and it's pretty clear that the reason Silas hadn't seen them in some time was because they're assholes.

He kept one hand on me through the entire dinner, constantly checking in with his expression and I gave him the energy he needed to get through it but when they started to get more drunk and we headed back to the longue, the night grew tense. After excusing myself to use the bathroom I returned, my easy path to Silas was blocked but I could hear them chatting.

"So what's the deal with her?" Troy asked, sliding his empty glass across the bar. I tried to get around the two people blocking me but there was no way without pushing.

"Drew?" Silas sounded confused.

"Yeah, did you pay her to be here tonight? Trying to make us look bad because you have a piece of arm candy?" Troy teased.

"Silas would never pay for a prostitute, he's too innocent. She's probably just a hometown whore he found to sucker into being his date tonight." Preston's comment ran down my spine like ice-cold water.

"We all had a red-head phase man, they're fucking psychopaths though. You just gotta have fun with it and let it go!" Troy yelled over the sound of the music and crowd.

"Yeah no," Silas was quick to shut him down. "Despite your idiot comments, she's my fiancé," he corrected them and the sound of him saying it made me feel a little better. It wasn't like he meant it, or that it was even true but he was defending me and that held some weight.

"Silas Shore, the serial hump and dump her?" Don laughed, "what? Does she have a magic snatch or something? There's *no way* you're committed to her."

I shoved my way around the couple blocking my view of Silas and his gaze instantly caught mine in apology. I inhaled, pushing a smile to my face and pretending I hadn't heard a word of their nonsense as I slid onto the stool next to Silas.

Without a word Silas pushed himself between my legs, his hands on my face and his body pressed against mine. Our lips collided with a fury I had never felt from him, like he was trying to remind me exactly how he felt about me with his touch alone. It sparked a fire that started in my chest and spread around my body wildly, making my skin itchy and my breath catch. He went down through the darkness with me until the music was nothing but a dull hum and the lights around us were nothing but blurred stars across our vision.

It was more than just a kiss, it was another mark.

One on my soul that only I'd ever know was there.

It was possessive, and threatening. *Mine.*

My heart thumped dangerously slow in my chest and I realize then as the feeling of completely restless euphoria ran through my veins that I'm royally fucked. Silas Shore had altered my brain chemistry.

When he pulled away I almost forgot to breathe, my lips felt fuzzy and it took a minute for everything to come back into focus.

"I probably shouldn't have done that," he whispered, brushing his face against my temple and looking at his friends who had all gotten a little quieter, stunned in silence by the extreme show of possession and public affection.

"Take me back to our room," I hummed, flexing my fingers and tangling them into the fabric of his shirt at his side. The display had my adrenaline pumping like it never had before and I needed more of him. I wanted to feel him everywhere. I didn't give a shit about the bar, or how crappy dinner had gone. Their remarks meant nothing suddenly and even my anxiety was subsiding where it would usually run rampant..

"Goodnight boys," Silas didn't even flinch from my soft demand. He turned to lead me away despite their jeers and calls for us to return. We entered the elevator and before the door even closed our lips were frantically called together again. His hands cupped my ass, tugging at the silky fabric of my dress as his mouth roamed over my skin. He grew more desperate with every floor passed and as the door opened on ours he hauled me up into his arms not quite ready to release me.

"Back pocket," he grumbled against my lips and I snaked my hand around to grab his wallet, slipping out the keycard and slapping it against the door as his tongue swiped into my mouth.

He set me down on the floor beside the bed and his hands were on the zipper of my dress without thought. The fabric slipped off me without his help, pooling at my feet as he backed away to admire me in the dim lighting of the room.

Silas's eyes darkened taking in every curve and line of my body. "Goddamn," he huffed, running a hand through his hair, "you're *everything*." He stepped forward again, pressing his body against mine as he kissed me more.

The back of my legs hit the edge of the bed and both of us tumbled downward in a mess of breathless laughter and more kissing. Silas settled between my legs, breaking the kiss to trail his lips along my jaw and down my neck. His hand roamed over my body, caressing and exploring every inch of skin he could find. He nipped at the sensitive spot where my neck met my shoulder, inches from the mark he'd left this morning making me gasp and arch into his touch.

It didn't take much for a pool of warmth to form between my legs with how he was touching me. Knowing exactly which spots would elicit his favorite noises and god had he earned every single one after that kiss in the bar. My mind was still fuzzy and my skin on fire.

Silas smiled against my throat when he felt my breath hitch, knowing what he was doing to me and surging forward with prideful excitement. He slid a hand between my legs, cupping me possessively and pressing his thumb against my clit.

"So wet already," he growled, biting down gently.

"You have that effect on a girl." I arched upward into his hand, needing more contact and furious at how many clothes he was still wearing. My fingers reached out, aiming for the buttons on his stupid shirt but he stopped me.

"Did you need something..." He trailed off, kissing a line down my chest and capturing a nipple between his teeth drawing a low moan from my throat. My impatience was only making his ego worse and the smirk on his face would be the death of me. "Are you in a hurry?" He teased.

I narrowed my eyes on him, wiggling free of his body weight and slipped up higher on the bed out of his reach. Watching as he sat back on the bed in disbelief and I propped myself up on my elbows. "No hurry, but I think you need to earn it. I deserve a little treat after suffering through that dinner with your horrible friends."

The corners of his mouth twitched upward in amusement, settling on his heels to admire me. "I think you're right." He started unbuttoning his shirt, maintaining eye contact as he undressed himself at the end of the bed.

"Slower," I whispered, planning on getting every last second out of his striptease.

Silas chuckled, slowing his motions and keeping his eyes locked with mine as he popped open each button. I wanted nothing more than to get my nails into the perfect skin on his chest but I was enjoying the show too much to care. Finally, he shrugged off the shirt completely, tossing it to the floor.

"Better?" He asked, his tone low and sweet.

"Better." I responded, the word making my heart race in a weird way it never had before. When he attempted to return I pressed my toes against his chest and my eyes flickered to his belt and pants.

A smirk formed on his lips at the commanding gesture, leaning back slightly he worked his belt open gradually, deliberately. "For someone who isn't in a hurry, you seem very interested in getting me naked," he said, unbuttoning his pants.

"I'm enjoying the show." A smile licked at the corner of my lips as he pushed the zipper down.

COURTNEY

Silas huffed, stepping to the end of the bed and pushing his pants down his hips revealing black boxer briefs that left little to the imagination. "Is this part of the show satisfactory?" He asked teasingly, gripping the hem of his underwear and pausing, waiting for permission to remove them.

"Could use a little more passion," I teased him. He rolled his eyes at me and inhaled slowly. "Sorry, sorry, no absolutely," I giggled, "please continue," I encouraged, sinking my teeth into my bottom lip.

He chuckled, a genuine smile spreading across his face as he finally pushed his boxers down, stepping out of them completely. He was hard, his length standing proudly against his stomach. Silas watched as my eyes flickered down and he bit back a smirk, clearly enjoying the power play.

"Oh she's quiet now," he purred.

"Show me that passion, Doc." I grinned, letting my legs fall open but he shook his head gently, a few pieces of hair falling loose as he raised his hand and did a roll over motion with his finger.

"On your knees, hands on the wall," he said, and I swallowed tightly. I was going to pay for making him strip but with a heated excitement I did as I was told. Rolling over and getting up on my knees I placed both hands flat against the wall and felt the bed dip behind me.

Silas positioned himself behind me, tracing his knuckle down my spine. "Tell me," he whispered in a low voice that made my body shutter. "How wet are you for me right now?" His free hand slid around my hip and down between my thighs just barely grazing me.

"Don't ask silly questions," I sighed, letting my head fall back.

He slid one finger inside of me, finding me wet despite my teasing. "Mmm," he hummed, "Don't move," his hand moved up to tweak on my nipples and I grinned hearing my favorite words. Silas slid between me against the bed, his hands wrapping around my thighs and forcefully pulling me down on top of his mouth without warning.

I gasped at the sudden intrusion of his tongue, my thighs shaking around his head and brushing against his scruffy jaw as he started to work my clit. "Fuck," I cried out, just trying to keep some control as my fingers curled against the wall.

Silas held my thighs open, his tongue swirling against me in slow, tortuous circles while his fingers curled inside of me. He was proving a point, slow, deep and dirty. He could be passionate. He hummed against me intentionally, making vibrations that had me fluttering tightly around his fingers.

"Silas..." His name dripped from me and I couldn't take it anymore, weakening attempting to pull away from the wall. But he was quicker, his arms wrapping around my thighs tightly, keeping me imprisoned between his mouth and the wall.

"Don't you dare fucking move," he growled sucking my clit hard, he was doing everything he could to work more noises from me. I pressed my hands flat against the wall to steady myself as I sank lower over his face as my legs started to go numb and the pressure twisted up through me like a warming coil.

My body tensed and Silas doubled down on his efforts, sucking and licking with relentless effort. His fingers curled inside of me expertly, hitting that spot that caused my legs to tremble uncontrollably.

"I need you," I begged him.

His fingers snapped free of me, making me whimper pathetically. His hand smacked my ass hard, just once but enough to make my body tense. "You can't even handle my tongue right now and you need *me*?" He taunted softly, spreading my thighs wider apart with his broad shoulders. He knew if he talked dirty enough, I'd get snappy. He was doing everything he could to keep me present and fuck it was working. I wanted more. I didn't have to be quiet here, there was no one listening but him and he wanted me to sing for him.

"Don't be mouthy," I gasped.

Silas smirked against me, knowing he was pushing all the right buttons. "Make me shut up then," he challenged, grabbing my hips and lifting me slightly so he could speak against my wet, sensitive core. "Fuck my mouth instead if you don't like my attitude."

I shook my head in disbelief and flicked my hips back in his grip.

He hummed in approval when I started to move against his mouth again, "that's it," he praised, his hands digging into my hips tighter. I whined slightly as his fingers dug so tightly into my skin I could feel the bruises forming while my body crumbled into the pleasure he was building with his tongue. An intoxicating combination that I couldn't save myself from as the orgasm broke inside of me, exploding like a firework.

He moaned against me as I came apart, the sound vibrating through my clit and prolonging the orgasm. Silas pushed his face deeper between my legs, his tongue continuing to lick, and suck even as I tried to push him away in search of relief. He didn't relent until I was shaking and completely spent against the hotel wall.

Silas pressed a soft kiss to my stinging ass cheek giving me a chance to catch my breath. "Look at you," he whispered against my skin, a satisfied smirk in his voice. He gently slid his hand up my stomach, steadying me against the wall as the feeling returned to my legs.

Still on my knees with my back to him I arched against him, letting my head fall to the side as his lips found my neck. He wrapped his arms around my waist and pulled me back against his chest. His lips trailing up and down my neck. I was boneless and pliant in his arms, completely wracked and breathless. Silas nipped at my pulse point, soothing the bite with a lingering kiss.

"Mmm," I purred, rolling my hips against him and trembling as his length, still hard and ready brushed between my legs.

He hissed sharply as my hips moved me along his shaft. "Damn it, Drew." He muttered softly, his hands squeezing my thighs. "I can't get enough of you." He accused gently, nipping my shoulder. His body was literal sin, I could never get sick of it. Every sharp line, strong muscle and perfect curve.

"Show me," I urged.

He growled softly, one hand sliding up to wrap around my throat lightly. He used the other to guide himself to my entrance, pushing in slowly. My body easily stretched to accommodate him like it was made only for him.

"Fuck," he groaned, bottoming out. He started moving his hips deeper, each thrust hitting that spot inside of me that made my legs shake. His hand on my throat tightened slightly, making my head fuzzy in the best kind of way.

"Just like that," I whispered each word and fell forward against the wall gently to give him a better angle. He moaned out as I bent forward, giving him more access. He pulled back slowly before snapping his hips forward, setting a steady pace.

"You're goddamn perfect," he mouthed against my shoulder, his breath hot against my already flushed skin. Silas used his hand on my throat to pull me back onto his dick each time he thrust forward, each time growing closer to his release. His body tightened around mine and his breath became ragged and shallow.

"Baby, I'm not going to last much longer," he groaned deeply, his hips moving erratically. His voice was strained as he thrusted again, holding himself deep inside as the rubber band snapped within him. His cock throbbed with a wave of pleasure before he pulled free of me. He shifted on the bed, his mouth finding my clit one more time, working out the second round of shockwaves as his hand pumped hard between his legs.

He pushed two fingers inside, but it wasn't the same. My body craved the fullness that his fingers just couldn't provide. His mouth suctioned over me, sucking hard. I was so oversensitive from the first orgasm that it took such little effort to draw out the second one. His teeth grazed my clit, sending fireworks bursting through me as he groaned loudly and spilled across the bed both orgasms hitting us simultaneously.

Silas moaned against my core, drinking down the release as my body spasmed with waves of pleasure. I was reduced to nothing more than a boneless, moaning mess. His hot release covered his hand and the bedsheet, evidence of his feral enjoyment. He slowly removed his fingers and sucked them clean before rising up, pressing kisses to the back of my thigh and round of my ass.

I clumsily pushed away from the wall and sank into the pillows away from the mess we had made. Silas followed, crawling up my body and wrapping around me. He nuzzled into my neck, pressing soft kisses to my shoulder and collarbone. His eyes were heavy with satisfaction as his arm tightened around my waist possessively.

"Let's test out that tub." He kissed my jaw and dragged me backward off the bed.

SHORE

I stood in the dugout listening to the stadium explode as Van crushed a ball to the right field. Perfectly sending it out of play and bringing Josh and Louis home. I should have been elated but all I could think about was Drew.

Under me, over me. The thought of her was consuming.

I had almost told her that I loved her.

I couldn't figure out when it happened or why, but the words had been on the tip of my tongue that night at the hotel. Only silenced by my fear of her running if I said them.

"Si!" A voice barked at me and I looked up to see Dean shoving a Portland player on his ass. I rushed out after Arlo, who was trying to keep anyone from throwing a punch but Van is too fast and his fist connects with Keller's jaw. They're shoving and screaming without reason over a misstep and a shove. Louis was trying to reason with Otis who played catcher for Portland and had his meaty hands tangled into the front of his jersey.

Collected from more than one source of hollered insults it seemed the fight had started because Louis ran over Otis at third.

"Put him down, Otis!" I cracked, stepping between them. Louis scrambled backward. "You were on the bag, what did you expect!?" I shoved him backward, "get back to your dugout."

"Fuck you, Shore!" He stepped forward but Van had gotten loose of the ump and Ryan. Jensen grabbed the back of Otis's jersey, Van dropped his shoulder and knocked him into the dirt with a massive thud.

"Get Mitchell off the field now!" The Ump barked.

"Jensen don't you dare!" Ryan's voice boomed as he went to block Van's body from another Portland player. Jensen, the idiot that he was, didn't listen and before he could be stopped, he drove his knee into the players stomach. "Get off the fucking field!" Ryan snapped and Jensen rose both hands in the air with a wicked, flushed grin on his face.

I hauled on the back of Van's jersey, ripping it at the shoulder but not doing anything to keep him from pounding Otis into the clay. It took both Ryan and I to get him on his feet and backward enough for him to listen to orders.

The jersey hung from his massive frame and he pointed across my shoulder with a hate-filled expression. "You're twice his fucking size Otis, that was a dirty fucking play!" He spat at him and Otis flipped him off.

"Hey!" I scrambled to get control as Van surged forward, "go before you get suspended."

Van's eyes never left Otis as he allowed me to walk him backward. Everyone in the stands was standing and watching the sudden blow up. The tension between the two teams was too high; they weren't going to make it through two more games. Not if they kept on going into them so aggressively.

I followed the three ejected players through the tunnel back to the locker room as Ryan figured out how to finish the game short of his best players.

Van tried to argue, ripping the shreds of his jersey off and throwing it in the garbage with a thud. "It's bullshit!" He whirled on me and I put my hands up, staring at him until he got control of himself. "Sorry, Doc." He inhaled slowly and I watched as his shoulders relaxed. "They do that to Lou all the time," he said, "and they always get away with it because he can't explain himself!"

"Louis is fine because he has you guys, but starting fights this late in the season over something so trivial is pointless and it's going to screw the whole team. If you get suspended, even one game." I looked around at the three of them, "that puts Keith in left field and that's a massive pocket." I warned him with an even tone. It would be much nicer than how Ryan would deal with him later. It was a stupid explosion but Van couldn't help it, the entire team was a powder keg.

Jensen was nursing a set of bruised knuckles next to Dean.

"You're a dumbass, you're acting more like Arlo everyday." I pointed at him.

"That team is out of line," Dean snapped back and I glared at him. On any other day he'd be cowering but he squared up and it only infuriated me more.

"Settle down, Tucker," I snarled. "I am not in the mood for your confidence."

"Whatever Doc, we're going to win this series and never have to see their faces again, I don't regret hitting anyone." He argued.

"Of course you don't because you don't see the consequences of your meathead actions. You think Keith in left is bad? Imagine Matheson on first!" I snapped. "Do you want to lose this series over a bench brawl? Smarten up!"

That was it, I couldn't take them anymore. I took off down the hallway toward the front offices and grabbed my keys. Ella could handle the last inning on her own, I needed to get out of here before I said something I didn't mean to a bunch of stressed out kids.

I guess I'm more like Charles than expected.

I had three missed calls by the time I slipped off my bike in the Nest drive way but I didn't care. It rang again while I was holding it in my palm and Harbor Correctional flashed across the screen. "Speak of the devil," I swore and shoved my phone away and went in search of the one person I knew could make it at least a little better. She was sitting at the counter on her phone, her hair falling over her face and I couldn't help myself. I wrapped my arm around her and pressed my face between her shoulder blades just to be able to breathe.

"Oh," she squeaked, wrapping her arms around mine. "There's still an inning, why are you here?" She whispered.

"They didn't need me," I lied.

"Hmm," she hummed, clearly questioning the legitimacy of my statement. She tapped her hand to the top of mine and I released her gently. "What actually happened?" She asked.

"I blew up on Dean." I stepped back and closed my eyes, feeling her eyes on me helped to slow my racing heart. "There's so much happening and he did something stupid... it might cost them everything."

"Sounds exhausting," she offered with a gentleness I wasn't expecting.

"It is... I am."

"How about a drive?" She suggested next and I opened my eyes to take her in.

"You know what... yeah." I nodded. "Where's Auggie?"

"In his room with Red," she said, looking confused.

"Get him too, we can steal the fastback," I declared, pushing a smile on my face for her. She stared at me for a second, skeptical but wandered away to get August moving. We were halfway to Pittsburgh when she finally questioned what the hell we were doing.

"Going to a Reds game," I said, turning off the highway. August snorted at his mother's expression from the backseat.

"Are you serious? I said drive, Silas. Not a road trip," Drew gasped as she took in the signs.

"Stadium is closed tomorrow, neither of us work and Harbor was too loud," I said with a groan. The responsibilities that fester there are suffocating me, one at a time. *I can't breathe.* "There was no reason we couldn't."

"None of us brought clothes Silas," she reminded me.

"This is my selfish act for the day," I said and that was all it took for her to understand.

She went quiet but her eyes spoke a hundred different concerned words. For the first time in months I felt bad for pulling her into all of this, regret stung like a hundred paper cuts. I opened my mouth to say something, to apologize maybe but she looked at August in the backseat and smiled. Warmth blistered at the edges of my frustrated thoughts, consuming the shadows in bright light.

It would be easy enough to go back to being a mess later, for now I was going to forget it all. I pulled us into the Pittsburgh stadium an hour later, and with only ten minutes to spare before first pitch. August was the first out of the car, his excitement was infectious. For a kid that had never shown interest in baseball he sure had started to care a lot more lately.

I bought him a Reds jersey against my better judgment and got Drew a cute white Pittsburgh hat that fit down over her head perfectly. I had to resist any sort of physical contact and even though August had a clue of what was happening. I wasn't going to go against Drew's wishes until she could find a way to have the conversation with him herself.

Until then, I sat next to her in the middle of a sea of pirate jerseys with my hand pressed against her thigh, hidden out of August's sight and soaked in one evening of feeling *normal*. No one here knew who I was, no one cared. The air smelled like hotdogs, peanuts and stale beer. Drew kept looking over at me as the game went on but never said anything about my mood.

"He'll throw a cutter," I said to August who was grinning ear to ear with a bundle of french fries between his teeth.

"How do you know?" He asked in grumbled English.

"Singer sinks into them sometimes to throw off the batter, he throws a lot of sliders and sinkers. Changing up his routine keeps people on their toes and usually results in an easy out," I said, and watched the field.

Drew's fingers tickled against my side in approval and I relaxed against the feeling of her as Singer threw the pitch and the ump called the out.

"You're good at that," August said, sipping on a drink bigger than his head.

"It's my job," I laughed.

"I thought you were a doctor," he snipped.

"I am, but I've spent a lot of time watching baseball. Once you know how a person operates it's not hard to figure out their next move." I explained. "Players are creatures of habit, they're always going to resort back to what they know."

"I like stars better." August grumbled. "Less complicated."

"Yeah, you're right, Kid." I agreed.

Drew snorted at his nonchalant response and leaned on her elbow into my space as she watched the game. With August's eyes on the game I used the opportunity to kiss her on the head and inhale her into my lungs momentarily. I wasn't sure I could ever thank her for the day, she had no idea how much her willingness to just go meant today. She waited patiently through every inning and when the game was done I took us for dinner.

She argued when I suggested staying in a hotel overnight but she was vetoed by August who found out about the two water slides at the pool. Perched on the edge of the bed she flipped through the pay-per view movies mindlessly as he changed into a swimsuit we'd bought him on the way over. She gave him a list of rules and I waited patiently on the other side of the room but as soon as August was out the door, I curled around her and pressed my lips to her neck.

"Are you sure you're okay?" She asked after a second. "We've been running a lot and it's not exactly your M.O."

I chuckled, breathing her in and matching my breathing to hers.

"Silas," she whispered, trying to encourage the answer out of me.

"I'm okay, Drew." The words came out shaky and I hated myself for it when her gaze tilted down to me.

"You don't have to be," she said in a small voice, "it's okay if you're not."

"I'm okay," I repeated to her, each time I believed myself a little less. My fingers dug into her and without words she pulled me into her lap.

My knees hit the floor as my face tucked into her stomach and I wrapped my arms so tightly I felt her tense. I hid my face, unsure what she'd catch if she took a look at me but knowing nothing good would come from it. I let the panic settle at the base of my chest willing it to fade away into nothing but a dull thrumming as Drew pushed her fingers through my hair.

I sat on my knees between her legs trying to get control of myself for too long, I could hear my phone vibrating across the room where I left it. Everyone wanted something from me and I was starting to feel the effects of it. My patience was waning, that much was evident in the way I treated the boys today. Yelling wasn't my style, and I had taken out my frustration on them without warning. *Shit.*

Drew waited patiently for me to relax and when I finally looked up at her she was staring down at me with an understanding expression that I probably didn't deserve.

"What happened today?" She asked carefully.

"Classic case of trying to do everything for everyone." A halfhearted smile formed on my face and Drew's fingers traced the curve of my bottom lip. My phone rang again.

"You should answer that," she whispered.

"No, that's exactly why I needed out, no matter how many times I answer it, no matter how many fires I put out. It won't stop ringing," I sighed.

Her hands cupped my jaw and her nails raked through the scruff as she tilted my head up to look at her. Without words she leaned down and kissed me, it was gentle, simple in the best kinds of way. Like rain after the hottest day or fresh snow. It was enough to push back everything and I realized in that moment where she went when she was hiding. It was nice there, dark and cool, away from the rest of the world.

Drew pulled back and I lifted up chasing the feeling of her lips for one more second of calm. She hummed but obliged the follow up with the same softness she had shown before.

"Thank you," I whispered. "For just going with it."

I wanted to tell her everything, her expression begged me for it but what I wanted to say and what she wanted to hear were two very different things. I wanted to tell her how much I hated putting her ring on my keys anytime she didn't *need* to wear it. How much I hated not being able to kiss her whenever I needed one.

How *real* everything had become.

COURTNEY

"Auggie, can I talk to you?" I sat across from him at the island as he picked at his cereal before school. He had three days left before summer vacation and he had sweetly made a bunch of plans for him and Daisy to hang out. The color had permanently returned to his cheeks and I got to see his smile more often than not.

He looked up at me and flinched.

"Sorry, not like that," I corrected myself, those words typically and repeatedly in the past had been used to start the conversation about moving. But that wasn't this. His shoulders relaxed a fraction but he stopped eating his food to listen to me. "It's about Silas."

"I know Mom," he practically cut me off, looking back at the manga he was reading.

"You know what?" I asked him.

"That you like him..." he said, flipping the page.

His honesty caught me off guard and I couldn't tell if I was confused or relieved that he wasn't more upset about it. I wet my bottom lip and inhaled slowly to give myself time to come up with a response that didn't give away my emotions.

"How do you know that?" I asked, I was going to be pissed with Silas if he had spoken to August behind my back about everything.

"You're happy," he said, looking up from his book with a soft expression.

"Oh." Something about the way he said it broke my heart. I *was* happy. Happier than I had been in a really long time but I didn't think it was so obvious that my thirteen-year-old would pick up on it.

"You're not as good at hiding things as you think," he added and it made me laugh.

"How do you feel about it?" I asked him, leaning over the counter to steal some of his breakfast.

"He's nice to you," August said.

"Yeah he is," I agreed and gave his spoon back.

"He tries too hard sometimes but the manga he brought me back from New York is pretty cool," he hummed, the way he was playing it off was nice. It felt nice to know that I wasn't entirely screwing all of this up. "And he buys my favorite pop tarts," August added.

"Oh is that all it took?" I shook my head and laughed.

"I'm happy here too, Mom." He said and my breath caught, my chest sore instantly from the weight set there. "So if you like him and it makes you happy. Then it's a good thing." August smiled but he shrugged, reaching out his hand to Red who slumped across the island like he owned it.

"So you aren't mad?" I asked him.

"No," he said, his fingers curling repeatedly across Red's mangy fur.

"And if it doesn't work out?" I pushed.

"You're doing that thing you tell me not to do," August said and I furrowed my brows at him. "Getting upset about problems that don't exist."

"Auggie," I sighed. It was serious. If anything happened with Silas our life would be upended, all of the happiness we were feeling now would be pulled out from under us...just like that.

"Mom," he mocked me, "stop making problems and just be happy."

His tone was low and too authoritative for a son talking to his mother but it made me smile and I gave him a small nod. *Just be happy.* Easier said than done.

"There you are!" Silas rounded the corner in a huff, blasting into the office. His Hornets polo was crumpled, and his shorts were lopsided like he had thrown them on in the dark. "We need to go," he said, giving a sweet smile to Susanna before turning to me. He had been like this for days after our impromptu road trip. Moving too fast, talking in circles. The Hornets had officially beaten Portland and I had hoped that it would ease his stress but the finals were here and he was even more strung out than before.

He was burning out and was too stubborn to admit that it could happen to him.

"Go where?" I laughed, filing a few papers away.

"Up to the cabin," he said, like I should know what's going on.

"I have to work today, we can't..." I turned and lowered my voice just for him, "run away again."

"No," Silas stopped me, "this isn't... I could have sworn I mentioned it."

"I am definitely out of the loop," I said looking to Susanna for help but she just kept working away at her desk.

"Cabin is important this weekend, promise. There's a reason." He looked at me, taking the stack of paper from my arms. "Susanna," he nodded to her and she waved him off as he pulled me from the office.

"Is that?" I asked confused as we wandered out into the light. August was sitting in the backseat of a black SUV I'd never seen, headphones in and scrolling through his phone without a care in the world. Silas popped open the passenger door for me and held onto the frame with a serious look on his face.

"Schools out, you're all packed. We're going to the cabin. Get in the car, Drew." Silas's voice dropped lower. "Please."

I looked at him for a moment, "this isn't a *'Harbor's too loud'* moment?" I asked him.

"It's a 'I want to take my girlfriend and her son to my family's cabin for the weekend' moment." Silas's smile was infectious and I couldn't say no to him when he was in such a good mood so I climbed into the car and let him close the door. I reached back and patted August on the knee to get him to look at me.

"What did I tell you about riding in cars with strangers?" I teased when he pulled his headphones down.

"Don't do it unless they promise money..." August joked.

"Seriously?" I laughed but drank in his soft expression.

"He wrestled Red into the kennel for this." August said with a smile as Silas climbed into the car.

"I have the war wounds to prove it," Silas grumbled, starting the engine.

"Oh you poor thing," I feigned concern and winked at August before turning around in my seat. I hadn't told Silas that I spoke to August, everything had been so insane that I never got the chance. He was coming home from the stadium after games and showering on auto pilot. He was too wound up and exhausted to even entertain sex, he usually just fell asleep curled against me. But I took a chance and reached across the divide to lay my hand upright for him.

He looked down at it in surprise and then over to me with a flicker of confusion as I wiggled them around for him. *It's okay.* I mouthed and he looked back down at my hand, pushing his fingers between mine and giving it a gentle squeeze.

And just like that every piece of the puzzle slipped together with such ease.

"Don't worry, I made a playlist." Silas reached over and scrolled through the menu, throwing on whatever monster he had created and Savage Garden flowed through the speakers causing me to laugh out loud. "There's no way you just laughed at the Savage Garden!"

"I don't know how I didn't see the whole *Dad Rock* thing before, it was right in front of my face the entire time," I scoffed in disbelief as he smiled brightly at me, enjoying the teasing. "You could have at least eased me into it."

"Oh, Garden *is* easing you into it," Silas chuckled and turned his attention to the road. The drive was nice, August spent most of the time playing on his phone and ignoring our adult conversations.

"You grew up out here?" I asked when the highways became nothing but thick forest for miles on either side.

"Yeah, they built the cottage for team building and weekend retreats but it became this place for my Mom to get away, and she's always hated the quiet so usually we got dragged along." Silas explained.

"Arlo?" I asked. It had been weeks of asking him questions I already knew the basic answers to. But I liked hearing his side of the answers, they were so different then what Arlo had coldly written in the binder.

"Yeah, and Nicholas... and their older brothers Lucas and Sawyer."

"There's four King brothers?" I asked, knowing the basics.

"Yeah, all four insanely talented baseball prodigies..." he sighed. "Arthur ruined them with the pressure, thinking he could make them even better but it only made them resent each other and the sport."

"Arlo still coaches though." I said.

Silas smiled and nodded, "it would take a lot more than drunk Arthur King and a few slaps to make Arlo hate baseball. He'll play and coach until the day he dies."

"And you'll be right there with him," I said and Silas's grip faltered on my hand slightly.

"That's the plan," are the words that came out of his mouth but they weren't believable. He was holding on to so much stress between the team, his grandfather, us, and the trial. It was insane to watch a man seemingly so soft and humble, stand up to the wind like he was made of steel. "Look," he said, directing my attention to the incredible structure at the end of the driveway.

"That's not a cabin," August said, leaning through the middle of the seats. "That's a resort."

"Had to be big enough for everyone," Silas said, like that was the natural explanation.

There were people and cars littered the driveway, so many it's impossible to count as they moved around the gravel talking to one another and hauling things from the backs of vehicles.

"What is going on?" I asked, turning to look at him as he parked.

"A wedding."

The panic that filled my body when the word wedding left Silas's beautiful mouth was biblical. It rose up my body and hit me in the chest so fast it felt like someone had run me over with a car. I inhaled sharply and stared at him, not registering a single word coming out of his mouth.

August climbed from the car and I froze, unable to form words to explain the fear coursing through me. Silas grabbed my face and brought us closer together, slowing his breathing down until I was able to follow his lead.

"Not ours," he said, his tone soft. "Ella and Arlo."

I let my tongue fall from the roof of my mouth and worked back the urge to sob in his arms. I swear my soul left my body.

"I'm sorry I scared you... I wasn't thinking—"

"No, no. It's okay," I choked out, pleading with my heart to slow down.

Silas looked like I had broken his heart and it only made how guilty and anxious I felt worse. It stung in the most agonizing way as he worked through his own disappointment at my reaction to calm me down.

"I'm sorry, I—" I stopped trying to catch my breath. "You wouldn't want that," I said quietly, "it's not what you want." I choked down the urge to cry as I tried to explain to him that taking this further than what we were doing...making the ring real. It was a mistake. I could barely manage my own emotions, the intrusive depression that threaded through my mind every waking hour. I couldn't trap him in life, which meant always having to look after me in some capacity. I wouldn't.

"Don't tell me what I want and don't want," he leaned forward, forcing me to look at him. "I didn't take your fear as a refusal, Drew. It's just another challenge." His gray eyes never left mine, his words slow and said with an intense intention. "Do you understand?"

I didn't. And I did. It was not that simple.

"Yeah." I offered and his lips curled into a smug smirk.

"The least you could do is say it with some conviction." He kissed the corner of my mouth and then my cheek and my nose, making a path across my face. "We do this slowly, at our own pace. The ring doesn't mean anything until you ask me to make it mean something. Alright?"

That helped, the next breath I took didn't feel as strangled.

There he went, making it better with such ease.

"Come on," he said, brushing the crazy strands of hair behind my ear with another quick kiss.

He led me through the chaos into the front doors and I paused to take in the incredible extensive inside. Large couches, high ceilings, with a huge kitchen and a wall of windows that looked over the lake. There was a set of stairs that led up and down, the sheer size of the building felt daunting but Silas never let go of me.

"Nice of you to show up, asshole!" Arlo groaned, leaning against the counter with Ella resting between his legs with a mug between her hands. "We were going to do this without you."

"You can't do this without me, prick," Silas snapped with a bright smile.

"Van was looking up how to get ordained." Arlo shrugged and Silas bulldozed across the kitchen only pausing for Ella to scoot out his way before he started wrestling with Arlo.

"Don't you dare give him a black eye!" Zoey yelled loudly from her spot on the couch with Van who was reading comics with Jensen, his girlfriend, and August... At least he was good at making himself at home.

I must have looked uncomfortable because Ella slid around the island with a second mug and handed it to me. "It's okay, they won't hurt each other... too badly."

"Thank you," I said, holding the warm tea to my lips.

"I'm glad you came," She said.

"I'm glad to be here," I said, she stared at me for a second and I couldn't tell if she was waiting for me to continue but I tried, "I actually didn't know until we got here..."

"That sounds like Silas," Ella sighed with the shake of her head. "Did he spring it on you and scare the shit out of you?"

"Ha," I huffed, "something like that."

"For a man that is so incredibly smart. He really is stupid sometimes. However," Ella paused, setting down her mug. "He did have me pick up a surprise for you."

"You guys shouldn't have done that, it's your d—" I started but Ella shook her head at me, crooking her finger for me to follow. Down the hall and to the left was a massive well lit bedroom with large windows and classic cottage touches.

"One thing you need to learn if you're going to be around us, is that nothing is a hassle and a day never belongs to just one of us." Ella opened the closet on the back wall and disappeared inside before I could argue with her that she shouldn't have been worrying about me on a day like today.

"And if Silas had brought you up here with nothing to wear, I would have had to find another person to marry me and the love of my life, because I would have killed him. So before you argue, this was in the best interest of everyone." Ella stared at me with a long bag in her hand and a better death glare on her face than I could have ever given.

"Consider me quiet," I said, holding up one hand in surrender. I set the mug on the table next to me and stepped closer to the bag Ella laid on the bed.

SHORE

"Beautiful." I pressed my palm flat to my chest and shifted in my uncomfortable dress shoes at the end of the bed as Drew appeared from the bathroom. The mid-morning light bathed her in a hazy golden light that made her glow like an angel. I swallowed tightly, my heart racing so fast in my chest I could have sworn it was ready to escape.

"Stop it," she said, turning to the large mirror on the wall. She fidgeted with the dark red satin around her breasts making sure it was hanging appropriately and not revealing too much but my focus was on the thin, wispy pieces of lacing that worked up the small of her back in a criss-cross pattern.

"I have something for you," I said, moving around her. My restraint was waning and it made it so much worse when she looked as perfect as she did.

"Silas the dress was enough," she hummed, fixing the pieces of her hair back behind her ear.

"It's from Auggie," I said to her and handed her the box. Inside on a simple chain was a small gemstone that matched August's birthday. It had taken him two hours to pick out and cost me a fortune but he was proud of himself for finding something that Drew would love. And by the look on her face, he had been right.

"He picked this?" She asked, her finger running over it. "It's perfect."

"Just like you," I said, taking the necklace out of the box and wrapping it around her neck so it rested on her collarbone. I took the chance to press a kiss to the back of her throat, looking across to the mirror just to see her smile. Her fingers came up and tangled into the scuff against my jaw holding me against her for a long, private moment.

I love you.

The words bubbled up again but stayed locked behind the wall of fear. Logically she would be okay, maybe there was even a small chance she felt it back and even if she spiraled from hearing them I could talk her off the ledge. But I selfishly didn't want to have to do any of that, I wanted to say and hear it back. So I stayed quiet, hoping that one day I'd look up and see it in her expression instead of having to guess.

"Auggie is in the living room with some of the boys, I need to get out there..." I said, finally releasing her from my grip. I pressed a kiss to her palm and stepped away to let her breathe, "save the first dance for me?"

"Of course." She confirmed watching me until I disappeared from her view. Everyone was making their way down to the forested path behind the house.

The dock was set up with a hundred bushels of lavender that softly rained petals in the breeze. Mom was standing with Arlo, in a dark green dress that matched the suits of the groomsmen. And Arlo was wearing all black, with a green tie and gold jewelry that seemed to drip from him. He looked handsome, his hair pushed back off his face and his eyes a lighter shade of brown than usual. I'd never seen him nervous but he was spinning his finger around his mothers wedding band on his pinky finger and staring off into the distance.

"Two steps at a time," I said to him, invading his space without asking and knocking my knuckles against his heart. "Take a breath."

Arlo listened and his chest rose slowly, the focus coming back to his expression as his jaw tightened. "You clean up nice," he said, swallowing tightly and looking over my dark blue suit.

"Ella said jewel tones." I gave her all the credit. Even the mention of her made Arlo's shoulders relax a touch. "We'll do this quick and you can go back to hiding in the shadows, asshole."

"Prick," he coughed out.

"Language gentlemen," Ryan cleared his throat in defense of my mother. I narrowed my eyes on him and he flashed a smug smile as the wind pushed around his graying dirty blonde hair.

"Mom," I nodded, my eyes still watching Ryan like a hawk.

"I got him, honey. You go." She kissed my cheek and I made my way down the dock past the team that was sitting and found my book. Everyone else took their seats, Drew sat with Josh in the second row looking nervous but radiating like the sun. Grandpa sat a few chairs away, chatting with Nicholas who had been stuck as his escort for the night. I hadn't wanted to turn the wedding into a chess piece but having him here, having him see me with Drew in this capacity was necessary. He had to know it was serious.

I just hated every second of it.

One by one the wedding party made their way down, Van, Dean, Lucas and Sawyer stood beside me as Mom and Arlo came down the aisle arm in arm. She kissed his cheek gently before retreating back to her seat and he carefully slipped into place beside me under the archway of lavender.

"Cael did good," he whispered, his brown eyes trailing over the arch.

"We knew he would," I smiled. He had helped Ella every step of the way there wasn't a single flower out of place, or a problem he hadn't solved. He was stepping into the role of event planner like he'd always belonged there and it wasn't hard to be proud of him, it was overwhelming and warm against my chest to see him thrive.

"Hey Si," Arlo said as the music started for Ella.

"You can't run now," I joked but he shook his head.

"Thank you for bringing Ella to me," he said, his eyes a little watery. I nodded as he tapped his fingers to his chest and turned his attention to the end of the dock. Ella stood there, her blonde hair pulled back off her face in soft curls that bounced around in the breeze. The smile on her face was luminous and one by one everyone stood from their chairs.

Her something blue stood beside her in a dark suit that glimmered in the sunshine with his hair shaved down. Cael beamed just as brightly as Ella as they walked behind Zoey who led the charge. Arlo cleared his throat as they approached, taking Ella from Cael who joined Zoey at the side. Our family, complete, and right where we all belonged.

"Ready, Blondie?" Arlo asked.

Ella nodded holding back tears as Arlo reached out and fixed a piece of her hair.

"As ever, Cap."

I gave them another second before taking a deep breath, slipping on my glasses, and doing the job they asked of me. Van dog whistled loudly as I pushed them on my face and Jensen hollered out something intangible as Addy tried to get him to be quiet.

"Settle down," I warned before clearing my throat. "Friends, family, and Hornets, we come together today, in the sight of you as witnesses to join Arlo King and Ella Miele in marriage. We gather around them now in this wonderful place, and we look on with love and hope as these two begin their new life together as one." My voice carried across the dock into the trees as everyone listened on. Getting through all the necessary lines before stepping back and letting Arlo and Ella take the reins.

Arlo rolled out his shoulders and it took a whole thirty seconds for him to speak but when he started I knew it was going to be good. "My sunshine incarnate," Arlo said quietly, the vows only for Ella. "My bossy blondie." He smiled and Ella was a goner, a heavy tear trickled down her face and Arlo reached out, rubbing it away with the pad of his thumb. "There's no epic speech coming because frankly I'm a little better at actions than words but *you* incite all the best emotions in me and I never wanna experience anything on my own again."

"How do I follow that?" She pouted.

"Don't let me win now," Arlo teased. I cleared my throat, digging out the piece of paper she had given me last night for safekeeping. "I should have known you two would be in cahoots."

"Shh, you have a whole hat full of names and secrets with Zoey," Ella whispered to him and unfolded it. Arlo steeled himself, but I proofread her vows, he didn't stand a chance. "A year ago I was lost, seemingly forever. Determined to punish myself and struggle through life alone because that's what I thought I deserved."

Arlo opened his mouth and Ella shook her head, "argue later, listen for once," she laughed as he sighed but surrendered to her demand. "And you'll only ever hear me say this once in our lives, Arlo King, but I was wrong."

That brought a smile to his face.

"You are the most stubborn, annoyingly pushy person I know. You have insulted me, pushed me away, chased after me, followed me home with your car, stole my books, *stole my heart.*" Ella hummed, "I was committed to walking alone, to spending the rest of my life apologizing to ghosts and sitting in the dark. But from the moment you laid eyes on me, you were committed to making sure I never did. You have been here, two steps at a time, incessant and convincing. Thank you for not giving up on me even when it felt too big, even when I slammed the door in your face."

I looked over at Drew who was staring through the two of them at me. She had that soft worried expression on her face and it tightened the string around my heart. Fear blossomed there, stinging the cuts left behind by the thread. I needed to try harder, for her. For us.

"Arlo I love you," Ella said softly, "you will always be my favorite."

Ella and Arlo were sitting at their table in the center of the baseball diamond. It was dressed in hazy lights that hung low into the center in long rows of buzzing bulbs. The tables scattered out over the field in a circle so everyone was included and Ella had refused to do a seating plan. *"Everyone can sit where they want."* She declared much to Cael's annoyance that day. But she had a purpose because now the whole thing felt like a family dinner. Cael had even brought Lorraine's chair up from the Nest and it sat in the corner, with her picture, along side one of Arlo's mother, and a basket overflowing with lavender.

Cael was getting restless but it wasn't until Ella nodded that he sprung from his chair, dragging it across the grass to rest by their table and clambering up on top so everyone could see him.

He tapped his glass of water a few times with the back of a knife but he wasn't loud enough for people to realize he wanted their attention.

"Shut up!" Arlo stood, his palms flat on the table and yelled like he always did.

The field went dead silent.

"Thanks princess," he said before clearing his throat. "Most of you know who I am, and honestly if you don't I'm not sure why you were invited..." Cael trailed off and Ella shook her head at him with a laugh. "And yes if you were wondering I'm her something blue," he waved to his seat but I'm also Ella's something borrowed," he smiled down at her, "a brother." She held her hand up to him and he took it gently in his own. "I never met Ethan but I've heard every story that could be told about him and there is one thing I know for sure. He'd be so proud of you."

Ella's nose scrunched up as she fought to keep from crying. "You showed up at Harbor with the intention of keeping your head down, finishing school and disappearing forever. But Harbor had different plans for you and I like to think that Ethan did too. Then you bulldozed your way into the Nest without expectations and took every single one of us under your wing. Peachy, we probably wouldn't have survived this long without your love. Arlo definitely not." He laughed and Arlo flipped him off. "When you asked me to be your something blue I obviously took it too far and decided that if I'm one, I'm clearly all four."

"Cael," Arlo grumbled loudly, "fuck off."

"I'm speaking," he hissed playfully at Arlo.

"Seriously?" He looked to Ella for help but she was too focused on Cael to care. "I hate you both."

"Something new was a little harder to get my hands on, I'm not an artist and I don't even have a paying job but I can get creative when I need to." Cael said the mischief was violent in his expression. He dug in his pocket and tossed a set of house keys at Arlo. "By creative I mean I roped Silas into a plan so I could spend his money."

"What are these?" Arlo asked but his gaze was on me at the next table.

"You can't live at the Nest forever, Ar," I said to him with a sad smile, the end of an era playing out right in front of us.

"If my best friends weren't rats, I could have tried," his voice was tight and angry but there was a smile on his face. He was grateful he just wasn't sure how to say thank you.

"We love you too," Cael laughed, using Ella for balance as the chair shook in the grass. "Mom would be proud," he got serious, looking at Arlo. "She always knew you were the best of us and she'd be ecstatic you found the best. This is also my chance to petition that your first born be named after me!"

"I'm going to strangle him." Arlo surged from his chair and Cael almost fell backward but somehow kept his balance against the odds. "Finish your speech so I can kill you."

Ella snorted, tugging on Arlo's belt to get his attention. One look from her and he was sinking back into his chair with a tight jaw, but Cael would live to see another day.

"The distance between us will be hard," he cleared his throat and looked around at the team now. Everyone sat quiet in the realization that it was all coming to an end. The family we'd been for nearly ten years, players coming and going, relationships forming and growing. Soon we'd all be on our own and the fear of solitude was horrifying for a group of people that had grown into themselves just feet from each other.

Drew squeezed my hand under the table, her touch bringing me a semblance of relief as Cael continued.

"But not impossible," he said. "Time pushes and pulls people around but we've always been a force to be reckoned with and that doesn't change. The Nest will always have new faces to nurture, new players to help. It doesn't end here. We will always be a family. Living under one roof or many, we'll always find home in each other and that's a promise." Cael tapped his fingers to his chest, holding them there. Ryan rose from his chair and mirrored the motion creating a waterfall effect of players that joined in. Soon the entire team was staring at Ella and Arlo.

Two fingers to the chest, a universal sign for I love you.
Something old.

"To Mom and Dad!" Cael yelled loudly and the entire room cheered.

COURTNEY

I sipped on the whiskey that Silas set in front of me. He was talking to Ryan about the games next week and I was completely lost. But it gave me time to take in my surroundings. The tables had been cleared and everyone was flooding the space created for dancing but he was very clearly done with the entire day. Cael's speech had been so sweet and it was wild to watch the way they cared for each other as an outsider.

Seymour had snuck in a conversation about how soon it would be Silas and I leading the circus and the thought was eating away at the back of mind like a rabid dog. I didn't want to think about that, I wanted to focus on the good I had in front of me at that moment.

August was dancing with Zoey who was teaching him patiently even as he stepped on her toes. Van and Dean were dancing next to them, trying to lead by example but seeing two grown men dance the waltz was only distracting August more.

It had taken no time at all for him to fall in love with them all and sitting there watching them, I understood why. They effortlessly made room for each other and anyone that needed it. We'd gotten unbelievably lucky. I took another sip, chasing away the feeling that rose in contest to my happiness. Scared of the possibility that if I screwed up with Silas, all of it would be stripped away from August.

He would hate me even more than he did usually.

"Come with me," Silas said, holding out his hand to me. I lifted my head to look at him and was met with such warmth. "Did you hear me?" He asked when I didn't move but I nodded and took his hand.

He said goodnight to Arlo, who was very sober and clearly practicing his restraint as Cael spun Ella around on the dance floor. I was glad for the rescue, I wasn't sure what to do with myself at parties and if left much longer I probably would have started clearing tables.

Silas kept my hand in his as he led me back toward the cottage, the closer we got the quieter it became and soon it was. Nothing but birds and breeze. It was oddly peaceful and even though it took us a while, me going slower in my heels, the walk was the perfect way to settle my restless heart.

"Where are we going?" I asked him.

"I'm sick of people, your son is occupied, and I want that dress in pieces."

"Silas!" My mouth fell open and I slowed my pace but Silas wasn't having the interruption, he dipped down and scooped me up against his chest, carrying me the rest of the way back.

He pushed open the back door and stepped into the empty cottage, not stopping even for a second before we were locked behind his bedroom door. He set me down, his eyes running over my body hungrily.

"You're being ridiculous." I licked my bottom lip and stepped back from him.

"I have waited *all day*," Silas said, "if anything I've been very well behaved and earned what I'm about to do to you."

"You looked handsome today." I ran my finger along the lapel of his jacket and he smirked.

"You like the suit?" He asked, his voice low.

"Yeah it's nice... although it would look better on the floor." My eyes flickered over his body as it tensed, loving how easily he reacted to my teasing. I shifted in my satin dress, the laces at my back tightening and pulling across my skin as I walked back toward the dresser.

"You think you're clever don't you?" he asked, his eyes darting to my lips as he quickly closed the distance between us, his large hands gripping my waist.

With my back to the dresser Silas lifted me onto it with ease, pushing up my dress and slotting his frame between my legs. I was fighting every urge not to kiss him. I wanted to light the fuse so badly but the need to see where the game took us was greater.

"It's part of my charm." I smiled.

Silas chuckled gently, his thumbs brushing against the skin of my thighs, "your charm is going to get you into trouble." His voice was low with warning, but his eyes were filled with amusement.

His fingers tightened against my soft skin briefly before releasing and trailing up higher until they hit the delicate lace of my underwear. He leaned closer, his lips brushing against my ear, "I wonder if you can handle the trouble I'm about to give you."

"Don't underestimate me." My smile grew and I surged forward, gently capturing his bottom lip between my teeth.

A sharp exhale left him as I bit down, his arm instantly wrapping around me to keep me in place. He turned his head, capturing my lips in a sudden, deep kiss, his tongue pushing past my teeth.

I pressed my hands into his hair, and leaned into the kiss without hesitation. One of his hands moved to my hair to hold me in place while the other continued to tease the edge of my underwear. "You always kiss me like you have something to prove, Drew. Breathe," he mumbled against my lips, "we don't have to rush tonight."

Silas's eyes fluttered closed at my slower pace, one arm wrapping tightly around me while the other spread my thigh as wide as it could in my dress. He slowly deepened the kiss, his thumb hooking into my underwear and pulling it slightly to one side. "I want slow kisses and soft touches," he hummed. "It doesn't always have to be fast and hard."

Something in his words rattled me to the core, I curled around him like I could melt into him. I needed to be consumed in the way he described. Slow. Overwhelming. With nothing to prove but everything to feel.

"Show me how." I whispered.

His eyes softened for a moment before he captured my lips again, this time slower and more deliberate than before. His tongue traced my bottom lip before slowly exploring my mouth. One hand slid up to hold my jaw gently, tilting my head slightly. "No biting," he whispered against my lips, smiling.

"I'm not the one that likes to bite," I hummed with a lazy smile.

He rolled his eyes, nipping gently. "Okay, maybe a little biting," he countered. He lifted me with ease, setting me on the bed and slowly pulled my underwear down, his knuckles brushing around my center. "Lay back."

I listened, raising my hands above my head and sinking into the bed as Silas pushed the fabric of my dress up around my hips. He looked down at me, taking in the sight before climbing onto the bed between my legs. He spread them gently with his knees, leaning down to pressed delicate kisses to my inner thigh. His hands gripped my hips, holding me in place as he began to move upwards slowly.

My body trembled under his careful touch, he was moving with intention, every kiss meant to tease. Silas noticed the shutter and smiled against my skin, deliberately avoiding my center to keep building anticipation. His lips trailed up my thigh toward my stomach where he paused to press a lingering kiss just below my navel.

"You're shaking," he whispered, his hot breath ghosting across my skin.

"You're teasing." I smiled down at him gently.

Silas looked up at me through dark lashes, a mischievous smirk playing on his lips. "Am I?" A single finger traced a line from my belly button downward, barely skimming my center but not quite touching where I needed him to. "Should I stop?"

I gently shook my head no, surprisingly I enjoyed how gentle he was being.

"Good girl." A smug smile formed on his lips, pleased with my response. He returned his attention to my thigh, pressing soft kisses higher up that time. "I want you wet and ready before I even touch you."

I was offering him a side of me he rarely saw, vulnerable and needy. I was completely at his mercy. Nothing to say, nothing to prove. Just ready for him to make good on his promise. My breathing grew heavy, reacting to his touches as my legs opened wider. When Silas finally reached my core I inhaled sharply, he blew a cool breath against my wetness, making my body tense without even a touch.

The air around us was heavy and felt different from all the times before. His fingers gently brushed against my clit, the teasing becoming almost too much. I needed to feel him, needed him.

"I want you," I whispered.

His pupils dilated at the statement, his voice hoarse as he replied. "Not yet," he said, pressing his face between my legs. He spread me open with his fingers, slowly licking up my center, his tongue focusing solely on my clit.

"Silas," I said, softer that time, reaching my hand down to touch his hair, "I need you."

He tensed, his fingers digging into my skin at his name. He pressed his tongue firmer against me, sucking it into his mouth and swirling his tongue around it. "Beg me," he muttered against me as his fingers worked their way deeper.

"I *need* you," I lowered my voice to try to convey what I wanted without sounding completely pathetic. He had a plan and it would all be ruined by my need to be closer to him at that moment. It was all too much, the cottage, his family, our life. It was weighing down on me and if he didn't tie himself around me soon, I would drift away at sea to drown in my fears of never being good enough.

He froze, pulling back to watch my chest rise and fall rapidly. "Alright baby," he hummed, reaching for the table. He was getting too good at finding condoms in the dark and I appreciated his consistency in using them for me. Other than the night at the hotel when we were both completely out of control, he'd never once pressured me into anything else.

Silas flipped the zipper on his pants, freeing himself without hesitation and rolled the condom on, his hands shaking slightly with restraint. He positioned himself between my legs, his arms caging me in as he looked down at me.

"Hold on to me," he commanded, his voice strained.

I wrapped myself around him, desperate for the closeness and gasped as he slid himself inside. Silas let out a low groan as he bottomed out, his eyes fluttering shut for a second. He stayed still, allowing me to adjust before he began to move. His thrusts were slow, like rolling waves and each time he returned to me I felt a piece of me returning back to where it belonged. It seemed so dramatic to say a person could fix you but Silas had, he still was, fixing me. Helping me. Encouraging.

He captured my mouth in a deep kiss as he pushed back inside, swallowing my soft moans. He pulled back to watch my face, no doubt reading me like an open book but there was nothing to find. For once I was just happy.

"Better?" He asked, his voice low and sweet.

"Better," I responded, losing myself in him.

Silas smiled softly, pressing kisses along my jawline as he continued his steady rhythm. His hand found mine on the pillow beside my head, fingers threading together. His gray eyes met mine and I knew exactly how he was feeling before he said it, but the brief realization didn't help the shock. "I love you," he whispered, picking up his pace.

I want to love you back.

I'm not good enough to love you the way you need.

The worst thoughts flooded in and made my vision of him hazy. I was losing myself and Silas in the process. I swallowed hard, and instead of responding I pressed myself against him tighter. Willing away the sense of dread that bubbled up. I kissed him in a deep and gentle way that said everything I couldn't.

Silas kissed me back but I could feel his heart aching at my silence. He knew I cared for him but with the words remaining unspoken I knew I had hurt him. He buried his face in my neck, his thrusts becoming more frantic and desperate.

I had done the one thing I was trying not to do. I had broken his heart. He continued to drag us to the edge, my pleasure mixed violently with sadness as he exploded like a firecracker. He came with a choked groan, his body tense above me as he spilled into the condom. He stayed buried inside of me for a moment long, his forehead pressed against mine as he caught his breath but there was a sadness in his eyes that hadn't been there before.

"Give me time," I whispered to him, pressing my hand to his face. "It doesn't mean I don't feel it too. Saying it is harder than expected."

Silas watched me for a moment longer but nodded, understanding but he was still hurt and it broke my heart to see him like that. Unable to just give him what he wanted.

I'd never be good enough for a man like him.

That much was clear.

SHORE

"Why aren't you in bed with your wife?" I asked him as he sank to the dock beside me. He handed me a cup of coffee and scowled.

"Because my *wife*," he emphasized, "saw you sitting down here like a kicked dog and made me leave my warm bed to check on you."

I chuckled, bringing the mug to my lips. "Sorry," I said after a minute.

"Make it count," Arlo said.

"I think I fucked up."

He didn't even flinch.

I had definitely fucked up, unreasonably so. I had talked myself into waiting to give her more time so she could come to the realization herself. But she looked so peaceful, so ready to hear it at that moment. My idiot head was clouded by how good she felt that I didn't stop to think about how terrified she probably felt trapped in that moment. Cornered like an animal.

"She's pregnant isn't she?" He asked, looking terrified. I was so lost in my thoughts I forgot to follow up.

"No, what the hell?" I scoffed, "I'm not some seventeen year old idiot with a wandering dick Arlo."

"Could have fooled me," he laughed.

"The lake looks nice and cold, want to go for a swim?" I threatened and he cracked a smile. The wind kicked up through the trees and rustled everything around. Usually it would bring some solace but the knot was tied so tightly in my chest that I didn't even know where to begin to get it undone.

"Only if you go with me," Arlo said. "What happened?"

"I told her I loved her," I confessed and Arlo looked at me like I slapped him.

"Idiot," he sighed, "one look at her and it's clear that she's cagey, Si. Even Ella said she's tough to crack. Anytime she tries to make small talk Drew bricks up and finds a way out of it. I can't even imagine how she reacted."

"Ar I was—" I stopped and did the motion with my hand.

"You said it with your fucking dick inside her?" Arlo barked, his laughter hopping across the quiet lake. "You're unbelievably dumb."

"If all you're going to do is call me stupid go back to Ella," I sighed, setting the mug down.

"I'm sorry," he said, trying to stop. "What do you want, Si?" He asked once he calmed down, his tone more serious than before.

What did I want? I inhaled slowly, completely fucking unsure.

"I want to keep doing what I'm doing," I answered. I knew that much. "I want to help everyone at Harbor." I didn't hesitate. "I want to support you guys, I want—"

"Her." Arlo finished my sentence.

"She's at the top of my list," I admitted. "Her and Auggie."

"So you didn't just say I love you, to say it?" He asked.

"No...maybe? No..." I went back and forth. "No."

"So you do," Arlo pushed with a cocky smile, "say it."

"Say what?" I rolled my eyes at him. He stared at me, waiting for it and suddenly the air felt thick and my mouth went dry. "I love her."

"I can't believe you're older than me," he said. "Do you remember when Mom died, what *your* mom said to me?"

"That was like ten years ago," I scoffed.

"Think hard," Arlo snapped, wetting his bottom lip.

It was so long ago that even trying to remember felt impossible but given our conversations surrounding Drew it could only be one thing. Fuck Arlo was an asshole.

"She told you not to let the world's disappointment harden you to love."

"If only you had listened to her we wouldn't be here," Arlo groaned.

"I'm not hardened and the world isn't disappointing," I brushed him off.

"It's not? You have a fucked up little brother, a dad in jail and your girlfriend is your fake fiancé because your grandfather thought it would be more fun to make a game out of your family's fortune." It really pissed me off when Arlo made sense. He was supposed to be the irrational one.

"I'm not hardened," I argued in a defeated voice.

"You're making it hard," Arlo said with a small shrug.

"I'm not making it anything," I groaned.

"Shut up," he clipped. "I'm not running in this circle with you again, if Drew is what you want, act like it. Stop pretending like she's the last priority. Are you ready to make a fool of yourself yet?"

"Not if it means losing family," I huffed.

"It seems to me like you're missing the point here, Si." Arlo licked his lips. "They are family."

"I hate when you do that," I said.

"What?" Arlo laughed.

"Make a good point," I groaned, "it's fucking annoying."

"If anyone can have everything Silas, it's you." He said, "you're the only one that deserves it." I watched him stand, shoving his hands into the pockets of his shorts. "Don't fuck this up because you think you don't."

"Go back to Ella, you're pissing me off." I said with a laugh and turned back to the rising sun. I hated how right he was about my feelings.

COURTNEY

"We're leaving aren't we?" August stood in the doorway of my room...Silas's room.

I shook my head with a smile as I ran my fingers through my hair, the half-packed duffle three feet out of sight in the closet. Red curled around August's feet, sitting beside him in the hallway while my son stared at me for a little while longer. Seeing right through my lie.

SHORE

It had been a week.

A week of dancing around Drew trying to pretend like I wasn't waiting on her every word. She was all smiles, all the time and I couldn't tell if I should be worried or happy about it. Not a single one of them seemed real. She kept checking out on me and was bright but distant. Like a light I couldn't reach no matter how much ground I covered.

It was frustrating but if she thought it was going to be enough to make me give up. She was wrong. I could be stubborn if I wanted to be, *especially* about her. I climbed off the bike, fixing the crinkles in my suit and brushing my fingers through my hair, my eyes turning up to the high-rise in downtown Lorette. My head was beating so fast in my chest it felt like it was in my throat and before even leaving the house I had sweat through two shirts.

Today marked the day I either pulled off the most idiotic plan, or failed miserably. I could only hope that the countless dinners, outings and horrible conversations had done enough. Preston would have gone straight back to his dad with gossip about Drew from the weekend in New York, cementing that even when the shareholders weren't paying attention we were very much in love.

Well, I was in love.

Drew was terrified.

Everything was tangled up too tightly to know what was real and what had been fake in my mind. The day I met her marked a challenge that I never expected to be so difficult. But every single knot we managed to undo proved that we were still very much tied together.

My phone rang in my pocket and I groaned.

Harbor Correctional

I picked it up only because if I didn't he would continue to call through the entire meeting and I couldn't have my phone vibrating in my pocket while I was attempting to lie my way into a fortune.

It went through the usual speech and I clicked one to accept the call and charges, "What?"

"You haven't been answering my calls," Charles said from the other end of the static filled call.

"Honestly after what you said to Arlo I don't give a shit what you have to say, Dad." I led with honesty. If my testimony was as good as the prosecution believed it was, nothing I said now mattered. He was screwed.

"Just like your mother, always so touchy." Charles clicked.

"What do you want?" I emphasized every word, sick of his games, sick of his stalling.

"At least one of my sons cares how I'm doing in here," he sneered and I stopped dead in my tracks outside the building.

"What did you say to him?" I barked.

"Oh now he's listening," Charles sneered, "good. If you think I didn't know what you were doing, sneaking around, building a case against me with the enemy. You're just as stupid as your mother too and you didn't learn anything. You cannot keep me here, Silas. I didn't do a damn thing wrong, all I did was fuck another woman. Infidelity is not a crime."

"On top of extortion, bribery, fraud, tax evasion." I added tightly, my heart pounding in my chest. What had he said to Josh, and why had Josh gone there without telling me. *Fuck*. Everything was falling apart and we had come so far to keep it together.

"I'm not involved in any of that," Charles denied, just like he had been for the last four months.

"What did you say to Josh?" I demanded.

"We had a good father and son talk," Charles snipped, but I could tell he was trying to get under my skin with every word. "Joshua doesn't blame me for anything, said his mother's vices were her own and that he wanted a chance to get to know his father. Told him I was ready to repent, to be the father he always needed."

"Hah!" I pulled the phone away from my ear, laughing wildly. "You dumb shit," I snapped, "what did you promise him?"

Charles went silent.

"Mm," I hummed, "did you tell him that you have money stashed away, that you'd take care of him. Make up for all those years of leaving him in that fucking drug den with his abusive mother to be raped?" I growled through the phone, getting dirty looks from the people around me moving about their days. "You think that after all of that abuse, being sold around for drugs because *you* weren't man enough to own up to your adultery, he was on your side? Are you fucking dense?" I scoffed, running a hand through my hair.

It felt amazing to blow up on him finally, so close to the finish line I'd done everything properly down to the very last second. Nothing would save him now. I hoped he rotted in that concrete box.

"He went there because the prosecution needed you to confess about more hidden offshore accounts and you, being the stupidest man in Harbor. Played right into their hands." I smiled widely, knowing he'd screwed himself royally. "It's almost poetic that you signed your own death warrant because you couldn't get over yourself!"

The silence was glorious.

"Yeah, Dad, you were so busy thinking you'd won this fight, that you were too smart to ever lose it. But guess what? You hurt the two most important people in my life, and I may have gotten a lot from Mom but I learned how to lie, cheat and screw from *you* and I used every single one of those things to make sure the only repenting you'll ever do is in an eight by eight cell."

"Son," he huffed.

"Ah, nope." I stopped him, my jaw grinding together at the sound of him calling me that. "It's Doctor Shore to you from here on out, and I'm not your fucking son." I didn't even give him the chance to respond before I hung up and dialed Josh's number.

"Are you okay?" I asked the second the call connected.

"What?" He sounded confused, "I'm walking into practice."

"Why did you go to see him?" I asked and heard him sigh.

"Because they needed me to do it and I'm not a baby, I'm fine," he said.

"You shouldn't have had to do that, he's a piece of shit—"

"I know, and everything he says is bullshit. Silas, listen... going there meant keeping him behind bars and you've done enough for all of us the last couple months to make sure that happened. You're allowed to let people take care of you, it was literally the least I could do." Josh's voice resonated through the phone, full of conviction. "I had a meeting with Riona right after, got it out. I swear I'm okay."

He said it and I actually believed him. Thank God for Riona.

"Did he call you?" was the next question out of his mouth.

"Yeah, to brag that you were his new favorite..." I sighed. "No more visits."

"Promise." He said quickly. "I uh...gotta go, Coach is screaming." He sounded confused.

"Yeah, yeah. Sorry. Go." I let him hang up and took a breath, looking around at the busy street, just trying to compose myself before coming face to face with the other massive problem in my life. *One down, two to go.*

Board members.

Drew Courtney.

Grandpa stood in the main lobby talking to one of his friends with a smile on his face and his good mood gave me hope that today would go over well.

"There he is!" Grandpa shook my hand, giving me a pat on the back. "What no coffee?"

"Came on the bike," I said, my voice tense.

"Time to learn a new party trick," Grandpa teased with a loud laugh.

I nodded. "How's the energy up there?"

"I can't promise anything but you've done good." He offered. "Everyone is waiting, you ready?"

"Don't have much of a choice," I joked, following him over to the elevator.

"Soon you'll have control of everything boy, how does it feel?" Grandpa asked, waiting for the doors to open. I went to answer but he coughed loudly into his handkerchief and worry gripped me. It wouldn't be long before he was gone and everything would be on my shoulders. It felt suffocating.

"Great," I lied as the elevator dinged open.

"Silas!" August's voice pulled my attention around to the front doors.

What the hell?

Arlo marched in behind him, "he was coming with or without me." He said when I opened my mouth to ask.

"She's going to run," he said, out of breath. My eyes flickered from August to Arlo who looked as confused as I felt.

"No," I said, "everything is good, Auggie. It's fine." I assured him, trying not to make a scene in the lobby. But August wasn't having it.

"It's not okay!" He said a little louder, "I've seen it a hundred times, I know when she's going to run and it's happening." He pushed. It broke my heart how scared he looked.

"She went to work today," I tried reasoning.

"She stopped singing!" August fought. "And she's packing, she thinks she's sneaky but I know it, Silas. You have to do something!"

Arlo shrugged, "he busted in before practice Si." I swallowed tightly. I couldn't let her run, she had to know she was safe here. She wasn't going to run... was she?

"This is my fault," I huffed. I told her I loved her and she's scared. I caused this.

I rubbed my hands over my face.

"Silas," Grandpa's voice was low and demanding. "There are people waiting for you."

Very important people. He didn't have to say it. I understood the weight of the two decisions. Losing Harbor versus losing everything. I couldn't lose her. Nothing else mattered because when she was with me, everything was alright. I didn't need money or control to save Harbor, to provide for my family. I looked at August and could see Drew in him, right down to the worry that racked through his body. It wasn't just about us anymore, I wasn't willing to lose either of them. They were everything. I swore under my breath and stepped toward Arlo and August.

"Don't be daft, boy," Grandpa snapped. "Get on this elevator."

"I'm sorry," I turned to him, sincerely sorry for everything before backing away and having them both follow.

"Time to make a fool of yourself." Arlo clapped my shoulder as we flooded out the front doors.

COURTNEY

"I printed extra of these," I said to Susanna and set the flyers for the Hornets summer fair on the counter.

We're leaving aren't we?

"Thanks honey," she said, tapping her fingers along her keyboard.

"Anything else you need from me?" I asked her.

I love you.

"Nope." She turned in her chair with a smile, "we should be good for the day. Why don't you go collect Auggie and take him out for lunch?"

We're leaving.

I love you.

"That's a wonderful idea," I said, forcing down the bile that rose in my throat.

Leaving.

"Get him some ice cream, on me," Susanna gave me a five and winked as I grabbed my bag from the floor. I turned back as I stepped through the front door and looked at her for a long moment.

"Hey Susanna?" I said, waiting until she popped her head up. "Thanks." It was simple but underneath it all I wanted to thank her for everything. She had been nothing but kind to me and I wish I could stop it but the darkness was back and every weakening thought rolling around in my head was screaming that I wasn't good enough.

The problem was living with Silas made it hard to sink into it.

My body was giving out just pretending to be okay. I was trying. Forcing myself out of bed every morning for the last week, the sound of his voice haunting my every step and I plastered a smile on my face and got in the shower.

I just needed to get us into a hotel and then we could get on the road in a week or two. It made it easier with August on summer break. He wouldn't be so angry with me. I had picked up my phone to call Bradley more than once. Thinking maybe it was time for August to go live there. I knew after this one he'd never look at me the same way no matter how hard I tried. No smiles, or treats could save me from the disappointment.

He'd hate me for this, for good.

But he had his entire life to live and I just needed away from Silas.

I couldn't love him the way he needed me to.

I wasn't good enough.

Last weekend proved it.

They were all too good for me, too kind, too loving. I was a black hole to Harbor.

He was going to sign those papers today, the shares would be his. His father would stay in jail after a long trial. He'd have Josh, Arlo... all the Hornets to get him through it and if I stay he'll be distracted. He'll have to spend more time taking care of me instead of what he should be doing.

"I uh...gotta go, Coach is screaming," Josh's voice broke through the nasty wall of depression thoughts.

"Hi," I said, forcing a smile. He pushed his phone into his pocket and eyed me. "You're going to be late for practice," I said, stepping out of his way.

"No I'm not," Josh said, looking me over and shifting on his feet. "Something is wrong."

"I'm leaving early today to take August for lunch, Susanna gave me the afternoon off." I explained, hoping that he wouldn't see through the lie.

"Weird," Josh hummed.

"Why is that weird?" I asked him, shifting the strap on my shoulder as he leaned against the door and blocked my way out. He waited a long time before speaking again.

"No reason," he said, pushing out of my way and letting me pass. "Drew," he said as I reached the door. "You aren't about to do something that's going to break my brother's heart are you?" He asked and the question burned like he had pushed a hot knife into my heart. Branding me with my own guilt.

"Just taking Auggie for lunch, Josh. Have a good practice."

He watched me for a second longer before taking his leave. I sat in my car and cried for nearly twenty minutes, trying to get it all out before returning to the Nest. August would be home, probably sleeping still and I could get the car parked before starting the fight with him.

I started the engine finally, looking up at the stadium one last time with the feeling that I needed to apologize to it. I wish it could have been different. I wished I could be better.

The gates to the Nest were open and I parked the car close to the door so I could easily get everything inside before they finished practice. I left my purse and the keys instead hoping that it wouldn't take forever and we could be on the road.

I wandered into the apartment into the bedroom for the duffle not bothering to stop to wake August. Pack first. Fight later.

"What are you doing?" Silas is standing in the bedroom in a full pressed dark suit. The one he had picked out for this morning's meeting. He was angry, his sharp jaw pressed tightly and his gray eyes darker than I'd ever seen them. He was painfully handsome and it forced me to close my eyes in a shallow breath.

"I came home to grab a sweater," I lied, moving toward the closet.

"It's ninety degrees outside," he said quietly, his eyes never leaving me.

"It's cold in the stadium," I tried but it only made him more upset as I wandered inside and started to look around, ashamed that all my clothes were in the duffel on the floor.

"Can you... can you stop for a second?" Silas's voice was low and calmer than I deserved. I got down on the floor and dug through my duffle, searching for a sweater and trying not to cry. "Drew." He raised his voice but not enough to scare me.

My shoulders slumped forward and I pressed my hands into the carpet to ground myself. The silence was deafening, so loud I could hear my heartbeat in my ears. I had let him down and worse, he had caught me trying to run away before he even had a say.

"I didn't believe him," Silas said, cutting the silence. "He had to beg me and I didn't believe him." He was talking about August, it was clear by his tone of voice. "I didn't think after everything that you would do this," he said. "This isn't you."

"You have no idea who I am," my voice was warning. He was pushing too hard and it wasn't going to get us anywhere. I didn't even have an idea of who I was. How was I supposed to explain it to another person? He knew what he wanted to know, what had interested him... what looked good to his family and friends.

No, that's bullshit. He sees you.

"What's going on Drew? And don't lie to me." He said, and I could hear the hurt in his voice when he said it.

I chewed on my lip, unable to face him.

"It's nothing, it's just time for us to go." I explained.

"Go where?" Silas asked.

"This is what we do, you knew that."

"Why won't you look at me? Talk to me!" Silas said. "All you have to do is talk to me!"

I turned to look at him, "you can't fix this."

"I don't want to fix it," he sighed, still standing at the edge of the closet. "I want to understand it!"

"I can't—" I opened my mouth and stopped.

"*Please.*" Silas dropped to his knees in front of me, the fabric of his dress pants stretching over the expanse of his thighs. "Try."

The way he said it broke my heart, it was soft and whiny. Like he needed the explanation to continue breathing. Honesty was the best route.

"I'm not good enough for you Silas," I said it, blunt and true, watching him flinch backward. He opened his mouth to talk but I shook my head, my jaw clenched tightly and my nose itchy as I held back tears.

"You have to be kidding me?" He fell forward on his thighs, his fingers curling into the fabric like he was resisting reaching out. "Is that what you think?"

"It's not a conclusion I came to on a whim," I sighed.

"It's not a conclusion at all," Silas balked. "Did you ever think just once, maybe you should ask me how I felt about you? Like really felt?"

"What? Between all the secrets and drunk sex?" I felt like screaming. This wasn't going to end the way he wanted.

His jaw ticked. "On the bike, at the stadium, at breakfast, dinner, the table, the events. Drew, do you really think that's all this is? After everything?"

"I'm just a travelling waitress, with a son and a diseased brain Silas, you're—*you*. Doctor, best friend, brother, son. You spend everyday coming up with new ways to help everyone, no one forgotten, no one left behind. You need someone who can take care of you. Someone who isn't sick. You're incredible at every turn and all I'm going to do is drag you down. My brain is never going to get better, it's always going to come back around. It sounds manageable now but it turns to resentment."

"Don't you dare compare me to him," Silas said sharply.

"I don't blame *him*," I argued, "I turn into a shell, there's nothing there. It's a black hole and it will destroy everything. Just let me walk away, let me handle it."

"Whatever the hell he drilled into your head, it's bullshit Drew." He surged forward, taking my face in his hands.

"It's not." I shook my head in his grip. "I've seen what it does and I can't stop it. It comes in and it destroys everything I've built without remorse. I won't let it destroy—"

"Us." He said sadly, rolling his tongue against his teeth. "So I don't get a say? You're just going to leave without a word."

"You deserve better." I argued. "You deserve to be looked after."

"Ha," Silas chuckled, it was hollow and defeated. "One selfish thing. I never would have been able to do that before you. I never slowed down enough to think about myself. You did that."

I shook my head, "you're only ever selfish for the bare minimum. A kiss, a touch."

"That's because the one selfish thing I do want, *scares you*." Silas's tone dropped, "you aren't allowed to leave me. I *need* you, that's selfish. I need you more than you need isolation. How's that for the bare minimum?"

He had played the card well and as much as it stung, he had asked... no, he had demanded what he wanted from me.

"You got what you needed Silas," I said trying to control my tone, "I have enough money for August and I to go, and you got the shares."

"No I didn't," he snapped.

"What?" I stopped. "What did you do?"

"August came to me, he knew you needed me and I came."

"Why would he... why would you do that?" My voice trailed off in shock. All that time spent working towards one thing. We were doing it for that and he just... walked away.

"You really don't see it?" He whispered, his voice strained and frustrated, "all this time you thought— did you ever believe a word I said?"

I wanted to say yes, but that tiny doubtful voice was loud.

"Drew," Silas hummed, "you asked me to keep reminding you," he inched closer.

"That was different," I argued. *That was sex.*

"No it wasn't. Here's me, *reminding*." Silas stopped me, "It started as a deal, Drew. But it hasn't been about that for a long time and you know it. I don't care how *often* you need me to be there, I don't care *how* you need me to be there. We can lay in bed for a week, we can stand in the shower for an hour, sit on the fucking kitchen floor and eat nothing but pancakes drunk off our faces. If it makes the noise quiet I will do anything you need. I'm not trying to cure you or rid you of it. I love you for all the dark corners and what you hide in them."

I stared at him, trying to catch my breath.

"I love you." He said, his voice more confident that time. "Say it back."

"It won't last," I said, unable to oblige. "Look at how horrible this is now... how much I'm hurting you."

"Drew I don't give a shit about that," he scoffed. "You tell me what you need, what usually helps. I'll see you through it and then—" He stopped himself. "Let me remind you how perfect you are, maybe eventually it will start to sink in and you'll believe it but until that day comes. I'll keep my promise, I'll keep reminding you. To stay, to smile, to love, to laugh."

His fingers dug into the edges of my jaw and pulled my face against his.

"Every morning, every night. You need it, I'll be here. But you can't shut down when you get scared, you have to promise not to run away. You get in that bed, *with me*, and I'll see you through it." He paused, watching me, "and before you say it, I know you feel it. I could see it on your face that night, you love me too. You're just too scared to admit it because it means you have to take a risk." He said, "it means you have to trust something over that fickle, mean brain of yours."

My eyes fluttered just trying to keep the tears at bay.

"Say. It. Back."

I love you.

I love you.

I love you.

"I don't want to hurt you," I choked out.

"This is hurting me." He was quick and honest.

"When the time comes and I inevitably fuck this up?" I asked, inhaling a rough breath. "Will you let me go then?"

"No more running. Let me take care of you when you can't take care of yourself." He declared like it was law. "I know you feel it. Say it, Drew."

SHORE

"I love you."

The world came to a dead stop. She had said it, and despite how long it had taken to convince her that she could. She had meant it. I could see it, her evergreen eyes were drowning in it.

"I can't believe you were going to run," I said, watching her carefully. I couldn't stand the chance of her disappearing in a blink. I watched her take a long deep breath in, tempted to remind her that we weren't lying to one another anymore but didn't.

"I'm sorry," she said, sitting back on the carpet, I followed her down sliding off my knees. Wrapping my legs around her and pulling her closer. I wasn't quite ready for the distance she was trying to create and selfishly I didn't give a damn that she needed. "Explain it to me."

She chewed her lip and I wanted to make her stop.

"*Please*," I asked.

"It creeps up on me," she inhaled again, trying to keep her breathing steady. "Like fog," she paused. "Eventually it consumes everything in these sticky, horrible thoughts."

I couldn't help myself, reaching out I pushed my hand through her hair and pressed it flat against the back of her neck. I could feel her heart racing beneath my palm and it took every ounce of self-control I had not to just wrap her up in my arms.

"It feels like quicksand," she said, "it starts in my chest and spreads until all I can do is lay in bed. It's pathetic and I didn't want you to see it."

Her lashes fluttered, heavy with droplets of water from her trying to hold back her tears. I stared at her for a long time, wanting to choose my words wisely.

"It's not," I whispered.

"It is." Of course she argued, I couldn't help the tiny frustrated growl that vibrated at the bottom of my throat. "It's not showering, not eating... I don't care about work..."

The next sentence died on her lips.

"Drew, it's survival." I said to her and she frowned, her eyebrows scrunching together tightly as she looked up at me.

"August would disagree. It's cruel, watching his mother spiral out of control. I'm not unaware of what it does to him and I've tried to get him to live with his fat—"

"No," I cut her off. It just slipped from me. The heat exploded in my veins at the thought of August not being around. I should have been concerned about the protective rage that bubbled beneath the surface but I kind of liked the feeling of it. "August sees it, that's not wrong. He's smarter than anyone gives him credit for but... he loves you."

"It's not fair to him," she said.

"What's not fair is *moving* him." I corrected her. "You just need help."

"I burn bridges, Silas. It's what I do. I have no other option," She said, stuck in a cycle of self destruction.

"Well now you do." I stared at her, drilling it home. "And all of this, it's not your fault. Do you understand me?"

She didn't. I could see it. Her jaw tightened and her eyes unlocked from mine to look at the floor.

"I'm just as much to blame." I said, adjusting my hand to her jaw to tilt her chin upward. "I said I love you, and I meant it. I did. But I shouldn't have dropped it on you like that, in a moment when you felt cornered. That was unfair and I'm sorry I scared you but I'm not sorry I said it."

Drew stared at me, tears filling her eyes.

"Arlo said something to me last weekend and it's been rattling around like a loose screw." I shook my hand beside my head and closed my eyes. "I was looking at my problems like a list. Like I needed to check everything off to get what I wanted. But the list is broken and it was keeping me from seeing what was right in front of me."

She sat so still, listening so carefully that if it weren't for her tiny, shallow breathing I'd be concerned her heart wasn't beating.

"You and August," I whispered, wetting my bottom lip. "You were the missing piece in our family. I just couldn't see it through the fog."

She inhaled sharply at the word and her lip trembled.

I pressed my forehead to hers, "You have a home here," I said to her, digging out my keys from my jacket gently I held them up, the ring carrying all the weight.

Drew's eyes flickered to it and back to mine. *It was now or never, baby. Don't say no.* I pleaded quietly, hoping by some grace of god that I had gotten through to her. That maybe she'd trust me enough to take care of her that she was able to set aside all her thoughts just for a second. *It's just me and you, Drew.*

"Make it mean something." The words came out more clear than anything and hit me dead center in the chest with such force I started to laugh, a smile spreading across my face faster than the heat across my body.

"Yeah?" I blinked, almost not believing that the speech had worked but she nodded.

I pulled the ring off the loop, "I'm never putting it back on there," I said to her, chucking my keys to the ground. I was sick of seeing them. "Do you understand me?"

"I promise to take care of it," she said, lifting her hand. I took it in mine to quell the shake there and slipped the ring back where it belonged. "To take care of you, to remind you to be selfish."

"I promise to take care of *you*, to take care of Auggie," I said. I didn't need to ask her anything else. The ring implied it all and we both knew it. "To remind you to be kind to yourself."

I kissed her then, taking her beautiful face in my hands and crashing against her like a wave against a rock. I needed it, and she sank into my arms chasing the same relief I was as her arms wrapped around my neck. I tugged her into my lap, kissing her until I couldn't breathe and as I pulled back gasping for air I peppered more to her damp face.

"I love you, Drew Courtney." I said, kissing her some more. "Do you hear me?"

"I hear you," she laughed softly, her tears still drying. "I love you, too."

"One more thing..." I said, turning my head away from her, "Auggie!" I yelled and Drew flinched.

"Silas!" She groaned burying her face in my neck as the footsteps came down the hallway.

"Can we stay—" he started and stopped. "Ew you guys!"

"Grow up," I teased, "you wanted to stay, this is how that happens," I laughed, digging my fingers into Drew's side playfully. She wriggled in my arms and fought back with laughter.

He wandered into the closet and sat down on the floor with us as Drew slid back onto her knees away from me. "I'm sorry you had to do that," she whispered to him, reaching out to touch his face.

August nodded, "it was nothing, and Arlo drives really fast so... it was kinda fun."

Drew looked at me in shock, her terrified mom expression making me laugh. "Alright, no more rides in the fastback for a while."

"Thank you," she sighed. "I promise that I'm going to work harder, Auggie. For you. For us."

"I love you, Mom." August said, collapsing into her for a hug. The two of them sat there for a while, Drew's face pressed against his head as her hand raked over his hair. "I'm never calling you dad." He looked at me when he pulled back, a serious look on his face.

"Auggie!" Drew gasped with a laugh.

"Silas is good," I said, pressing my lips together in a tight line and giving him an approving nod. It made me think of Ryan and a very important conversation the two of us needed to have *very soon*.

"We good now?" Arlo's voice was a shock and the three of us turned to see him standing in the doorway with Red in his arms, his fingers pressed into the cat's ugly fur.

"What the—" I almost swore and curbed myself. "You didn't leave?"

"I wasn't gonna leave the kid to sit upstairs alone," Arlo said it like that was the most obvious answer. "Besides it was good I didn't, he came down here the second Drew barreled up the driveway."

Drew looked over at August.

"I had to make sure you were listening to him!" August raised his shoulders in a shrug. I shifted on the carpet to toss Arlo a look and Red hissed at me.

"I hate that cat," I grumbled.

"That's our cue, A-man. Let's get back to the stadium and make the boys run dead sprints until they puke," Arlo said, understanding that I needed some more time alone with Drew. I had told her I loved her and right about now all I wanted to do was *show* her.

"Sounds fun," August said. Drew kissed his cheek and let him get off the ground, her eyes following him as they disappeared.

"Sorry," I said to her as we heard the apartment door click shut.

"Don't be," she inhaled, "It's a weird feeling being able to trust...everyone."

"Get used to it," I whispered, closing the gap between us. "Except Cael," I said with a laugh. "Never trust him."

"Noted," she giggled and let me kiss her senseless until we were nothing but a puddle on the closet floor.

SHORE

"Are you sure you want to do this?" Drew's brows pinched together as she fixed my tie. No matter how many times I tied it, she always fixed it.

It had been a month, the longest month of my life. Immediately after the blowup, Charles' lawyers pushed for a quick resolution. He had held steady on his not guilty statement until the sentence was laid. Twelve years in prison, with a chance of parole after five. It wasn't the best, but it was enough.

I had asked Josh the same thing that day.

"*Are you sure?*" *I asked, as Josh shifted uncomfortably next to Dean who looked more like his bodyguard than boyfriend. Both had dressed in clean, new suits. Dean's broad chest rose and fell at a steady, sturdy pace at Josh's side who was pulling at the collar of his shirt.*

"Stop asking me that fucking question, Silas." Josh growled. "I'm here. I'm ready."

"They're going to show her picture in there," I said to him and his eyes snapped to mine.

"They prepped me," he reminded me harshly, "so stop."

"Boys, stop fighting," Mom's voice broke through the buzzing of the busy court building. Ryan was standing behind her, his hair and beard trimmed and his suit pressed perfectly. I clenched my jaw and sighed. "Your tie is crooked," she said to Josh and stepped forward.

I watched him breathe in once and hold it as Mom invaded his personal space with the utmost care and fixed it. She stepped back to admire him, reaching out to give Dean a pat on the cheek.

"You're a good man," she said to him and Dean finally cracked a smile.
"Are you ready for today?" I asked her and her smile faltered.
"If Josh is, I am." She said, her eyes never leaving him.
"I am," Josh answered her.

"I have to, I haven't spoken to him since the trial ended and Mom said he's making himself sick with guilt over what happened. If he dies and..." I trailed off. If Mom and Josh could be brave and face Charles. I could face Seymour.

"I'm just checking in," she said, pushing up on her toes to kiss me. "Just be patient with him."

"Since when are you a Seymour fan girl?" I teased her.

"I'm not, he's sick. He deserves a little grace." She argued gently.

Drew, after much deliberation and a little fighting, decided that she would go to therapy. I had suggested Riona but she refused, wanting to keep their relationship at a base level for as long as August was still spending time with Daisy. I helped her pick one from beneath the blankets on our bed. A spot I had willingly gotten very familiar with in the week that followed our blow up.

I learned quickly that once she was in it, there was no getting out. She just needed the quiet, the time to prove her own thoughts wrong and if need be, the space to restart. I gave her what I could, and took over the role of August's sole guardian. He joined a summer workplace program at the shelter with Cosy, and Ella had lent him her bike to go to and from.

I was grateful for how much weight the rest of the Nest was willing to bear as we found our way through everything. Cael graduated Harbor with a smile on his face and Ryan cheering from the front row as he walked across the stage. Everything seemed to fall into place like it was always the plan.

Drew pressed her hand flat to my chest, done fussing with my tie.

"You should wear the other one, if Mom sees that she'll have my head." I said, brushing a knuckle over a tiny faded purple spot on her collarbone.

Drew looks down at the mark and smirks before running her hands over the white sundress she was wearing. "No," she hummed. "I like this one."

Opening my mouth to argue she lifted my hand to her lips and kissed it. She hadn't meant the dress... *fuck*. She always knew exactly what button to press.

I knotted my hand into the back of her hair, bundling the red strands between my fingers and tipping her head back to steal a kiss from her stubborn, pretty lips. She tasted like sugar and the second she pulled away a tiny whine left my throat as I followed her to steal another.

"On second thought, let's stay home." I wrapped my arm around her waist as she turned to leave, pulling her back against my chest. My lips were quick to find her throat.

"Silas if we're late I'm throwing you to the wolves," she giggled and squirmed but it only made my grip tighter. My hand pressed down her stomach and inched into the soft fabric, pinching it in my fingers until I could feel the soft skin of her thigh.

"I'll be quick," I whined.

"You're never quick," she wiggled free, stepping back out of my reach and leaving me restless. "Deal with that and meet us outside." She pointed to my hard on.

"Seriously?" I huffed as she giggled and left me standing in the closet alone.

"Do I really need to wear this?" August tugged at his tie, mirroring Josh's action beside him.

Drew tilted her head to the side, no doubt thinking the same thing I was. How similar the two of them looked and acted without sharing a shred of DNA. She looked over her shoulder at me and all I could do was laugh.

"If I have to, you have to." Josh grumbled. "You owe me," he snapped at me.

"For what, Mom invited us both!" I tucked my hand into the pocket of my pants and wrapped the other one around Drew's waist. "Let's get this over with," I muttered, leading her into the house behind Josh and Dean.

"Holy shit," August swore.

"Language," Drew hissed at him gently as his voice echoed in the foray.

Josh stifled a laugh and Dean got August's attention to pull him into the living room. Seymour stood at the other end in the door of his office staring at me.

"Go," Drew encouraged, patting me on the chest. "I love you."

The sound of her saying that never got old. I wrapped my hand around hers feeling the ring in my palm and slowed down my breathing to match hers. "Don't let August and Josh bully Dean," I said, trying to keep calm and Drew shook her head, only letting go when I was ready.

I shoved my hands in my pocket and made my way into the office, Seymour shutting the door behind me.

"Before you take a chunk out of me Grandpa, I don't regret my decision." I leaned against one of the chairs as he circled slowly and sat down. He coughed for a second, bracing himself on the arm. He was looking worse every day and it wouldn't be long before we were holding another funeral.

I was so unbelievably sick of death.

"Sit down," he barked when he finally got finished with his coughing fit. I unbuttoned my jacket and sunk into the chair across from him. "The first time you walked that woman into my house you lied to me."

"Grandpa," I sighed.

"Don't try to tell me you didn't. I'm old, not stupid." Seymour snapped. "It was clear that you had found Ms. Courtney in an attempt to fool me."

I brushed my hand through my hair and nodded, "that's correct but not the whole story."

"I know. Your Mother figured the rest out before you left the drive way." He shook his head. Of course Mom had known, and the entire time. Her coming to the apartment, taking Drew to lunch... It had all been a show from the two of them.

"It was stupid of you to leave before that meeting." He reached for his glass of water. It was the first time I'd ever seen him drink anything besides scotch in my entire life.

I buckled down, pressing my heels into the floor and preparing for the fight.

"But I see you boy." He said. "I see the love and I'm proud of you for holding on to it."

TRUE HONEY

Seymour had never been one to mince his words. He was honest, true and despite his addiction to hard liquor and cigars. He was a good man. I just wasn't sure of his angle. Usually it was pretty clear but I couldn't for the life of me figure it out.

"Okay Grandpa, you're going to have to explain," I leaned forward.

Seymour chuckled, "we are in this mess because your father never valued love." He tapped his fingers on the table. "He always put money over it. I have to confess something Silas," he said. "There was no deal."

"What?" I balked.

"You are a hurricane, son. The quiet kind, that consumes constantly. You're always moving, helping everyone, solving problems. I knew you'd jump at the chance to help if I asked, if I made it serious." Seymour explained.

"So what... you aren't dying?" I choked on every word.

"Of course I'm dying!" He laughed so hard it turned into a long, painful cough. "The shares have been in your name since the day I found out I was." He got out once he finished. "They were never in jeopardy, your father is never getting out of jail. Harbor was never in trouble."

I stood from the chair, circling it and pacing the room once before I came back and gripped the back of the chair. "If it wasn't for the shares then why the hell—"

Seymour smiled at me. "You needed to slow down," he said. "I know you think I'm some cranky asshole, but I did this because I wanted you to take the time to find someone who loved you for you and not because of this," he looked around at the room, dripping in riches.

"Are you insane?" I sighed, staring at him in complete shock.

"Money isn't what built this family, Silas. Money isn't what built the Hornets. And if I was going to trust you to take care of them then you need to learn that lesson the hard way." Seymour smiled. "You needed less distractions so you could find someone to take care of you, while you took care of everything else."

"You did all of this to get me a girlfriend?" I scoffed.

"I did all of this because you were turning into your father and I wasn't going to die with the fate of my legacy in the hands of a man slut." Seymour coughed.

"Who taught you that term?" I groaned and straightened out, trying to work through the shock of what that lunatic old man had done. Tricked by a man halfway in the grave. Arlo was right. I'm an idiot.

"Joshua calls you that," Seymour laughed painfully.

"I'm taking him out of the will," I hissed only making him laugh more. "Ok stop before you die please, Mom would never forgive me." I handed him the glass of water.

Seymour opened his mouth to argue when there were footsteps down the hall. A soft knock on the door echoed out before it popped open and Drew stepped inside. It was like she knew it was her mark, timed perfectly with her bright smile and big heart. The sun poured in around her from the big open window behind her and made her glow the warmest shade of gold.

"Dinner's ready," she said, looking between me and Seymour completely oblivious to her timing.

"We'll be right there, darling," Seymour said, rising from his seat. Drew nodded and backed from the room. "Do you get it now?" He asked me.

I was still staring at the door with a smile on my face and my heart racing from the sight of her.

"Yeah I get it." *God, did I ever.*

EPILOGUE
SHORE

"Drop a little on the left," I said, pointing to the wall. Silas had gifted me a painting of the New York skyline for our wedding anniversary. It was massive and looked just like the view from the hotel we had stayed in the last time we were there. Arlo and Silas stepped back from it and stared with their heads cocked sideways. "It's still crooked."

"I told you we need the human level," Arlo snapped, crossing his arms over his chest.

"Van has his final exams today, we just have to figure it out." Silas shrugged, making his best friend growl something under his breath.

"I have a better idea," Cael said from the doorway.

We all turned to look at him, leaning there in a baby-pink cropped t-shirt and a pair of jeans. His hair was growing out again and there were streaks of blonde that had lightened from the sun.

"We go get dinner and hire someone to hang that monstrosity," he suggested.

"You mean, I take you all for dinner and pay for all of that…" Silas sighed, his hair was longer too, it curled at the edges and the gray was more prominent now behind his ears and in the base of his beard. He stretched in his tight black long sleeve, and it raised against his stomach showing off my second favorite part of his body.

They had been doing odd jobs around the new house all day. It was weird not to live at the Nest after being there for almost a year and Silas was adjusting decently but we wanted a space that was ours. It wasn't fancy or oversized, made just for the three of us. Close to the high school and the stadium.

It helped that we hadn't been left alone in a week, the team was helping us move and it was an open-door policy. I was starting to think that Silas set no boundaries on purpose because he didn't know how to be without them. Our living room was a mess with blankets and sleeping bags after their three day camp out on the floor.

The back of Silas's neck was dripping in sweat that pooled down between his shoulder blades and showed off the edges of all his strong muscles. I licked my bottom lip to keep from biting it at the sight of him.

I pressed my face into my hand, hiding the blush that spread across my cheeks as I sat on the edge of the bed. Silas eyed me and raised his eyebrow, a smirk growing on his face while Cael complained that he was being a fun vampire.

"On second thought, my card is on the counter. Treat the team to something nice, go all the way to Lorette…" he said, never taking his eyes off me. "Take your time."

"And take Auggie," I added quickly as Cael spun out of the door frame with a victorious yell.

"You're both disgusting," Arlo grumbled. "Use protection."

Silas chucked his work gloves at Arlo as he wandered out of the room.

I leaned back on the bed, propping myself up on my elbows.

"We've haven't been alone since they all came home from Pittsburgh, that was six days ago Silas Shore," I said, my voice lacking patience. "Please use your time wisely."

"I plan to." He stripped from the sweaty shirt and threw it aside.

"Thank-you," I giggled as he came toward me. I scooted back on the bed using my feet to push me but he grabbed my ankle, tugging me back to him for a hungry kiss. His lips were demanding as he pushed my legs apart with his kneel, positioning himself between them. He unbuttoned the shirt I was wearing slowly, peppering kisses down my neck and chest. His hand palmed my breast, bringing it to his mouth to suck the soft skin of one, and then the other.

It was slow and torturous.

"I know I've seen you every day this week but I missed you," I whispered, roughly pushing my hands into his hair.

Silas chuckled against my skin, his hands moving to my waist. He slipped the pants from my hips, ridding me of both them and the underwear in a quick, gentle movement.

"Enough talking, let me remind you why you missed me so much." He smirked, his hands moving to my thighs. Without warning he flipped me to my stomach, a tiny yelp leaving my lips as his hand came across my ass.

"I can manage that," I said lazily, rubbing my hands in a wide circle on the mattress until they were tangled into the fabric above my head.

Silas unbuttoned his jeans, the sound of them falling open making my body tense as I waited patiently. He ran a hand over my ass cheek before spreading it apart and pressing his face between them, licking me in one long, deep stripe from behind.

"I love this view," he murmured, his teeth finding skin and sinking in deep enough to make my hips rise off the bed toward him.

All his marks from the week before had faded and now that he had started, there was no stopping him until he had his fill. Silas bit down harder, marking my ass again. His hands gripped my hips tightly as he moved back to my center, licking and sucking at my clit. He was eating me out with a hunger that matched his earlier promise. "Fuck, you're so responsive," he breathed out, tickling the sensitive area without even trying.

My fingers dug into the sheets, unable to stay still as his tongue worked in firm circles that wound the cord inside my core tight. My body tensed and without warning he plunged two fingers inside and began to pump them back and forth while his other hand reached around to rub my clit in rough circles. Determined to make me come undone before we even got started.

"Come on, Baby." He encouraged.

My hips lifted at his words, my knees rising and digging into the mattress to keep me from shaking as he worked the orgasm from me relentlessly. As I came he didn't stop, his fingers continued to work inside of me pressing against that sensitive g-spot perfectly. He added a third finger, stretching me wider as my juices coated his hand and dripped down my thighs.

I practically collapsed against the bed when it rolled through me, my body completely wracked with pleasure. Silas's tongue licked a long strip up my thigh cleaning the skin, ending with a line of kisses over the curve of my ass.

He positioned himself behind me, his cock pressing against my still sensitive core. He didn't give me a moment to recover, thrusting inside of me in one hard stroke. Three months after our courtroom wedding, Silas had gone out and gotten a vasectomy. We had talked for a long time about the effect it would have on me to go through that again. And he didn't care as long as I was sure. He booked the appointment the next day claiming that he had enough kids to look after and all he really wanted to do was and I quote, stuffed completely full of him, *'I want to fuck my wife raw.'* And boy, did Silas Shore know how to keep a promise.

"God, I'm spoiled," I said out loud as he began to fuck me relentless, the sound of skin slapping against skin and the bed creaking under the weight of his blows filled the room. With everyone gone there was no reason we had to be quiet and fuck it was incredible.

"Look at me," he demanded, hooking one of my arms behind my back, changing the angle and hitting me even deeper as I turned my face to look at him over my shoulder.

Silas's jaw was clenched, his eyes locked on mine. He wanted to see my face, always watching to make sure I was there with him even after all this time. His hand wrapped around my hip, pulling me back onto his impressive length with each thrust. "*Keep* looking at me, Drew." He demanded, his voice strained and breathless.

As we grew closer to the edge his hand reached out and he pulled me back into his lap. His chest against my back as he guided me up and down his shaft. His hand pressed flat to my lower stomach, applying just the right amount of pressure.

I collapsed against him, swearing under my breath as I rested my head on his shoulder and cried his name to the ceiling. I could feel him in my fucking stomach when he did that with his hand and he knew exactly what he was doing.

His mouth found my shoulder and his smirk grew against my skin before he sank his teeth into the untouched surface. Silas continued to control my movement, pushing me down onto his cock harder and faster. His hand stayed possessively pressed against me as I came apart completely, nothing more than a trembling mess in his arms.

"Like riding a bike." He teased.

"It's only been six—" my words were cut off by a long moan when his hand found my clit.

"That's it baby," He said in a smug voice. He bit into my shoulder harder, leaving another delicious mark that he soothed with his tongue immediately after. Silas's hips moved faster and I clenched around him as the orgasm started to flood up from my core, "tell me just how much you missed my dick," he purred.

I could feel how close he was with every thrust, his muscles contracting tightly against my back. The bed buckled beneath us dangerously but Silas never stopped. His breathing was ragged against my neck, his movements becoming erratic as he chased his own release. The bed creaked loudly with each snapping thrust, the frame threatening to give out but Silas was too far gone, completely consumed. His need to claim me completely clouding his common sense.

"So much," I coaxed him faster, holding on tighter.

With a deep growl that vibrated from the base of his throat he wrapped a strong arm around my waist to keep me in place. His other hand moved from my clit and gripped my hip pulling me back onto him forcefully with each thrust. The entire bed was shaking now, the head slamming against the wall.

I fell over the edge first but Silas was frantic to follow. I came completely undone around his cock and he lost all control. He hammered into me wildly, chasing his release. He buried his face in my neck fucking me through my orgasm. His movements became even more aggressive as he finally spilled out, emptying himself inside of me. The bed gave out with a loud, echoing crack, collapsing lopsided beneath us.

"Silas!" I yelled in breathless laughter, slipping forward on the newly created slope.

Silas caught me around the waist before I could slide off completely, pressing kisses to my sweat-slicked back. He was still inside of me, tensing with aftershocks. The collapsed bed frame lay in tatters as we tried to catch our breath.

"I've got you..." he purred, pressing a kiss to the tiny bruise on my shoulder.

"How do we uh...get out?" I said quietly, my heart racing.

He chuckled softly, still breathing heavily. His arms tightened around me as he gently shifted, trying to ease out without collapsing further into what remained of the bed frame. "Carefully," he murmured against my skin. "Don't move too fast."

Once free of him, I turned slowly in his arms, wrapping my legs around his waist. He kissed me gently and carefully lifted me up, staying in the center of the bed as he stood. He carried me carefully out the bed, his arms securely around me as he stepped over the cracked frame. He nuzzled another kiss to the side of my head before setting me on the ground with shaky legs.

"Well, that was... unexpected," he said with an amused smile.

"I can't believe we broke the bed." I looked over the damage and then up to Silas with concern but he didn't seem to find the problem. He was ecstatic with himself.

He grinned proudly, completely unfazed by the destruction he caused. In fact, he looked pleased with himself. "I broke the bed *fucking* you," he stated and crossed his arms over his chest as he admired the damage.

"You would be proud of yourself." I pressed my flushed face against his sweaty bicep and closed my eyes.

Silas laughed gently, pressing a kiss to the top of my head. His arms shifted to wrap around me. "I am *very* proud of myself," he grinned ear to ear against my hair. "Hey," he whispered and tilted my chin up to rest on his chest. He admired me with those soft gray eyes and I could have melted into him right there and then. "We needed a new one anyway."

ACKNOWLEDGEMENTS

I've been doing these for a while now, and you'd think that eventually I would get better at them. I don't. I cry every time. I truly believe that the acknowledgements of a book shows the soul of an author. It's all the thing things that helped us get through all the writing, editing, formatting, and design. It's like giving an acceptance speech, except half the time no body reads them or cares because, "Aubrey you thank the same people over and over again." I do. That's true.

But saying thank you is important.

My husband for example, works way too hard so I can sit in my office and type funny things into a computer that make everyone laugh. He comes home high strung, stressed out and has to stare at the ceiling for an hour to regulate himself before hanging out with our kids so I can start my second job as an author. He's the reason I get to do this everyday, so of course I want to thank him every time. He earned that for being a reason that romance books get written. For showing me that the bar doesn't have to be in hell and most of the things we believe are princess treatment are simply just love and partnership. I know he's reading this, because he's part of the handful that does every time. I also know that I wouldn't wanna do this life with anyone but you. Love you more than Sonic and Mario. I win.

To my friends and family that are always supporting me, showing me love, spreading the word and reading these books. My Worms, my Freakshow, my HT, the Golden Girls... Thank you. I love you. You've seen me through a lot of struggles in my life and I can't begin to explain how much it means to me that you continue to support me through this next chapter. I promise I'll make it worth it.

To my team, Rory, Bec, the street team and the betas, Netty, Beth, Mattie, Sarah, Jes, Lizzy, and Tiffani. You guys are the main reason these books go anywhere. From the first stages of writing, to the cover creation, and editing. You read endless hours of unedited crap, tell me I'm pretty and still want to be my friend at the end of the day. I couldn't do this without you. I don't want to! Thank you for helping me grow and always having my back. I love you forever.

The dream team, MK and JJ. You two single handedly keep this shit show rolling. You are the voices of reason and the conductors of chaos. Perfectly balanced and somehow it works to create this perfect dynamic that has taken my career from good to incredible. You're both, in your own ways some of the strongest women I know and every day is truly a fucking pleasure knowing you because I learn so much from both of you. My life would be very boring without you. Thank you for believing in me when I don't believe in myself and for kicking my ass when it needs to be done.

And to Jess, because there is no Aubrey without her, a song because I'm feeling sappy and need a Tuck Duck: If I could be a duck for a day, I'd be a drunk duck because I love to drink. If I could be a duck for just one day, I'd be a duck that drinks a lot and that drink would be whiskey. I love how they fly away from all of their problems, like alcoholism...awe and if i could just be one, one day I'd be a drunk tuck duck. And I'd be Jake..... tonight. I love you twinkle toes. Please never leave me.

www.ingramcontent.com/pod-product-compliance
Lightning Source LLC
Chambersburg PA
CBHW020515080526
44583CB00013B/605